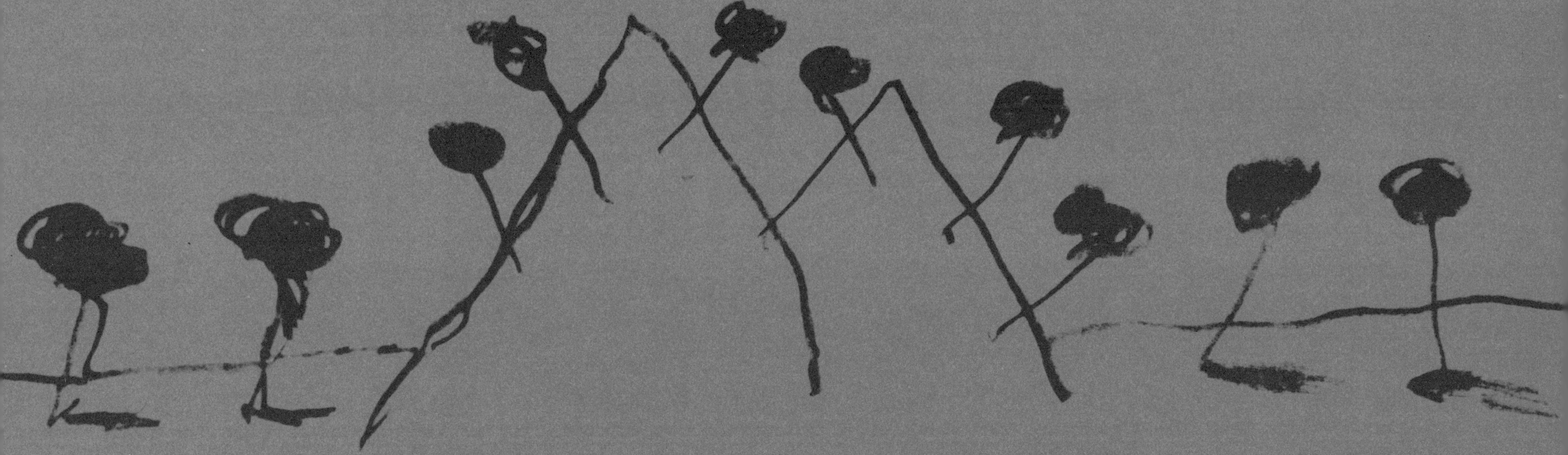

To Carter and Paul

To help keep memories alive

Meg and Ted

Seoul
Christmas 1982

The Australian Landscape and its Artists

The Australian Landscape and its Artists

Elwyn Lynn

Bay Books Sydney

First published 1977
Reprinted 1979
Published by Bay Books Pty Ltd, 157–167 Bayswater Road, Rushcutters Bay, New South Wales 2011, Australia
Printed in Japan by Toppan Printing Company.

Registered in Australia for transmission by post as a book

ISBN 0 85835 143 9

Artists and Paintings

The end-paper drawing, entitled 'Junee', was created especially for this book by Sidney Nolan in March, 1976.

Acknowledgements

The generous assistance given by artists, owners, collectors and institutions is gratefully acknowledged; I should like to thank the following people who kindly permitted paintings to be reproduced: Miss Pamela Bell, Mr Kym Bonython, Mrs Shay Docking, Mr Guy Grey-Smith, Mrs Caroline Hagan, Mr David Heysen, Mr Robert Juniper, Mr Rudy Komon, Mr Desiderius Orban, Mr John Rigby, Mr William Salmon, Mr Michael Shannon and Mr Oliver Streeton; I should also like to record my appreciation of Mr Sidney Nolan's gesture in providing the end-paper drawing and of the co-operation of those who wish to remain anonymous. I should like to express thanks for the help given by The Macquarie Galleries and The Artarmon Galleries, both of Sydney, and of the following galleries and institutions whose specific assistance is indicated with the captions to the paintings: Art Gallery of New South Wales; Art Gallery of South Australia; Australian National Gallery, Canberra; The Australian National University, Canberra; The Dixson Galleries, Sydney; National Gallery of Victoria; Newcastle City Art Gallery; Perpetual Trustee Company Limited; Red Hill Station Pty Ltd; The University of Sydney and The Western Australian Art Gallery; and to Douglas Thompson for his advice and assistance with the photography.

Introduction

'No tree, to my taste, can be beautiful that is not deciduous. What can a painter do with a cold olive green? There is a dry harshness about the perennial leaf that does not savour of humanity in my eyes . . . All the dearest allegories of human life are bound up in the infant and slender green of spring, the dark redundance of summer, and the sere and yellow leaf of autumn. These are as essential to the poet as emblems, as they are to the painter as picturesque objects; and the common consent and immemorial custom of European poetry has made the change of seasons, and its effect upon vegetation, a part, as it were, of our very nature. I can therefore hold no fellowship with Australian foliage . . .'
Barron Field: 'Geographical Memoirs', 1825

'The drover, the shearer, the bullock driver, and even the bush-ranger, to the utilitarian person, seems [sic] to be all that is needed as a keynote for Australian landscape, but yet for me the background calls for something that will better express the lonely and primitive feeling of this country. A feeling more suggestive of some melancholy pastoral to be rendered in music, and perhaps rather beyond the limits of painting . . .'
Sydney Long: 'Art and Architecture' Sydney 1905

'As far as we in Australia are concerned, a country young in the arts, we enjoy a certain innocence, I say enjoy because it may have certain advantages. Because of our youth and continental detachment it is more likely that we may be able to say something of our own in our own tongue as a contribution to the international language of art. Of all the British Dominions we have developed the most stimulating painting. We are in the process of building, and that is rather exciting, for although our cultural inheritance is European, we are physically removed from Europe, and our immediate influence is formed by our environment and is subject to the national characteristics we have formed.'
Russell Drysdale: 'Impressions of a Painter in Europe Today', lecture to the Art Gallery Society of New South Wales, published in 1959

Interest in landscape painting in Australia persists not because its landforms demand to be recorded, interpreted and celebrated, but because the landscape has provided a stimulus to and the occasion for the development of a variety of styles and approaches to art. It could even be claimed that in no other country is it so ideologically habitual for artists — even some of the most geometrically non-figurative — to relate their paintings to the landscape.

Such a consistent involvement with the relation of art to landscape has been regarded by many as a provincial and regional compromise whereby peripheral cultures, according to scarcely examined sociological notions, accommodate and, it is implied, debilitate the impulses from metropolitan centres. So narrow have such views become that their proponents are surprised when an indigenous culture emerges, because their guiding interest is not to detect what is newly created but to identify influences.

It is clear enough that there is an alternative reading of the history of modern painting; the orthodox history that what is significant has emerged from the Paris-New York axis and that Expressionism, Northern Europe and the Barbizon School are distributaries from the mainstream of metropolitan art has been seriously challenged by those who regard decorative or austere formalism as inadequate. A pervasive reading is that the best modern painting has more and more discarded its relationship to the other arts, especially literature, in the pursuit of expressing itself in terms of its own media, shape and surface. That has been true of some painting, but its theoretical adherents have promoted the banishment of topography, realism, verisimilitude and the deliberated evocation and symbolizing of emotion and atmosphere. Art with associations is suspect because it gives rise to considerations, it is said, that are aesthetically irrelevant.

In 1949, when Sir Kenneth (now Lord) Clark wrote his 'Landscape into Art', he wondered if landscape painting could ever regain its dominant position. Fifteen years later, in North America and Europe, it appeared to be almost eclipsed; in Australia it continued to shine fitfully. However, in recent years there have been two significant shifts in theory and practice; more significant than the rise of a new realism has been a physical return to nature by artists' making rings of stones on the moors, digging holes and planting mirrors in the drylands and drawing spirals in the snow. Those feats are related to the reassertion of a perennial aesthetic issue of how subject, feeling and structure are connected. To banish depictions of the objective world is not to be relieved of this fundamental problem.

Formalistic attitudes became so inhibitory that commentators and critics grew reluctant to write of anything but tensions, balanced harmonies and spatial deployment. Associative description was expelled along with associative painting; to describe the roots of Russell Drysdale's tree in *The Rabbiters* as 'tortured, clutching fingers' was questionable even if one had a precedent with Vincent Van Gogh writing in 1882: 'Now I tried to put the same sentiment into the landscape as I put into the figure: the convulsive, passionate clinging to the earth, and yet being half torn up by the storm. I wanted to express something of the struggle for life in the pale, thin woman's figure as well as in the black, gnarled and knotty roots'.

The impression gained from some writers is that Australian art has been impoverished by its predilection for landscape and associated painting; that its more recent distinguished painters — to mention only Arthur Boyd, Russell Drysdale, Sidney Nolan, John Olsen, John Perceval, Lloyd Rees, Roland Wakelin and Fred Williams — are harmfully *retardataire*. Australian art, it has been implied, being but provincial, must necessarily lessen the quality of the metropolitan art from which it derived or gained impetus. Commentators made more of how artists were bound by the visual conventions they brought with them or 'borrowed' than of the results of their confrontation with a new landscape of frequently exotic or seemingly featureless flora and landforms.

The facts hardly support such a view of artistic dependence. Artists cannot approach the world with the purely innocent eye that William Salmon knows it is vain to long for and even a 'naive' painter like Henri Bastin is knowledgeable enough to dedicate a painting to Henri Rousseau, 'Le Douanier'. Conrad Martens saw the antipodes both as a Romantic painter and a sharp-penned topographer; John Glover greatly modified his usual practices to cope with the sparseness of a new foliage and added precise descriptions to the catalogue of works he sent back to London. Other painters did find the actual landscape in full accord with their European experiences, for Eugen von Guerard's *Mount Kosciusco* in the Australian National Gallery, Canberra, caught at a tenebrously Romantic moment, breathes the secular religion of Caspar David Friedrich's landscapes. One could hardly accuse S.T. Gill and Julian Ashton of being confined to the exercise of stale conventions, for, illustrators as they were, they created authentic records replete with the flavour of the scene and of the exemplary nature of the event. William Piguenit, who grew up in sight of Hobart's ever-changing Mount Wellington, could find examples enough on the Darling or Nepean Rivers in New South Wales to satisfy his desire to paint the dramatic transformations of nature by storm, cloud, mist and flood, without recourse to exact European predecessors.

An allied attitude that painters needed to *justify* their approaches by their applicability to landscape has affected the contribution made from the late nineteen-fifties by the Abstract Expressionists. They have been depreciated for having treated abstraction as a form of landscape painting, even if one of the most influential American members of this school, Willem de Kooning, was stimulated by the pastoral, calling one of his paintings *Rosy Fingered Dawn at Louse Point*. Australian painters like John Olsen did not diminish Abstract Expressionism or French Tachisme but absorbed it into a vigorous local tradition of expressionist landscape at a time when that tradition was asserting itself. It was a local tradition exemplified in and encouraged by works such as Russell Drysdale's *Road to the Black Mountains* of 1952 or thereabouts, the spontaneous flow of ridge and valley in Sidney Nolan's Central Australian landscapes and, more emphatically, in those umbrageous creeks in Arthur Boyd's territory and the vortexes of paint that swirled in John Perceval's vision, for though The Antipodean Manifesto of 1959 did denounce the elegant formlessness of Abstract Expressionism in the name of the image (that, they said, had been the basis of art since the cave-man), the Antipodeans and the Action Painters had more in common than either side was ready to admit.

The belief that art could be uninfluenced and the result of the largely innocent eye seems to have emerged with the Heidelberg School that convinced Australians that their landscape was blue, golden and sunlit, except when David Davies turned the lights down low. The School had been influenced at a distance by mainly hearsay Impressionism but it was the result of the conviction that Australian landscape was rather shadowless and dappled with light from thin foliage. In his 'Lecture on Landscape Painting', 21 July 1856, Conrad Martens enunciated some pre-Impressionist principles that were appropriate to painting the local landscape: 'Never make use of cast shadows for your *darks*, but on the contrary keep them as light as possible, which will preserve the breadth as well as give the appearance of air and sunshine'. The Heidelberg School was a summation of those modifications in conventions that had occurred since the eighteen-thirties.

The appreciation of Australian art and especially of its contribution to landscape painting has been blinkered by rather simplistic theories of influence, it often being sufficient for a critic to detect an influence for a work to be dismissed as 'lacking originality'. To some writers paintings became simply eclectic inventories and artists forgers who could not quite decide on what to plagiarize! Influence, as Goran Hermeran has demonstrated in his 'Influence in Art and Literature' is more complex and subtle. The artist may borrow an attitude rather than a form; when Sidney Nolan said that his paintings were Henri Rousseau and sunlight, he was exhibiting knowledge of — not a dependence on — a naive mode, for he relished Rousseau's directness and immediacy and not his botanical configurations. Louis Buvelot and Hans Heysen have paid tribute to the Barbizon School that flourished thirty miles south of Paris from the eighteen-thirties, but it was the attitude engendered by the School that attracted such painters, not the massing of looming, clustered trees as in Theodore Rousseau or the succulent grasses and fugitive light in others. The Barbizon School, coming by way of the static compositions of Gaspard Poussin and Claude Lorraine and the silhouetted, contoured trees of Dutch seventeenth century landscape painting, found a definite, real and native landscape for their pictures. They sought a tranquil, harmonious cohesion to glorify the bucolic; they avoided the spectacular and the theatrical. Such were the elements in their approaches that influenced nineteenth-century Australian painters who, however, found Barbizon painting a little still, airless and lacking in vibrancy, but they felt that this school suited the Utopian temper of the times that saw virtue in the contemplation of homely hill, riverbank, forest and field.

The Barbizon School was concerned with the idea of a *typical* landscape that changed its appearance with the seasons and the weather; it was a naturalistic school whose notions of harmony and appropriateness coincided with those of the early Australian topographers, though the latter were concerned with the harmony of the scientific aspects of climate and country. What they had in common, and this deeply affected Australian landscape painting for one-hundred-and-fifty years, was a concern with the essential qualities of a specific environment whether it was rural. urban or coastal.

It was this feeling for natural coherence that was able to adapt modes derived from Cubism, a task made easier by the fact that the influence of Paul Cézanne was one that received a general and unusual blessing in Australia. Naturally enough, Cubism influenced urbanscapes more directly, especially in the work of Sali Herman, Godfrey Miller, Jeffrey Smart and Rah Fizelle. It has not shared the impact that another local tradition has made: expressive realism; that is, to generalize, the paintings by the Antipodeans. Like the Australian Impressionists, they knew of European Expressionism principally by hearsay — and a few reproductions; cut off from some influences by the Second World War they forged an approach somewhat reminiscent of the imposing grandeur, gloom, melancholy and resonance found at times in Louis Buvelot, Eugen von Guerard and William Piguenit; this did not, of course, prevent them from looking over the hill at the sunny fields of Heidelberg and Templestowe.

The Antipodeans have so often been presented as holding the fort against the barbaric hordes of abstractionists, that their furtherance of a local tradition in literature and painting — the melancholy, loneliness and alienating nature of the bush, a haven of real and imaginary monsters — has been underestimated. This underestimation has been associated with the lack of appreciation of local traditions and influences, for Australia's artists of the landscape have been as much aware of their own environment and its depictors as of overseas influences. The river in Nolan's *Riverbend* could flow through no other country; no one has epitomised the disparate flora of the sparse landscape as Fred Williams; few can evoke the beneficent symbolism of Arthur Streeton's *Still Glides the Stream and Shall Forever Glide* or the symbolism of endurance in Clifton Pugh and Russell Drysdale.

This book, while stressing the individuality of artists of the Australian landscape, traces, as well as a comprehensive survey allows, various traditions in style and attitude. Illustrations have been arranged so that twenty-five artists of established importance (though I have rather wilfully elevated Blamire Young on what Ern Malley called 'the vertical banners of praise') with three reproductions each are in approximate chronological order. Reproductions of work by twenty-five other artists who have been allocated one each have been interspersed sometimes chronologically but always to make a comparative point. In this way the persistence of similar attitudes, themes, approaches and purposes is indicated. The text contains a number of cross-references which emphasise this intention.

Since the theme of the book is the reaction of artists to art and landscape, preference has been given to observations by artists themselves.

That a vigorous and continuing art of landscape has not only survived dismissive and crudely formulated theories of influence but has also absorbed modes and attitudes from abroad and perenially revivified local traditions is clear. One suspects that this book will coincide with a growing and laudatory reappraisal of Australian art; in particular, the art of Australian landscape which we have presented in its moments of grandeur, relaxed intimacy, harsh vigour and Arcadian hedonism . . . but there is seemingly no end to the moods and styles that the landscape has promoted and prolonged. André Lhote, in the 1939 introduction of his 'Treatise on Landscape Painting', suggested that to appreciate the achievements of landscape painting we should 'reflect on the necessity of dominating our fragmentary impressions so that we may bring about this rich conglomeration of different elements; trees, rocks, meadows, lakes, clouds, flocks, waves, capable of summing up the universe in a more or less revealing lightning flash'.

Elwyn Lynn,
Sydney, New South Wales, 1977

John Glover

John Glover, born at Houghton-on-the-Hill, Leicestershire England 1767. Arrived in Tasmania 1831, where he died in 1849.

If his influence had been greater, and it survives in artists like John Olsen and Frederick Williams, John Glover might claim from Louis Buvelot the title 'father of Australian landscape painting'; but he was more interested in catching details than in transcribing the spirit and atmosphere of a new land. That in itself is remarkable for he came to Australia with a reputation based on the broad areas and subdued melancholy of some of the work of Claude Lorraine and Gaspard Poussin whom he admired. He retained their pellucid skies, their pervasive and indirect sunlight and the practice, as in *Patterdale Farm*, of bracketing the scene with trees, or anchoring one end of the picture with an imposing building, as in *Hobart Town from the Garden Where I Lived;* but his work was more transparent with suffused light and much more linear. He saw Tasmania as a Utopia of pastoral peace; as John Olsen wrote: 'For Glover, nature was passive and nostalgic'; and it is natural that the trees in *The River Nile, Van Diemen's Land* should resemble a decorative frieze.

Nostalgic he was, but he made these changes in his vision at the age of sixty-three; Desiderius Orban accomplished something similar when he arrived in Australia at fifty-five, and Sali Herman when he went to Sydney at forty. In the preface to the catalogue of his exhibition which was sent to London in 1835, Glover wrote: 'There is a remarkable peculiarity in the trees in this country; however numerous they rarely prevent you tracing through them the whole distant country'. His aim was expressed in his poem:

'Here with pensive peace could I abide
Far from the stormy world's tumultuous roar . . .'

Patterdale Farm, which he established on the River Nile, near Launceston, Tasmania, was named after another property of his in Cumberland, which was once owned by William Wordsworth.

The deliberate detail and uncompromising clarity still provide the shock that they once did; in 1839, John Lhotsky, a visiting critic, deplored the lack of anything really primitive and original and of botanical exactness, but G.T.W. Boyes wrote in his private diary in 1831 that the trees were painted 'with hideous fidelity to nature'.

The truth, as often, lies between the two views.

The River Nile, Van Diemen's Land
Oil on canvas; 1837; 76.2 × 114.4 cm.
Acquired: 1956
National Gallery of Victoria.

Hobart Town from the Garden Where I Lived
Oil on canvas; 1832; 73.65 × 149.8 cm.
The Dixson Galleries, Sydney.
Vertical line to right of painting is where the canvas was joined or bent in the past.

Patterdale Farm
Oil on canvas; c.1840; 77.0 × 114.5 cm.
Acquired: 1974
Art Gallery of New South Wales.

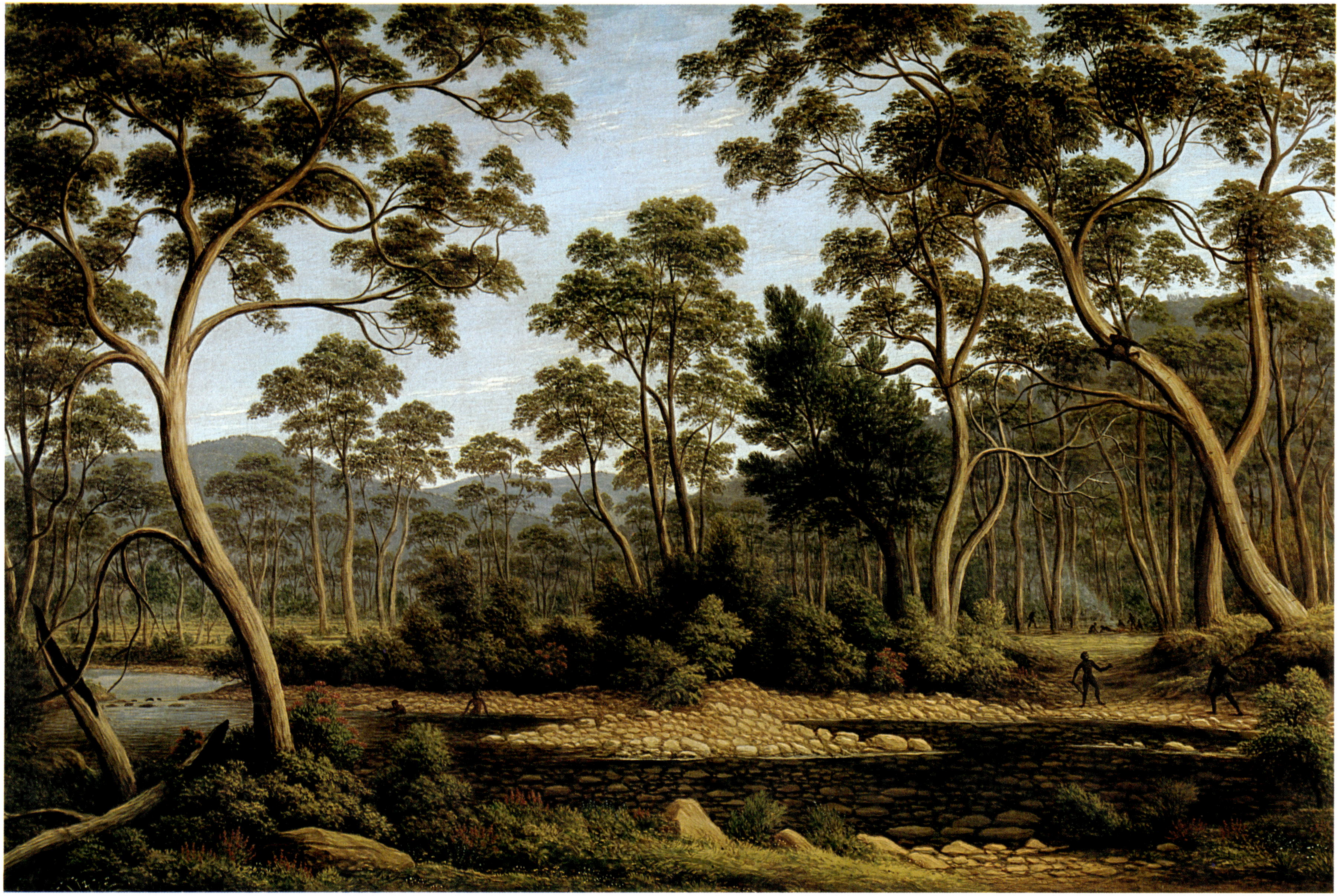

The River Nile, Van Diemen's Land

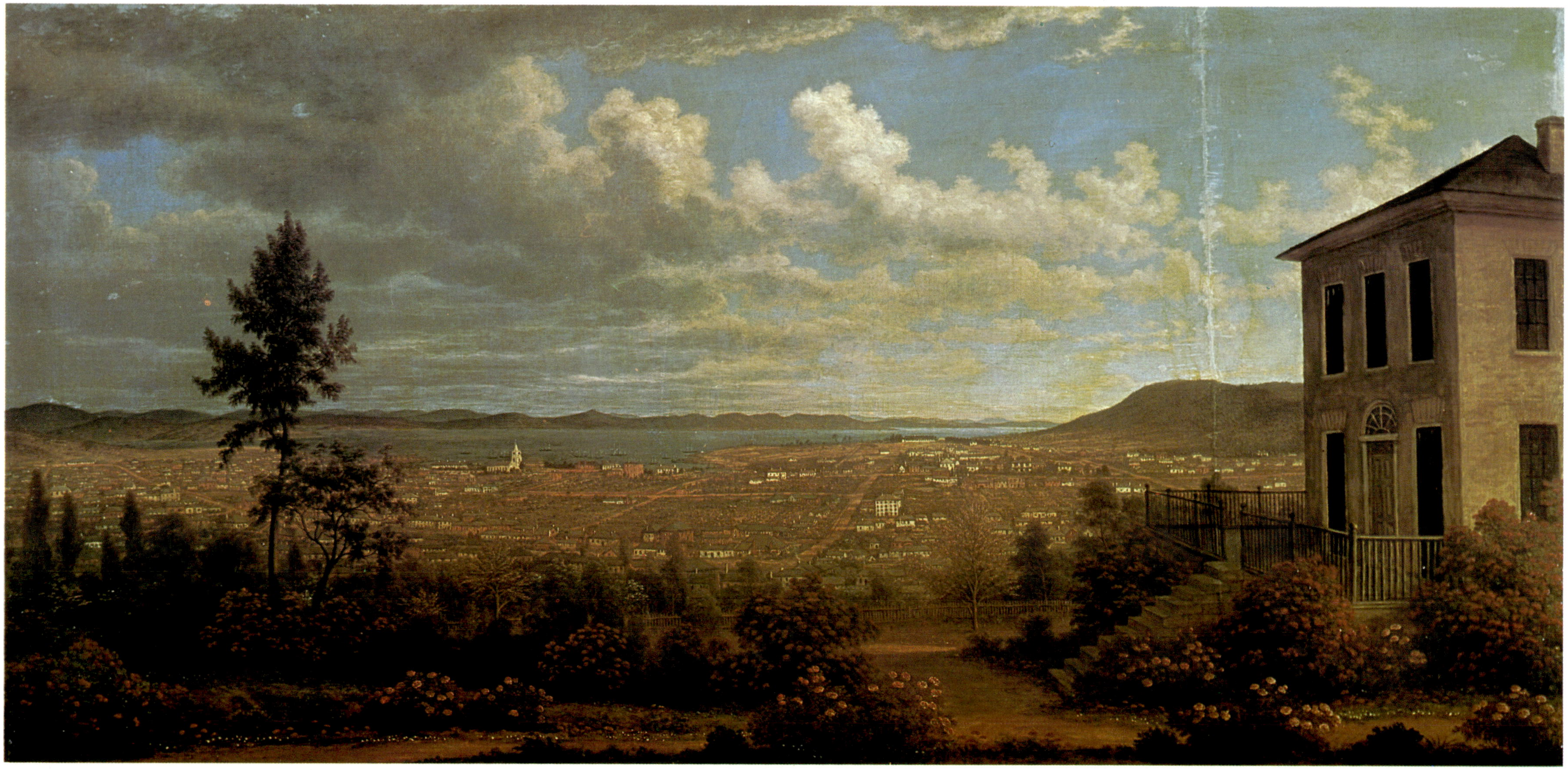

Hobart Town from the Garden Where I Lived

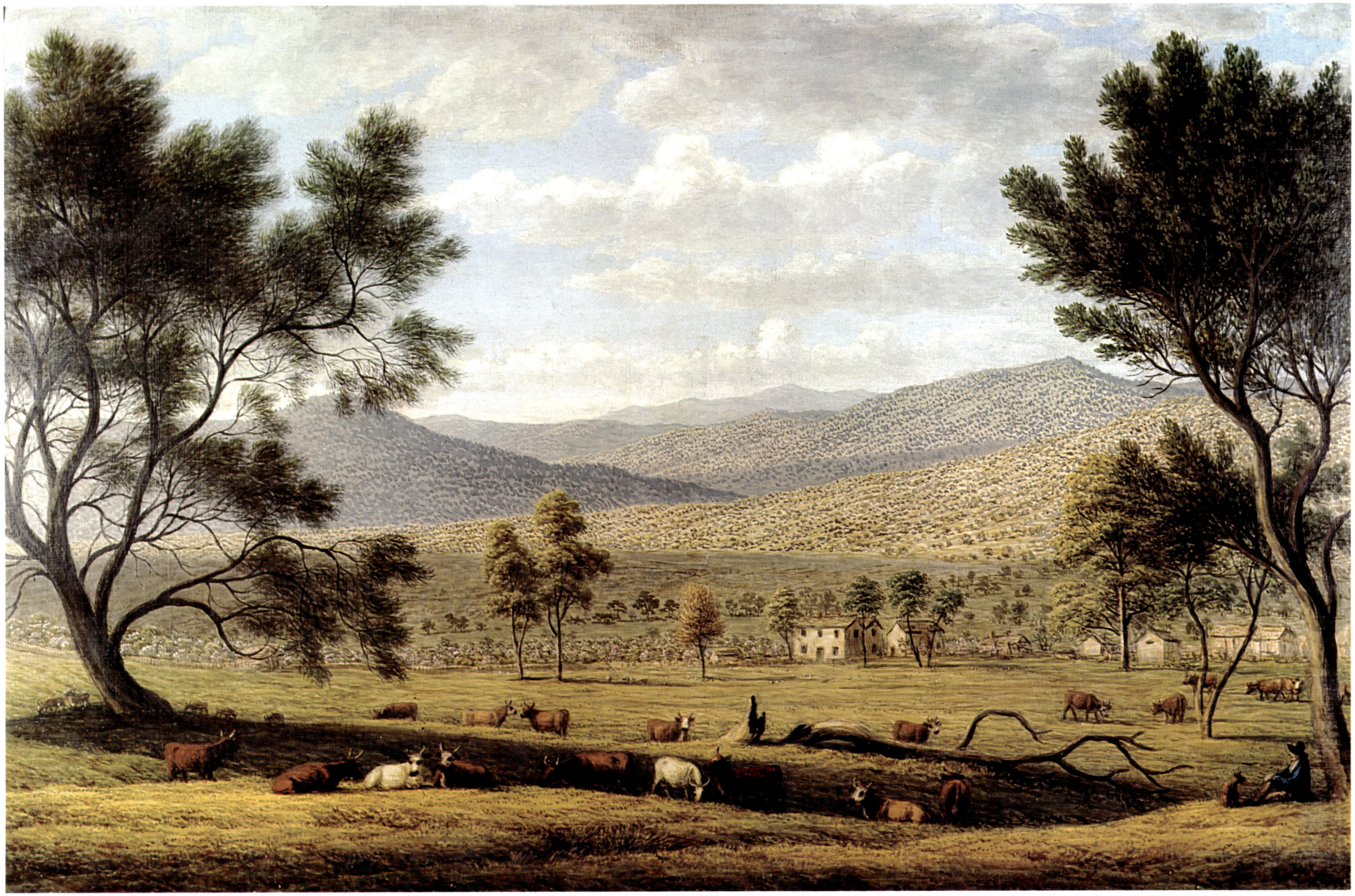

Patterdale Farm

Louis Buvelot

Abram-Louis Buvelot, born at Morges on Lake Geneva, Switzerland, 1814. Arrived Melbourne 1865; died in Victoria 1888.

How did Louis Buvelot achieve what Marcus Clarke praised in 1874 in *Waterpool near Coleraine*? Clarke wrote: 'With true artistic instinct, he has selected a subject which at once touches that sense of the poetic which dwells in awakened memories and suggested contrasts of past with present. It is a hot summer evening, and the sun sinking in an unclouded splendour of pure light more dazzling than the crimson glories of a heavier sky, glows already on the rim of the rising pasture land'.

Buvelot deeply influenced Walter Withers, Julian Ashton and also Frederick McCubbin who partly supplies an answer: Buvelot was able to 'lift the scene from the dreariness of the commonplace to the charm of the picturesque' and added that he, 'the last of the pioneer Artists, is the connecting link between them and that group of young Artists who sprang up in the eighties'.

The artists 'who sprang up in the eighties' formed the Heidelberg School and Buvelot's main influence, aided by the teaching of Julian Ashton, a near and helpful neighbour, was the adoption of open-air techniques and an emphasis on the subjects of the French Barbizon School of the eighteen-forties: rural scenes, noble trees, but without grandeur; no menacing mountains, but settled pastures; no chasms fit only for theatrical cataracts and bandits, but rich, comforting and tamed scenes blessed by the balmy evening or fresh morning light.

Buvelot's paintings were given a dignity, not much revered by the Heidelberg artists, by the use of broad masses of trees shown often as shadowy silhouettes with their foliage fretted at the edges in a way that Buvelot must have learnt from photography, for when he first arrived in Melbourne he set up a photography shop in Bourke Street.

We know little of his work in Switzerland and in Brazil where he lived for eighteen years, but it was his recognition in the Australian landscape of the prevailing and insistent azure and range of golds from bleached grass to brazen sunsets, that impressed Streeton, McCubbin, Withers and Roberts.

The Woolshed near Camperdown
Oil on canvas; 58.7 × 94.2 cm.
Acquired: 1967
Australian National Gallery, Canberra.

By the Creek
Oil on canvas; 1871; 39.2 × 60.5 cm.
Allan R. Henderson Bequest, 1956
National Gallery of Victoria.

Between Tallarook and Yea
Oil on canvas; 1880; 106.7 × 167.7 cm.
Presented by T.W. Stanford, 1902
National Gallery of Victoria.

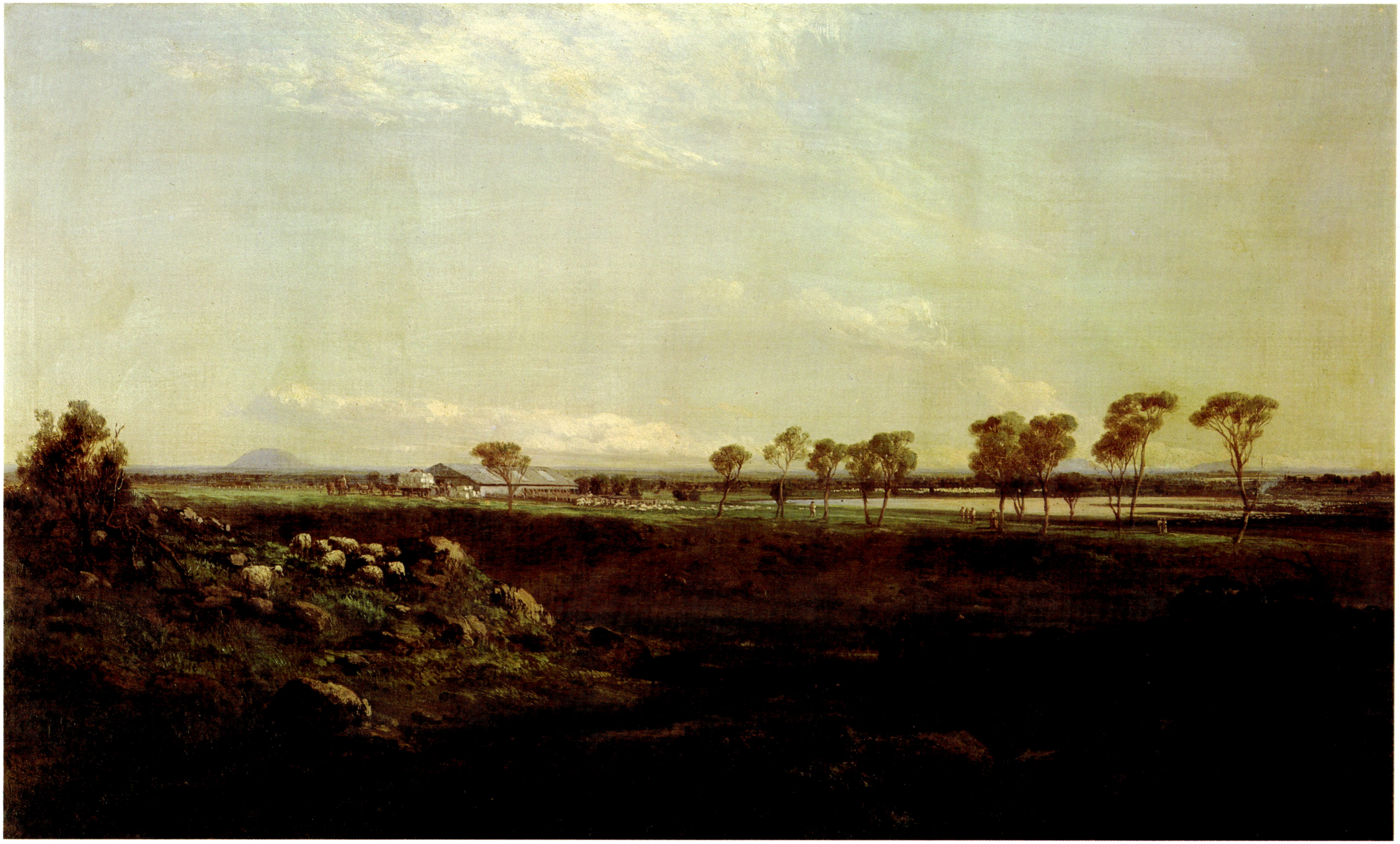

The Woolshed near Camperdown

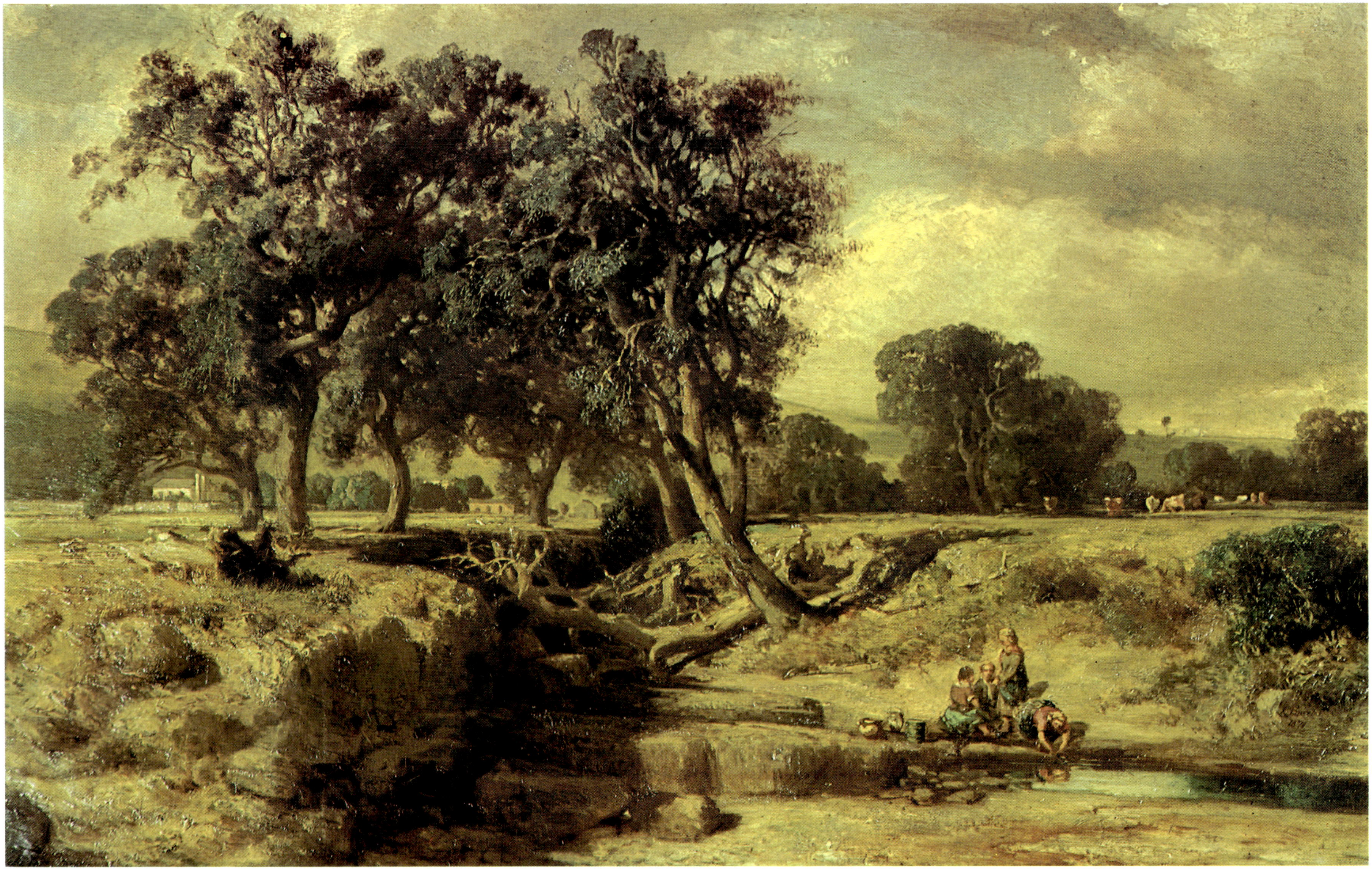

By the Creek

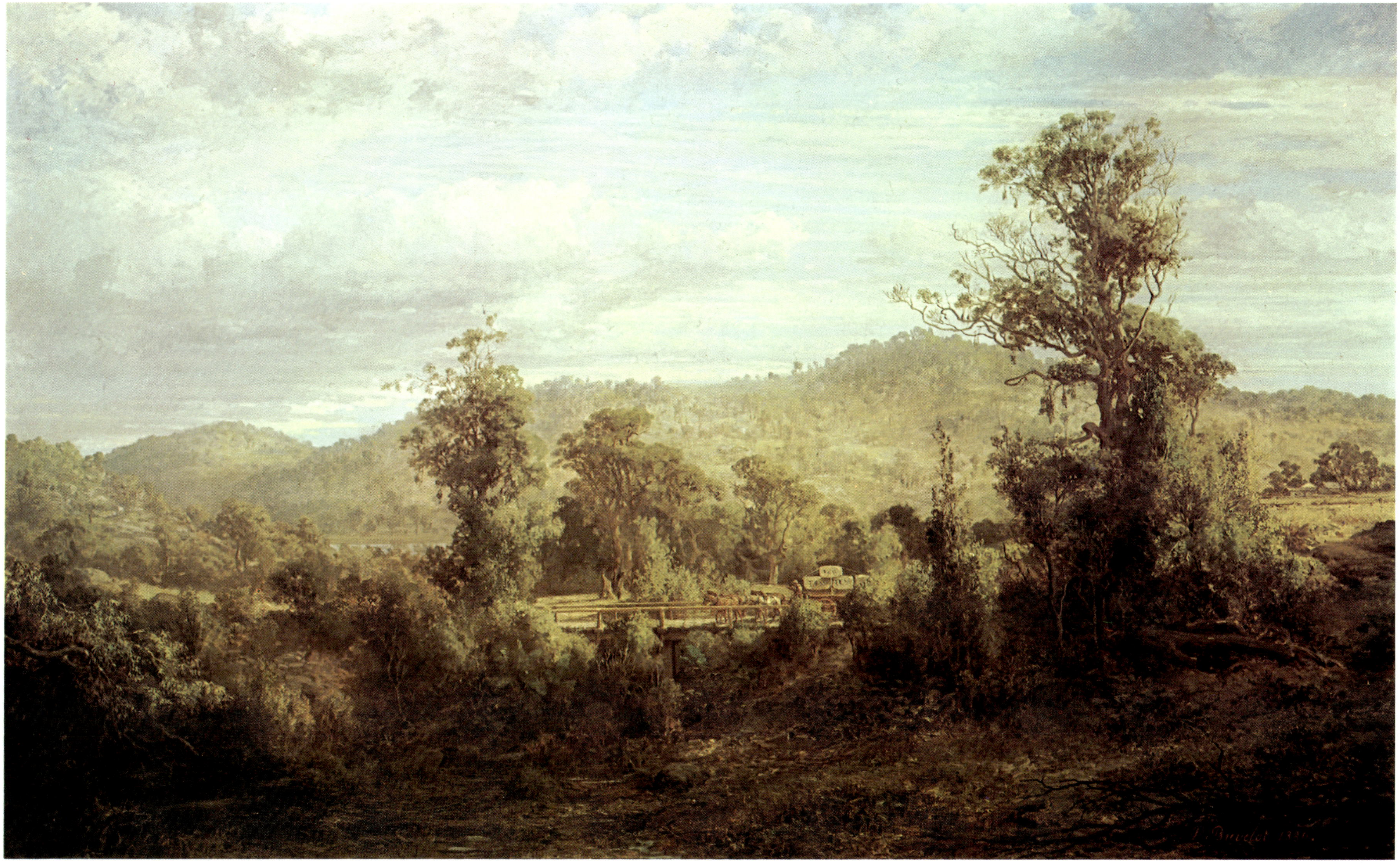

Between Tallarook and Yea

William Dobell

Sir William Dobell, born at Newcastle, New South Wales in 1899; died in Newcastle, 1970.

When, in 1948, William Dobell won the Wynne Prize for landscape painting, it came as a surprise. Not only did he win the Archibald Prize for that year with a portrait of Margaret Olley and with quite a different approach, but he also revealed an interest in the Australian landscape that few expected, for it was thought that he had left his heart in the worn streets and crowded parks of London.

Actually, he found refuge in such landscapes — *Storm Approaching, Wangi,* the Wynne prize winner, and *The Westerly Breeze* were both painted in 1948 — after the debilitating trial of 1944 concerning the portrait of Joshua Smith: and Dobell brought something entirely new to landscape painting and something that deeply influenced his last works. He sought a liquescent flux, a bleached combination of breezes, trees, water and land; the world went white with the wind. It filled the paintings with a ghostly presence that was to lead to his self-portrait of 1965-70 rising, as it were, from ashen, creative fumes, to such white, whispy paintings as *Kindly Man* of 1968, the year of the Opera House painting.

Dobell's method was beautifully attuned to his subject; the Opera House was being fashioned, was arising like an unpredictable monument in Sydney Harbour and was, on a grand scale, explaining the ways of creation to man; so Dobell had it waft up like reality in a dream; he wanted it to partake of the sublimity of the heavens, to enliven the imagination, to be wondrous yet be human and intimate, not remote and austere. To find parallels to his aims one has to turn to Francesco Guardi, Antoine Watteau and Giorgio Morandi — to those artists who allowed reality to verge on the immaterial so that it both arose from and melted into waters and skies. Dobell has made his Opera House a symbol and metaphor of tentative, creative feelings. Conrad Martens' paintings are less visionary but he and Dobell evoke the Harbour as a source of mystical vitality.

The Opera House
(Second version, unfinished)
Oil on hardboard; 1968; 121.9 × 109.2 cm.
Possession of Red Hill Station Pty. Ltd.

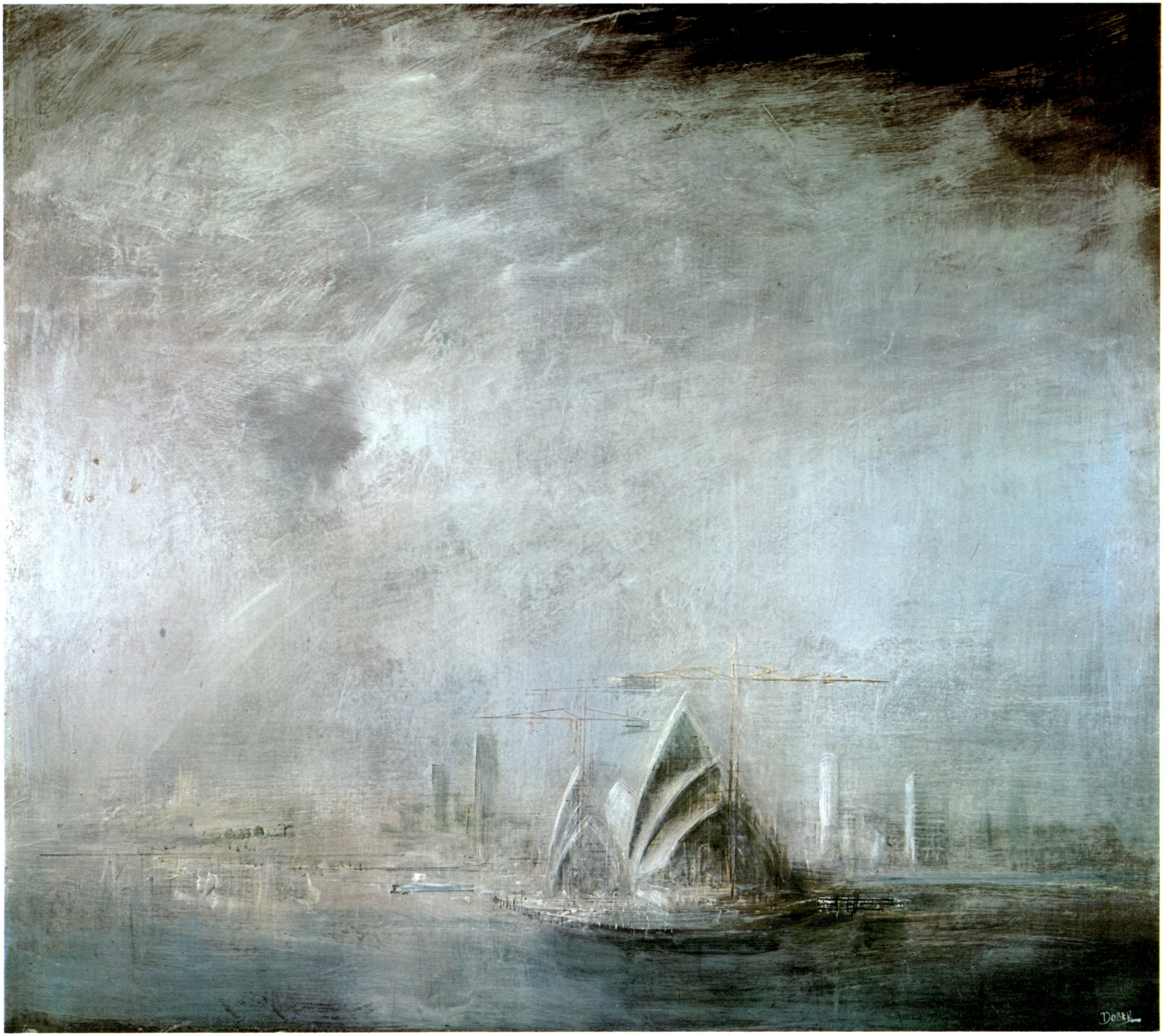

The Opera House

Conrad Martens

Conrad Martens, born Crutched Friars, London, 1801.
Arrived Sydney 1835, where he died in 1878.

There are two Conrad Martens and they often unite; one is the precise recorder of topographical facts, a scientific art that he learned in his two years on the coast of South America in *The Beagle*, on which he was befriended by Charles Darwin; the other is the admirer of James Mallord William Turner, for Martens was moved by the romantic grandeur of cliffs lit by vivid light and of skies shattered by storms. Lionel Lindsay wrote: 'The Turnerian Elevation of Theme was part of his mental texture', but Martens' luminous and opalescent rendition of the sublime was always domesticated by close observation and topographical precision. He could be as close an observer of nature as Darwin, who wrote of his journey to Govett's Leap in The Blue Mountains in January 1836 '. . . early in the day the gulf was filled with a thin blue haze, which, although destroying the general effect, added to the apparent depth at which the forest was stretched below the country on which we were standing'. As *Apsley Ranges* demonstrates, the mountain mists lent themselves to imaginative dreams of sublimity.

Yet, Martens, who was Australia's first consistently intellectual art-theorist, knew that there was no precise convention for rendering nature, whether sublime or scientific.

In his 'Lecture Upon Landscape Painting', he implied the importance of the inventive freedom that should be given landscape artists: 'And here I cannot but express my perfect conviction of the many and great disadvantages under which all labour who aspire to art in this distant country for it is through the *medium of art only that we learn to see nature correctly*'.

Later he added something that indicates why he had such an influence on The Heidelberg School of Arthur Streeton, Tom Roberts and Charles Conder, because his theory of shadows foreruns that of the Impressionists: 'Never make use of cast shadows for your *darks*, but on the contrary keep them as light as possible, which will preserve the breadth as well as give the appearance of air and sunshine'.

It was a generative formula for the broad, frontal and luminous landscape of Australia, but it was not immediately influential, for Eugen von Guerard and Louis Buvelot were happier to depict tenebrous, massy trees and monumental mountains, but when William Dobell approached Sydney Opera House recollections of Martens' sublime, veiled by mists, seem to have stirred his fancy.

Almost a hundred years later the same foreshores that had fascinated Martens inspired Lloyd Rees.

Incidentally, in April 1835, Martens settled in Cumberland Street, The Rocks, that area of Sydney which is the subject of Julian Ashton's painting. It is less than half a mile from where the Opera House was built.

A View of Sydney and Botany Bay
Watercolour on paper; 45.1 × 64.8 cm.
Acquired: 1947
National Gallery of Victoria.

A View of Sydney from Rose Bay with Native Figures
Watercolour on paper; 1836; 45.1 × 64.8 cm.
Acquired 1950
National Gallery of Victoria.

View on the Apsley Ranges, New England
Watercolour on paper; 1874; 52.1 × 74.9 cm.
Commissioned 1874 by the Trustees.
Art Gallery of New South Wales.

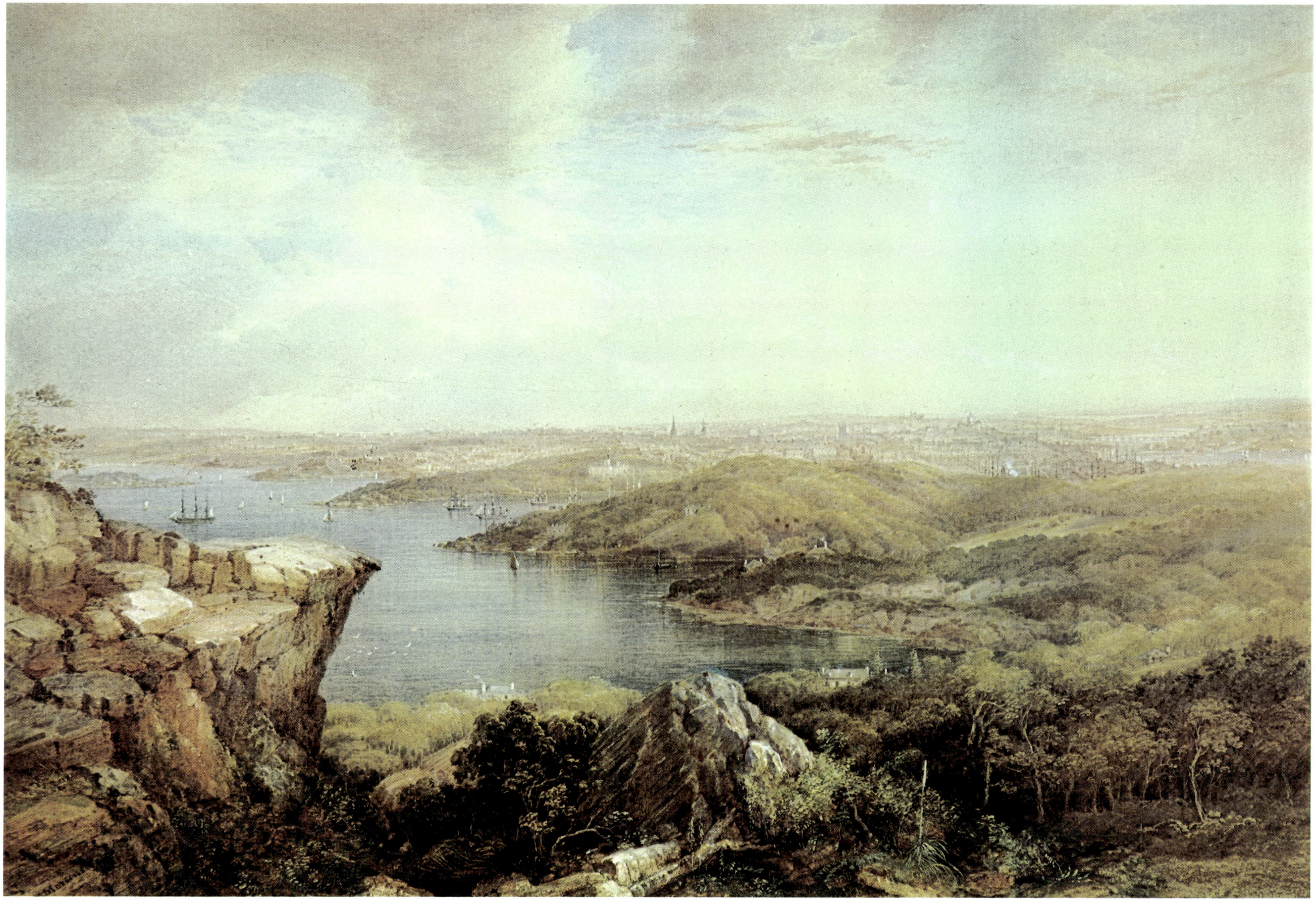

A View of Sydney and Botany Bay

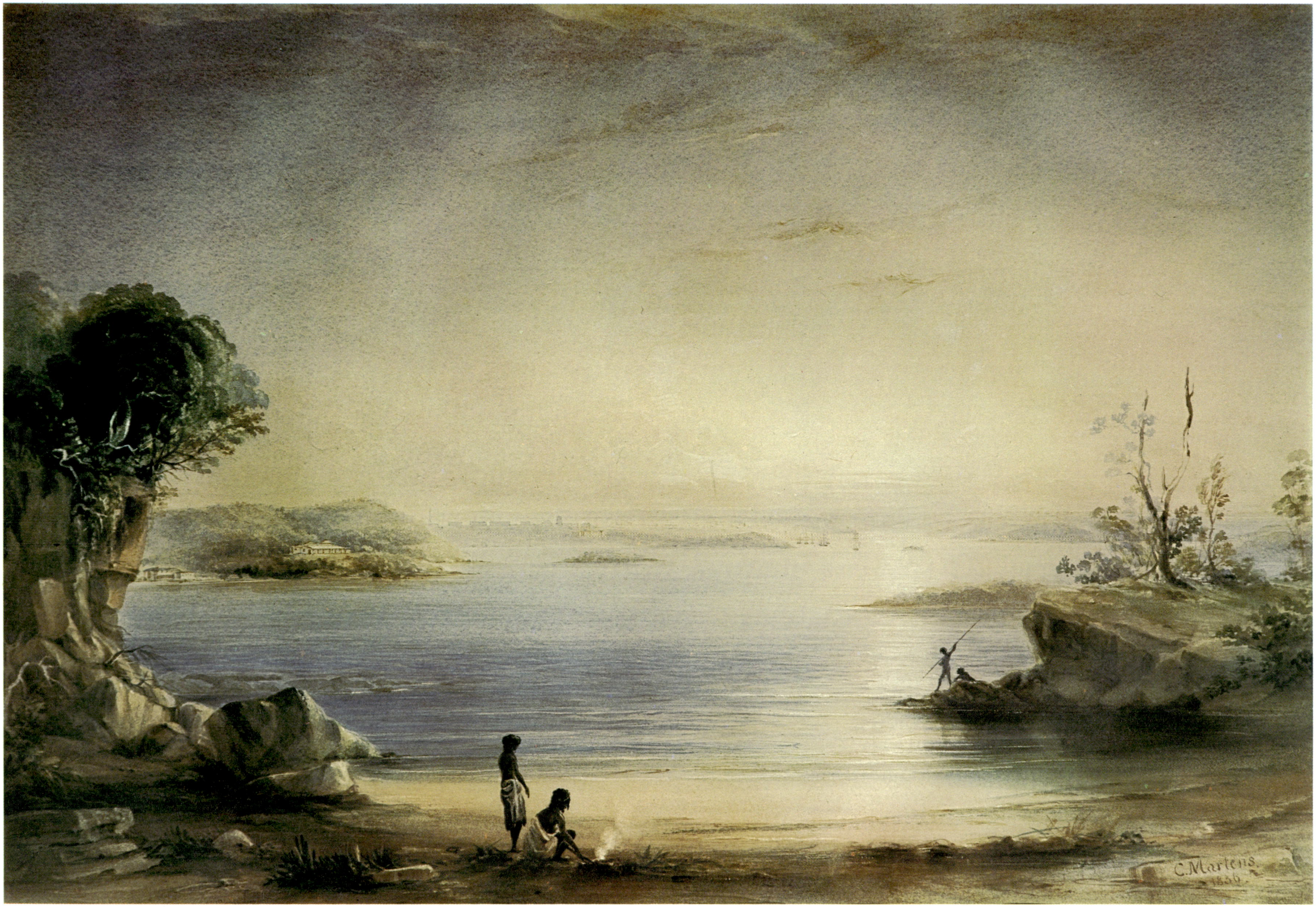

A View of Sydney from Rose Bay with Native Figures

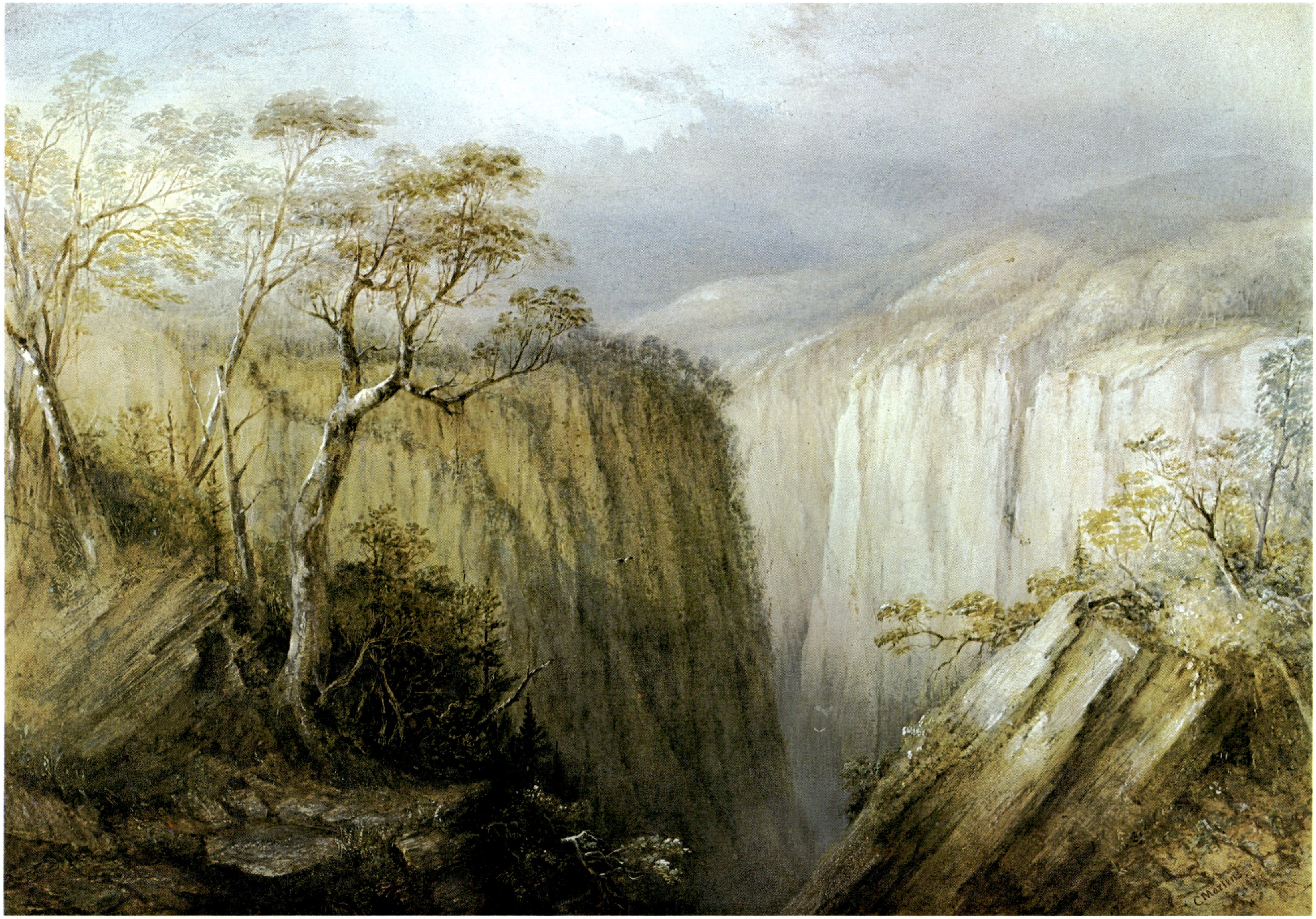

View on the Apsley Ranges, New England

Eugen von Guerard

Johann Joseph Eugen(e) von Guerard, born in Vienna, 1812. Arrived in Melbourne, 1852. Died in England, 1901.

Eugen (he did not use the final 'e' that was wished upon him) von Guerard was one of the most meticulous and painstaking of Australia's early painters. His detail, possessing none of the wilfulness of John Glover's, is often so insistent that one feels enclosed, but he has such a command of the broad and majestic sweep of a landscape, sometimes touching on the sublime, as in *Mount Kosciusco*, at Canberra, that, in comparison, Thomas Baines is a recorder of the exotica that arouses not awe but surprise.

A View of the Snowy Bluff on the Wonnangatta River is a fine play of detail against broad rhythmical movements, a triumph in the relation of foreground to middle distance and distance. It allows the light to play fitfully on rock, hills and clouds but never capriciously or fancifully for it clothes like a skin rather than enlivens like an illumination. None the less his control of massive movements was unparalleled at that time and reflected the thoroughness of his studies in Dusseldorf and his travels in Italy.

His approach was a curious blend of bountifulness with melancholy.

That slender tree on the left of his view of the Snowy Bluff indicates that he could use the forest inventively and that it was not a slight artistic pedantry that led to his being preferred over Louis Buvelot as the first Master of Painting at the Art Gallery School of Victoria when it was founded in 1870, and, after all, he did teach Tom Roberts. Furthermore, his attention to natural detail offered a way out of the sublime and noble.

That he was a closer observer than his formula sometimes permitted is evident from this vignette in his diary of his trip to the Australian goldfields to which he had gone from London with a group of Frenchmen in 1853: 'We occasionally passed human habitation, and one day met a poor fellow who had been attacked by bushrangers and robbed of his horse, and all the money he possessed, and then tied to a tree . . . The poor fellow's legs and arms were terribly swollen from the tight ropes'. But those subjects were pictorially fitter for S.T. Gill and Sidney Nolan.

The contrast with Buvelot is well made by Frederick McCubbin: 'Where Von Guerard and Chevalier went in search of mountains and waterfalls for their subjects, Buvelot interested himself in the life around him, he sympathised with it and painted it'. What von Guerard may have lacked in sympathy he made up for in dedicated scrutiny.

A View of the Snowy Bluff on the Wonnangatta River
Oil on canvas; 1864; 95 × 152.5 cm.
Acquired: 1965
National Gallery of Victoria.

Mount Kosciusko
Oil on canvas; 1866; 107 × 153 cm.
Acquired: 1870
National Gallery of Victoria.

Mount Kosciusko
Oil on canvas; 19 November, 1867; 66.2 × 117.0 cm.
Acquired: 1973, private collection, Mexico.
Australian National Gallery, Canberra.

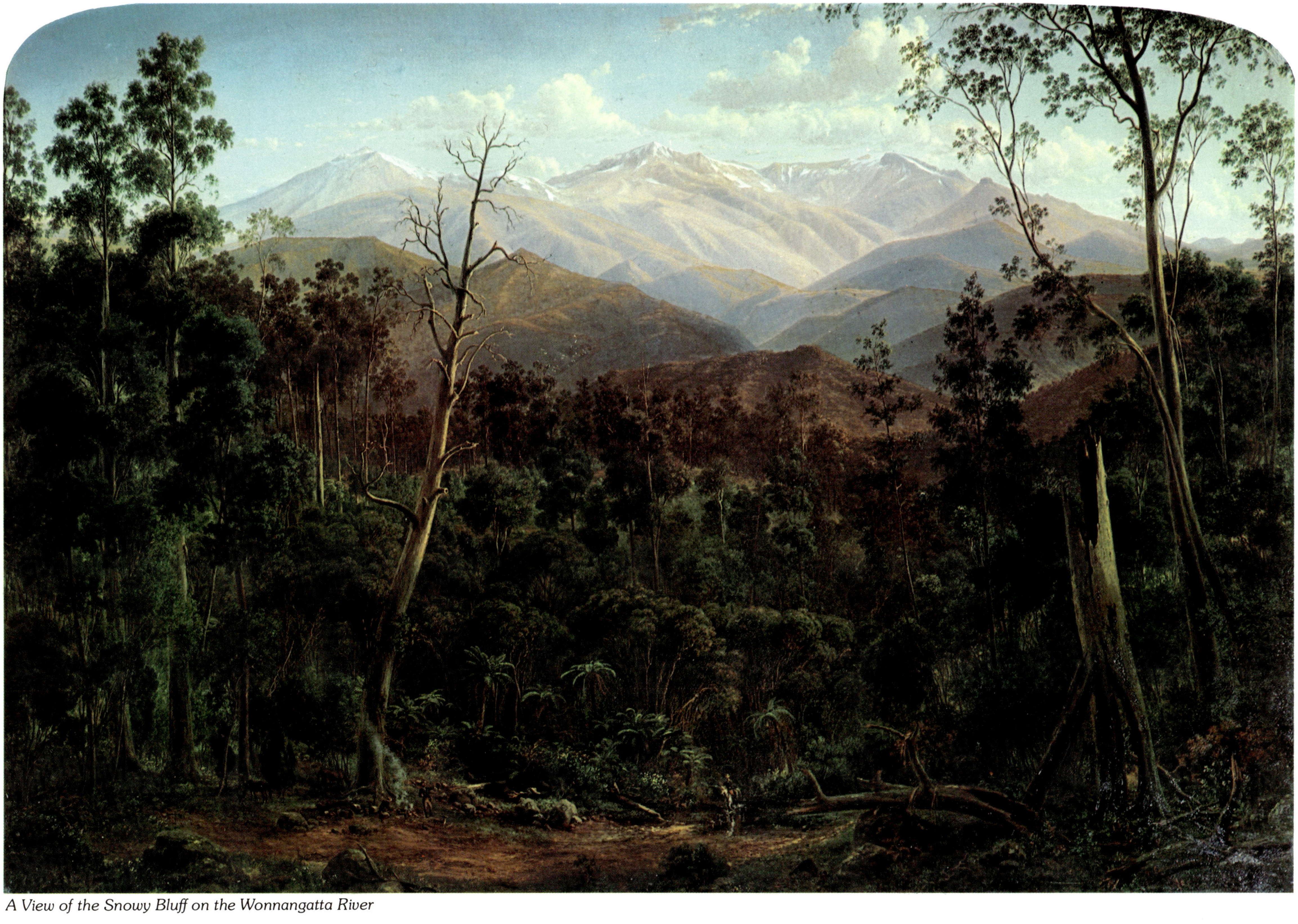

A View of the Snowy Bluff on the Wonnangatta River

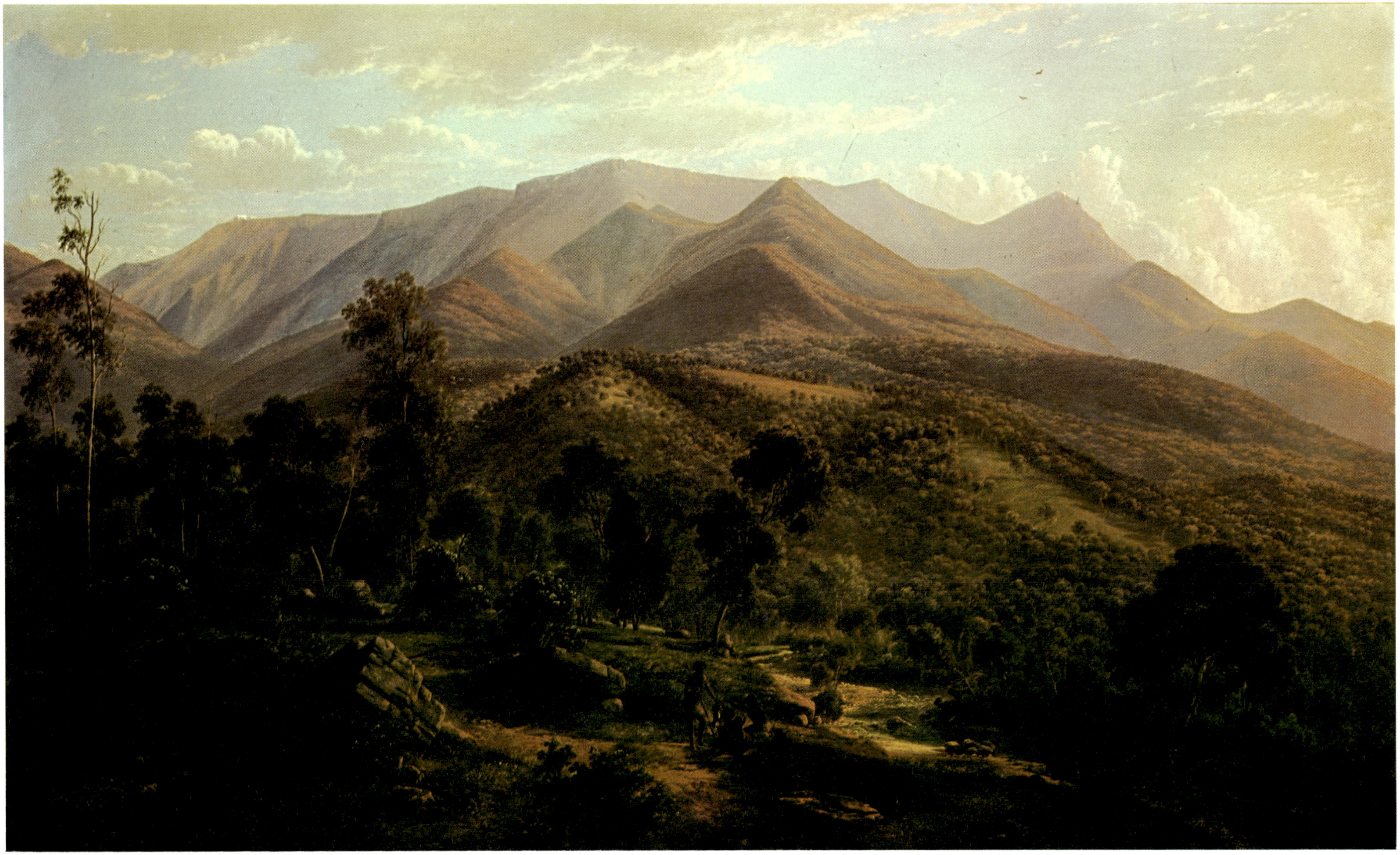

Mount Kosciusko

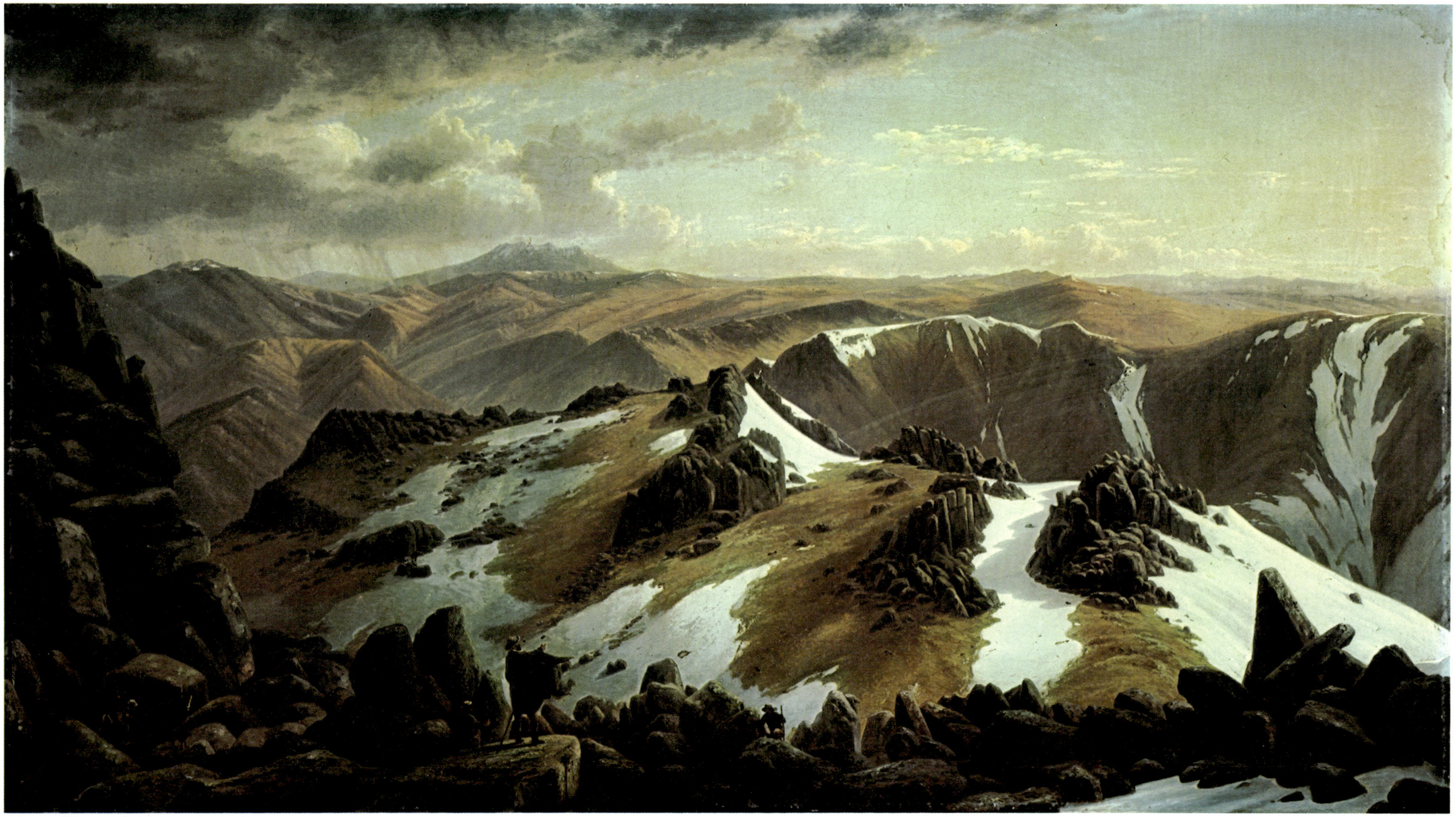

Mount Kosciusko

Thomas Baines

Thomas Baines, born Norfolk, 1820. Visited Australia from 1855-57. Died in Durban, South Africa, 1875.

Thomas Baines came to Australia in 1855 as artist and storeman to A.C. Gregory's expedition in search of Ludwig Leichhardt. Baines was already a well-trained observer of landforms, trees and animals unfamiliar to Europeans. In 1842, he had gone to Cape Town and had accompanied explorers into the interior of Africa. Nine years later he was artist-draughtsman to the British forces in the Eighth Kaffir War. Helen Luckett of the Southampton Art Gallery considered that 'when Baines, whose early Cape Town paintings were influenced by Western art, left the Cape he responded to Africa with a lack of inhibition and a freedom which established him as a leader of a new school of painting altogether; a colonial school which, although it owes its parentage to European art, has a quite separate validity'; the critic, Terry Ingram, wrote: 'He was it seems some kind of equivalent to Australia's John Glover'.

Baines' work in Australia was praised by Gregory and he was lauded on his return to England. Because he was considered an artist who was, as well, an accurate and scientific geographer, he was elected a Fellow of the Royal Geographical Society. The fact that his four Australian views are framed together tends to indicate that they were considered precise reports of aspects of the landscape.

However exotic the flora and curious the incidents in his work, Baines exemplifies the transition of artist from illustrator and reporter to landscape painter, for his quartet achieves both aesthetic and scientific harmony. Ecological unity had to prevail over the presentation of nature as a set of botanical specimens sometimes supported by a scientifically irrelevant background, however aesthetically appropriate that background might be.

Baines returned to South Africa and joined Livingstone's expedition to the Zambesi, but was dismissed for petty pilfering. Though the justice of the charge was questioned, his reputation suffered, but not so much that admiration was withheld from his Mashonaland drawings and paintings. He is now highly regarded in South Africa and was given a retrospective exhibition at Rhodes National Gallery, Salisbury, and at London's Fine Art Society in 1975.

The exotic yields to familiarity; in Jock Marshall and Russell Drysdale's 'Journey Among Men' (1962) a drawing by Drysdale of the gouty-stemmed baobab tree is described as 'most extravagantly droll'.

Expedition to North Australia (Four Panels)
Oil on canvas; 1868; 102.9 × 145.5 cm.
1. *The Victoria River* 457 × 66.0 cm. 2. *Gouty Stem Tree* 45.9 × 66.3 cm. 3. *Stampede of the Pack Horses* 45.8 × 66.2 cm. 4. *Pandanus at Quail Island, Paterson's Bay* 45.7 × 66.5 cm.
Acquired: 1975
Australian National Gallery, Canberra.

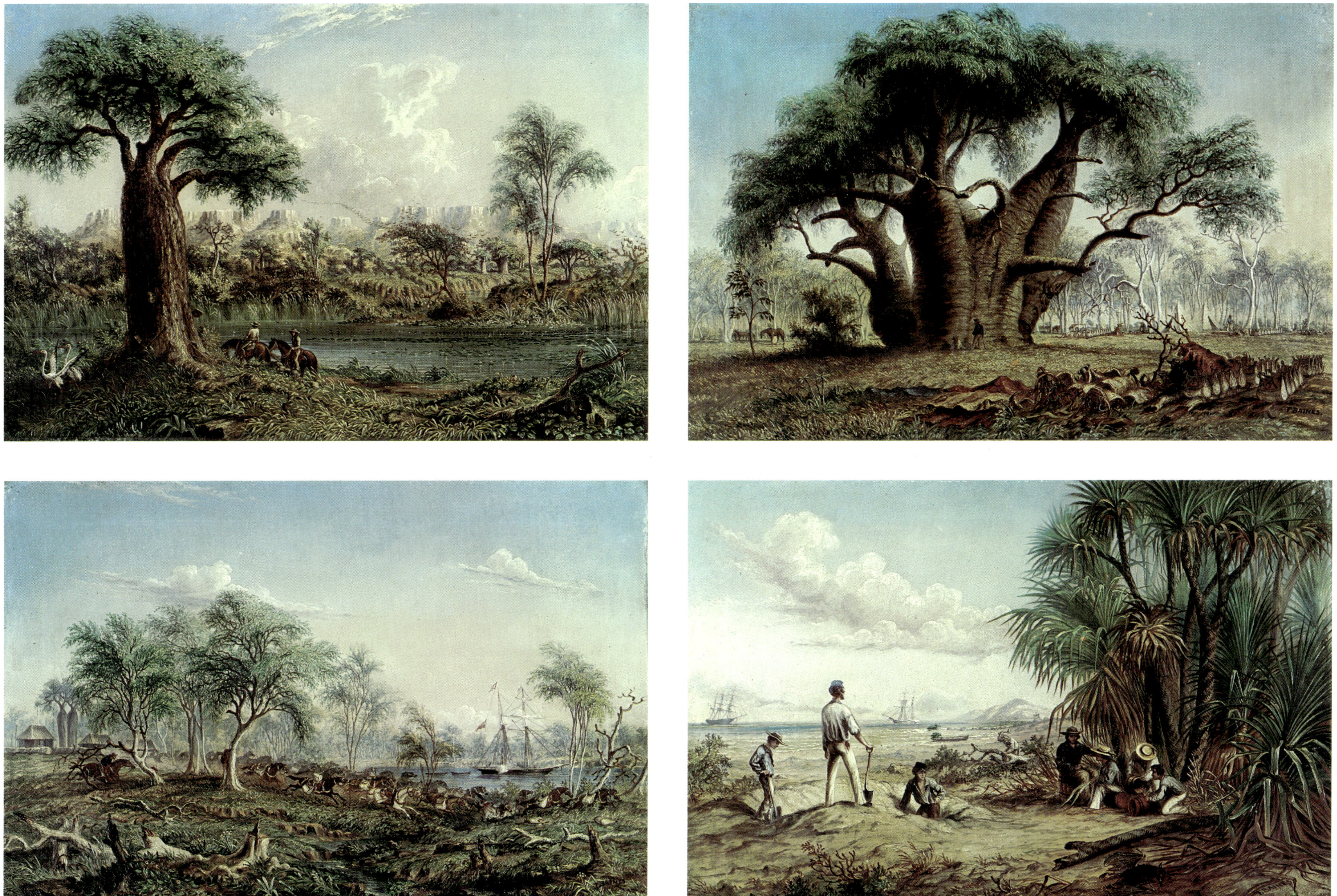

Expedition to North Australia (Four Panels)

S.T. Gill

Samuel Thomas Gill, born Somerset, England, 1818.
Arrived in Adelaide 1839; died in Melbourne, 1880.

For three-quarters of a century, until Donald Friend, Sidney Nolan and Brett Whiteley, S.T. Gill had the sharpest pen in the South. He recorded with sprightly directness the social activities of the colony, first in South Australia, where he had accompanied Horrock's expedition in 1846, and then on the goldfields of Victoria. Camps, mountain ranges, grog tents, herders, shops, street scenes, funerals, skeletons, the equipment of the mining fields and explorers along with topography were registered as he had promised when he set up a studio in Adelaide in 1839: 'Correct Resemblances of horses, dogs, etc., with local scenery etc., executed to order. Residences sketched and transferred to paper suitable for home conveyance'. He did not always keep his promise, and happily his delineations are often satires and caricatures, but never so insistent that factual evidence is obscured. He was, in fact, a visual journalist of the vernacular — whether purely objective or humorously derisive. Heroes of the Outback there may be, but they are presented as men among men, and behind his factual and ironic reportage is an early sign of the democratic temper that was to flourish in the Heidelberg School. His ideal could have been the poor old beggar in the sung ballad, 'Bullocky Joe':

'A better poor old beggar
Never cracked an honest crust,
A tougher poor old beggar
Never drug a whip through dust

His team got bogged on Five-mile Creek,
Bill lashed and swore and cried,
"If Nobbie don't get me out of this
I'll tattoo his bloody hide".'

Gill was first admired for his records of the goldfields where he went in 1851, but it was the record rather than the art that was appreciated, somewhat like the fate of the popular print in Japan in the Nineteenth Century, now sought both as art and reportage.

Such lack of recognition no doubt contributed to his decline into drunkenness; the corpse found on the steps of the Melbourne Post Office in 1880 and given a pauper's grave was that of S.T. Gill.

Mount Gambier
Oil on board; 1852; 22.5 × 30.3 cm.
Presented 1958 in memory of Arthur H.S. Piggin by his family.
National Gallery of Victoria.

The Overlanders
Watercolour on paper; c.1865; 33.6 × 56.2 cm.
Acquired: 1946
Art Gallery of New South Wales.

Botany Bay in 1874
Watercolour on paper; 1874; 16.5 × 37.5 cm.
Presented 1914 by Mr J.H. Connell.
National Gallery of Victoria.

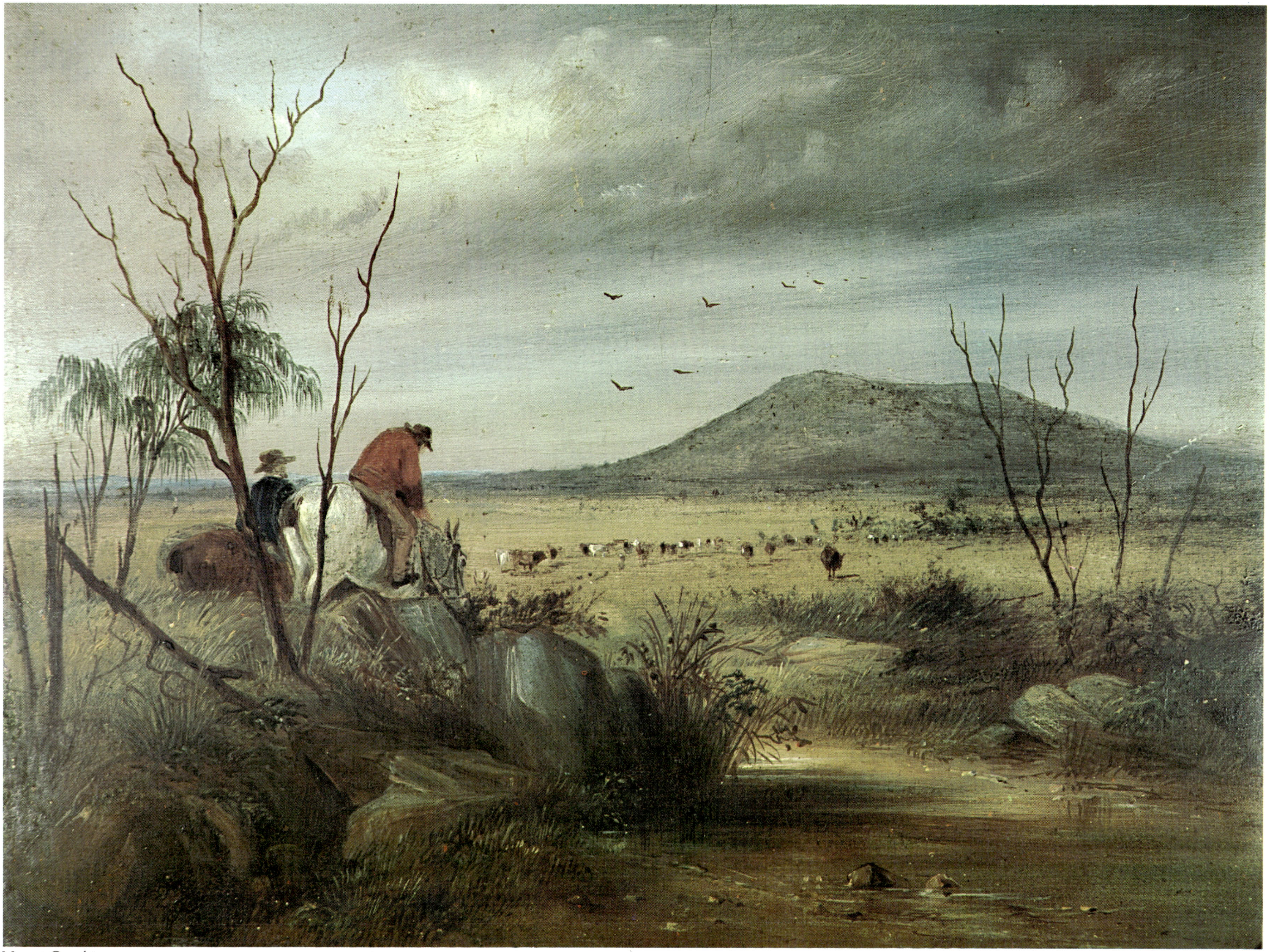

Mount Gambier

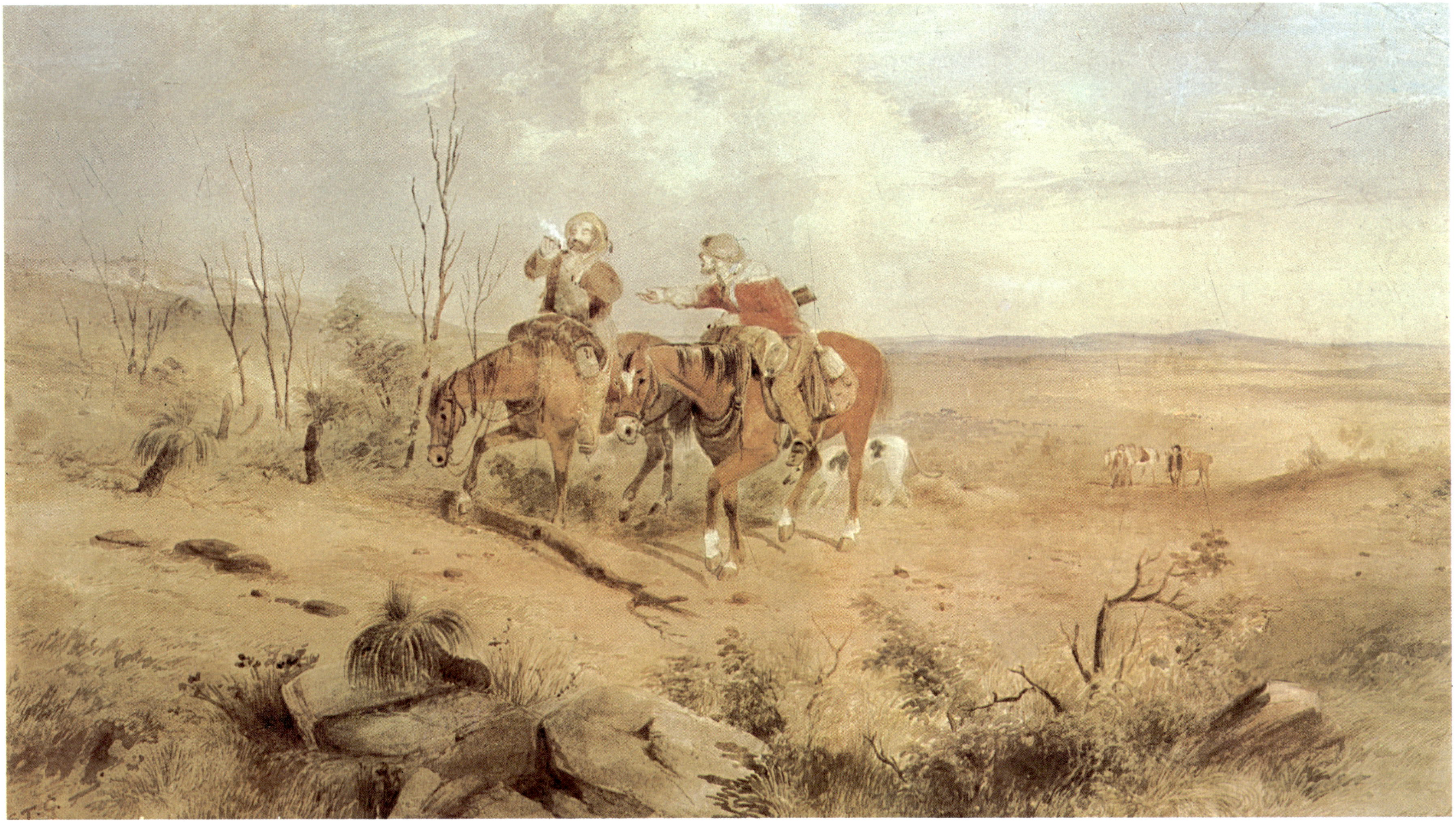

The Overlanders

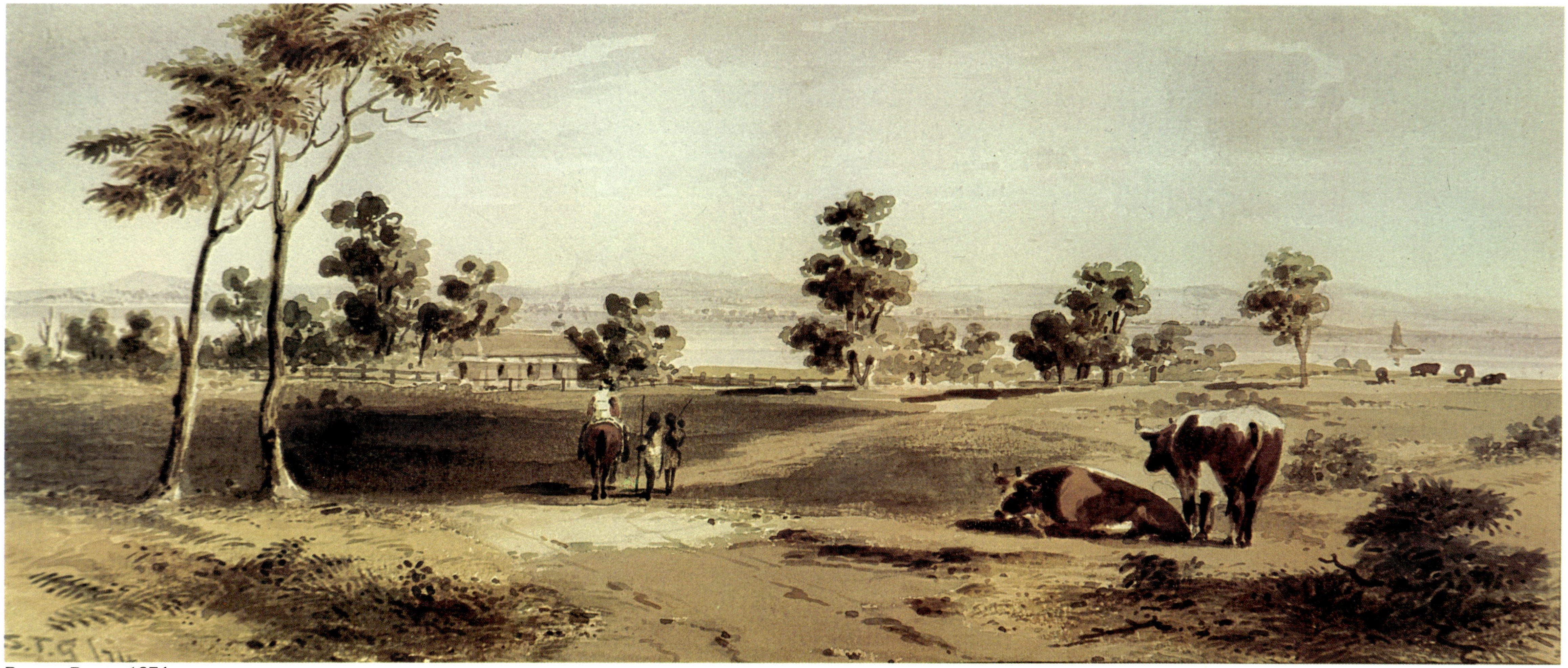

Botany Bay in 1874

Lawrence Daws

Lawrence Daws, born Adelaide, 1927. Lives in the Glasshouse Mountains, Queensland.

Lawrence Daws trained as an architect and studied geology at the South Australian School of Mines and at Adelaide University; he has always been interested in the structure of what lies on and below the earth. His earlier paintings were divided by undulating lines so that objects, houses and people were caught in a net of all-embracing rhythms.

In 1948-49 he conducted an oil survey in New Guinea and perhaps that primitive world deepened his interest in Jungian psychoanalysis and the theory of symbolism, because he seems to have concluded that the rhythmical net was not enough to hold the world together and so he painted a series of works in which mandalas float as discs and rings over a world that is disordered and desolate. The mandala brings all that is disparate and unresolved to an harmonious and paradisal state, a notion reinforced by Daws' habitually beautiful surfaces.

Jungian theorists are also interested in the traumatic and symbolic effect of great disasters that appal and fascinate mankind. Daws has done a series of paintings on such themes with tiny figures fleeing, somewhat in the manner of Juan Genoves, but Genoves depicts the terror of totalitarian states; Daws is entranced by the effects of calamities like mine disasters and train crashes.

After he returned to live in Australia in 1970, he spent a month south of Kalgoorlie and saw a photograph in the Marvel Loch Hotel of rescuers and rescued in the 1913 mine disaster. In a letter Daws notes, 'The imagery of transformation probably had more to do with the upheavals of leaving London after ten years and re-establishing contact with Australia, than the actual disaster'.

With S.T. Gill, as in *The Overlanders*, it is human personality, even if just plucked from the mass, that counts; with Arthur Streeton's *Fire's On, Lapstone Tunnel*, human beings are merely Impressionist notations, but in Daws they are mankind fleeing across a greyed land from the unknown with a brown and gold cloud advancing like a modern aerial missile. Daws' science has been transformed into vivid science-fiction and his Jungian interests have produced a many-faceted Surrealism.

The 1913 Mine Disaster
Oil on canvas; 1970; 121.9 × 121.9 cm.
Courtesy of the Rudy Komon Gallery, Sydney.

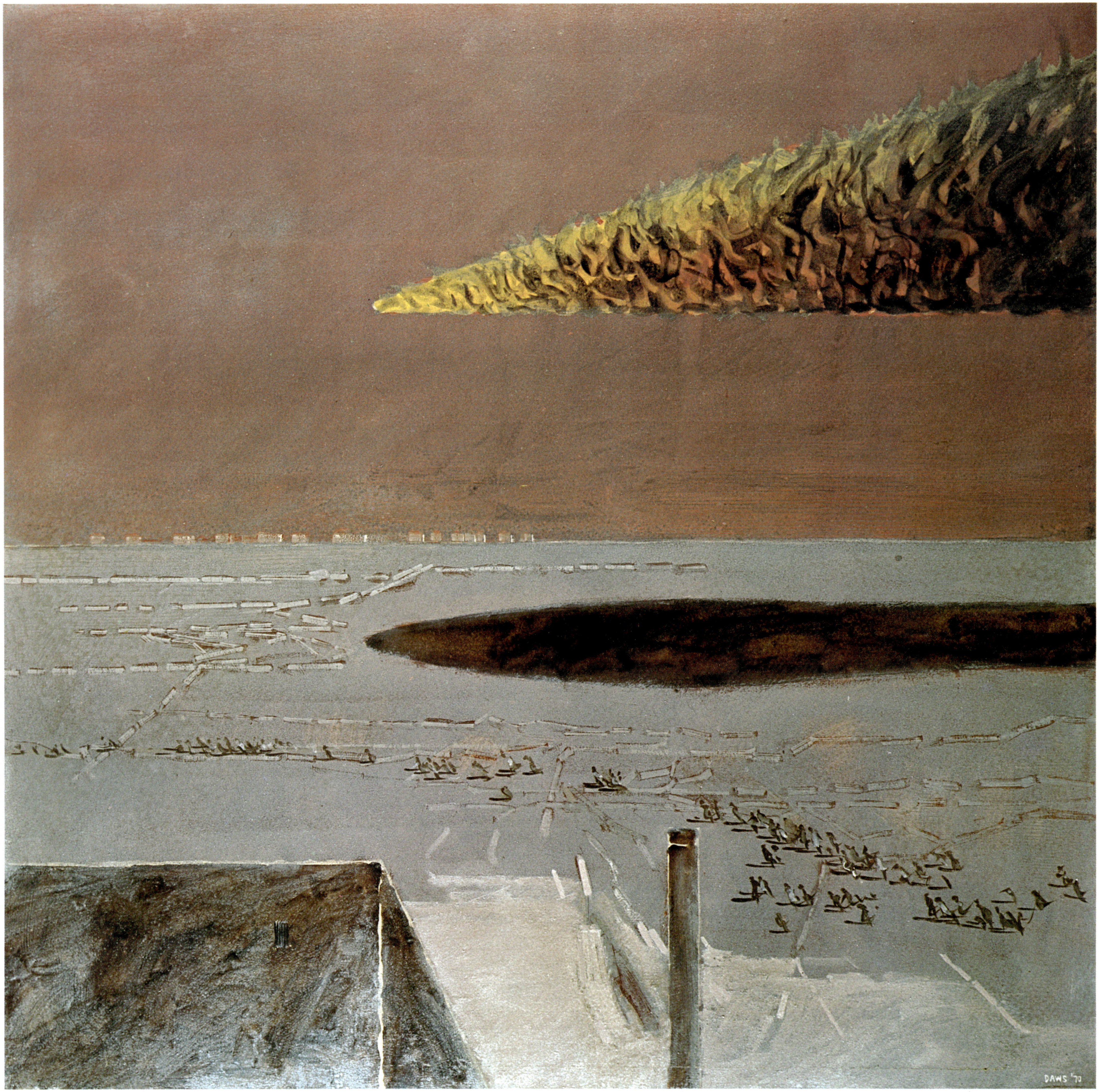

The 1913 Mine Disaster

William Piguenit

William Charles Piguenit, born Hobart Town, 1836; died in Sydney, 1914.

Although William Piguenit relished the majestic, imposing and mysterious, he was entranced by the river-flats and low horizons of the inland, where, as with sixteenth century Dutch painting, the only background was the rolling or tattered clouds. Piguenit, a largely self-taught painter, has been considered rather academic with 'the dust of the schoolroom' thick upon his work; and yet, in the local context, he was more revolutionary than is generally conceded.

He won the Wynne Prize for landscape painting in 1904 with *Thunderstorm on the Darling* four years after the prize had been established, but in 1895 he painted from sketches and memory his *Flood in the Darling 1890,* without a single towering tree in the Dutch or Barbizon manner, without a foreground sapling or reed to rivet sky to water and without the traditional play of foreground against distance and middle distance. The low horizon with its suggestion of infinity predicts the Wimmera paintings of Arthur Boyd, the Queensland Outback of Sidney Nolan and the Surrealistic remoteness of Russell Drysdale.

Piguenit's horizon is a silver slice of light emphasized and enclosed by the row of brownish trees; it just divides the watery, patchy sky from the expanse of waters so vast that reeds and birds are reduced to notations. No other Australian painter has achieved such an effect of opalescent wetness. Nolan's river is slow and opaque; Streeton's stream is luminous, but Piguenit has caught the irridescent transience of the flood.

Something of the same limpid light bathes Mount Wellington, Tasmania. Piguenit's longing was for the mist that veiled and enhanced, but he was also enraptured by intimations of concealed violence as in *The Upper Nepean;* there is the same central sliver of light that he saw on the Darling, but it reflects vehement skies. Despite the massy rocks the scene looks insubstantial, and this has been achieved without the usual theatrical contrivances of late Romanticism — those frail bridges, huts on crags and haze-enshrouded castles.

Mount Wellington from New Town Bay, Tasmania, 1872
Oil on canvas; 1879; 46.4 × 69.2 cm.
Acquired: 1972
National Gallery of Victoria.

The Upper Nepean
Oil on canvas; 1889; 90.5 × 129.9 cm.
Acquired: 1889
Art Gallery of New South Wales.

The Flood in the Darling 1890
Oil on canvas; 1895; 122.5 × 199.3 cm.
Acquired: 1895
Art Gallery of New South Wales.

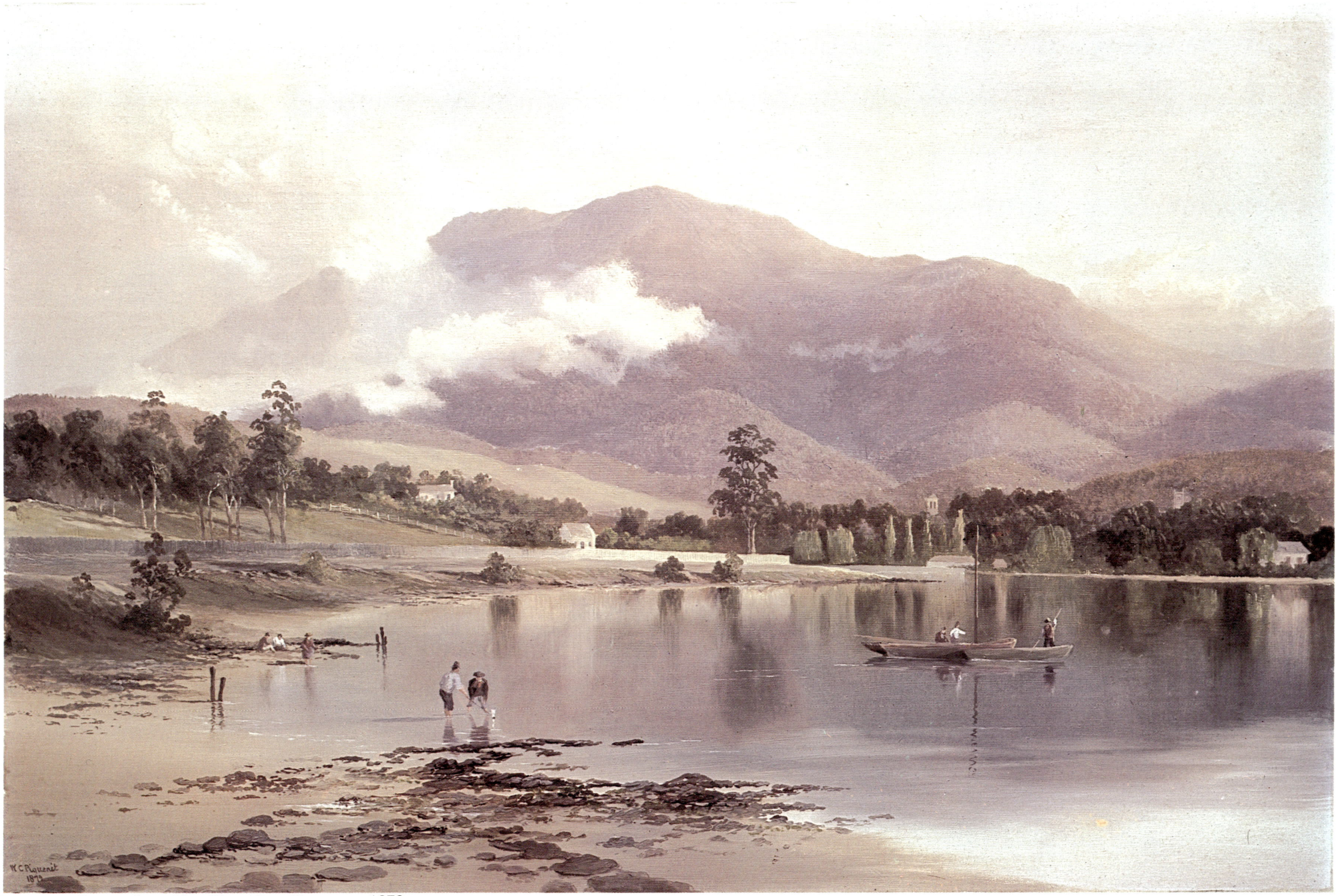

Mount Wellington from New Town Bay, Tasmania, 1872

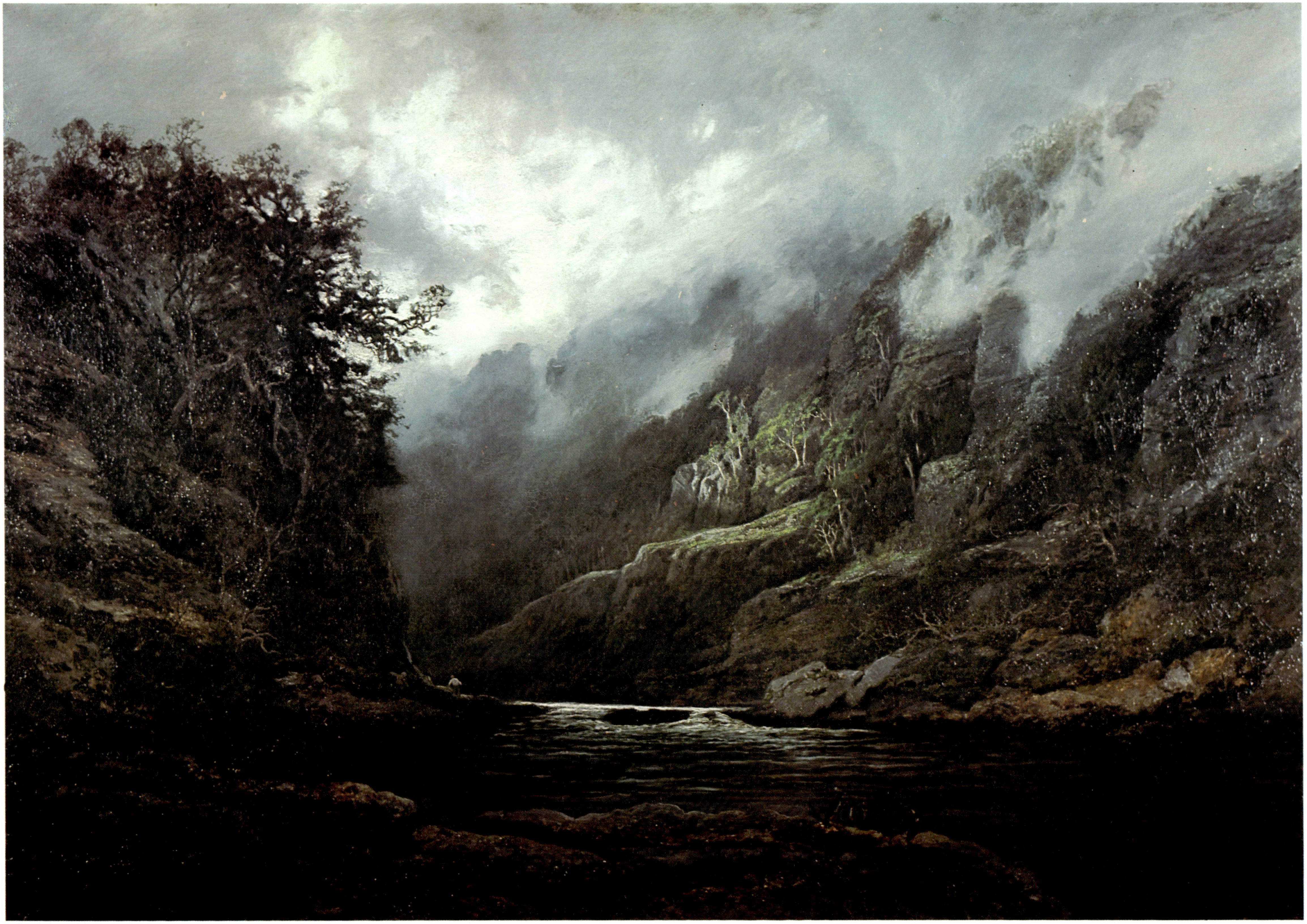

The Upper Nepean

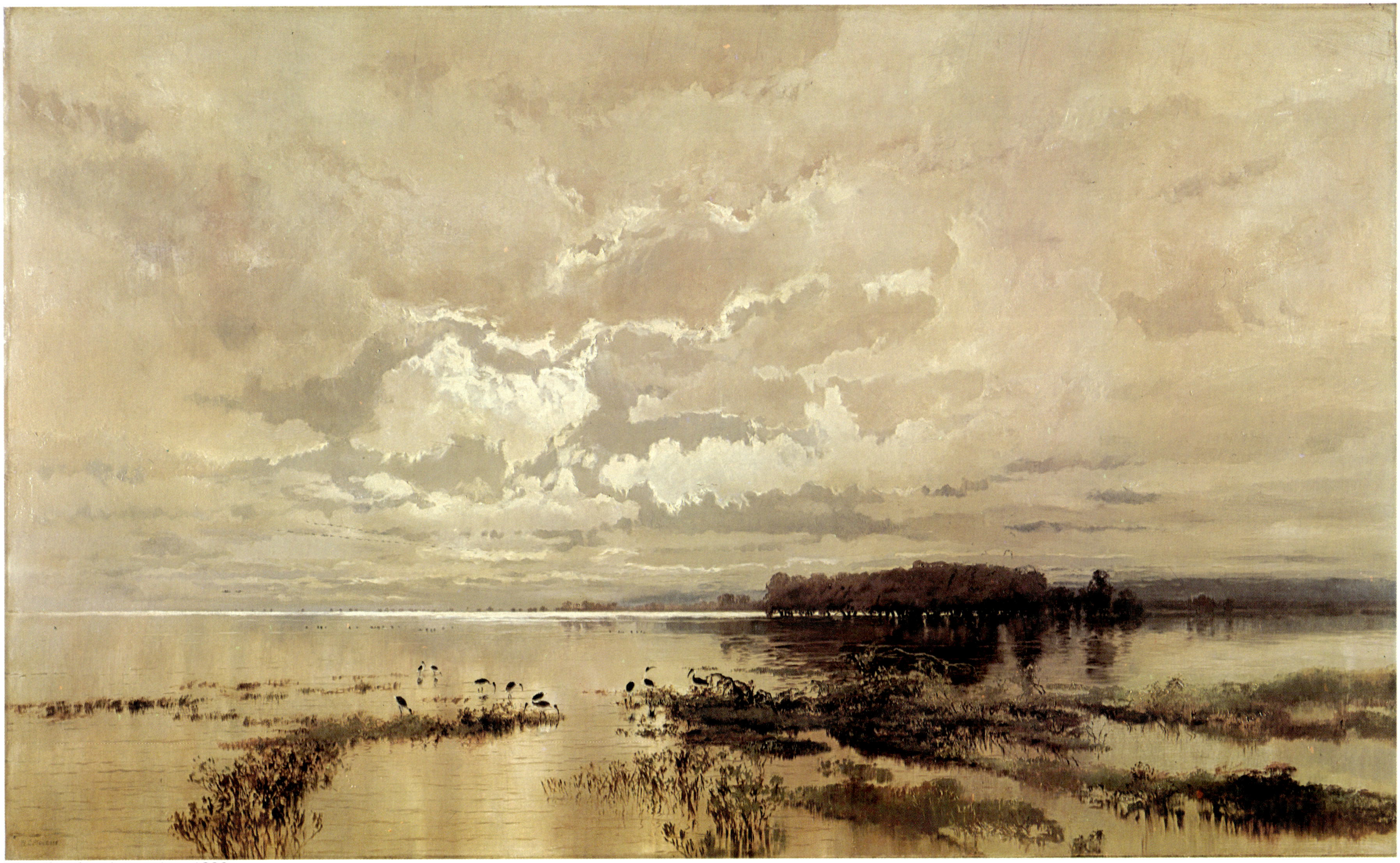

The Flood in the Darling 1890

Robert Juniper

Robert Juniper, born Merredin, Western Australia, 1929; lives in Western Australia.

With *Murchison Sand Plain* Robert Juniper won the 1975 (awarded in 1976) Wynne Prize for landscape painting and so brought more emphatically to notice an artist whose work is rarely seen in eastern Australia. He has thoroughly identified himself with the landscape and life in the West; after he had spent from 1936-49 in England he returned to Western Australia to work on a farm.

Like his fellow Westralian, Guy Grey-Smith, he combines abstraction with figurative imagery but he is a close observer of the general aspects of a place or region. Having established the identifiable characteristics, he adds intimate minutiae — rocks, seed pods, grasses, sand dunes, stunted trees, thick tussocks and wind-blown leaves. Such thematically decorative additions activate the broad areas of the painting by multiplying focal points and leading the eye easily across what is often a chaotic scene.

Juniper establishes the atmosphere of a location and then, lest it appear too summary, adds specific notations; in contrast, Guy Grey-Smith reduces the view to essential blocky masses with only a stray touch of colour resembling decoration. Juniper's vistas are sun-drenched, golden and bleached, shifting like the sands, capricious like the winds; they are created from a modulated and subtle flux of forms and hues. The burnt blond and amber hills recall Blamire Young, but Juniper's views are not controlled by strong horizons for the rhythms are loose and easy and often, as in *Murchison Sand Plain,* earth and sky are not asserting their differences.

The whole painting seems to be afloat as untrammelled seed pods, blackish and brown spots and grasses sweep across the facade of the painting. The sky looks freshly swept. It is a proliferating, pollinating period that one feels will be momentarily stilled. It is a landscape drenched with golden pollen. It has resemblances to *William Piguenit's Flood in the Darling 1890,* for the Piguenit is equally vast, similarly fluid and transitory, and equally a prelude to transformations of the landscape.

Murchison Sand Plain
Oil on canvas; 1975; 181 × 181 cm.
Possession of the artist.

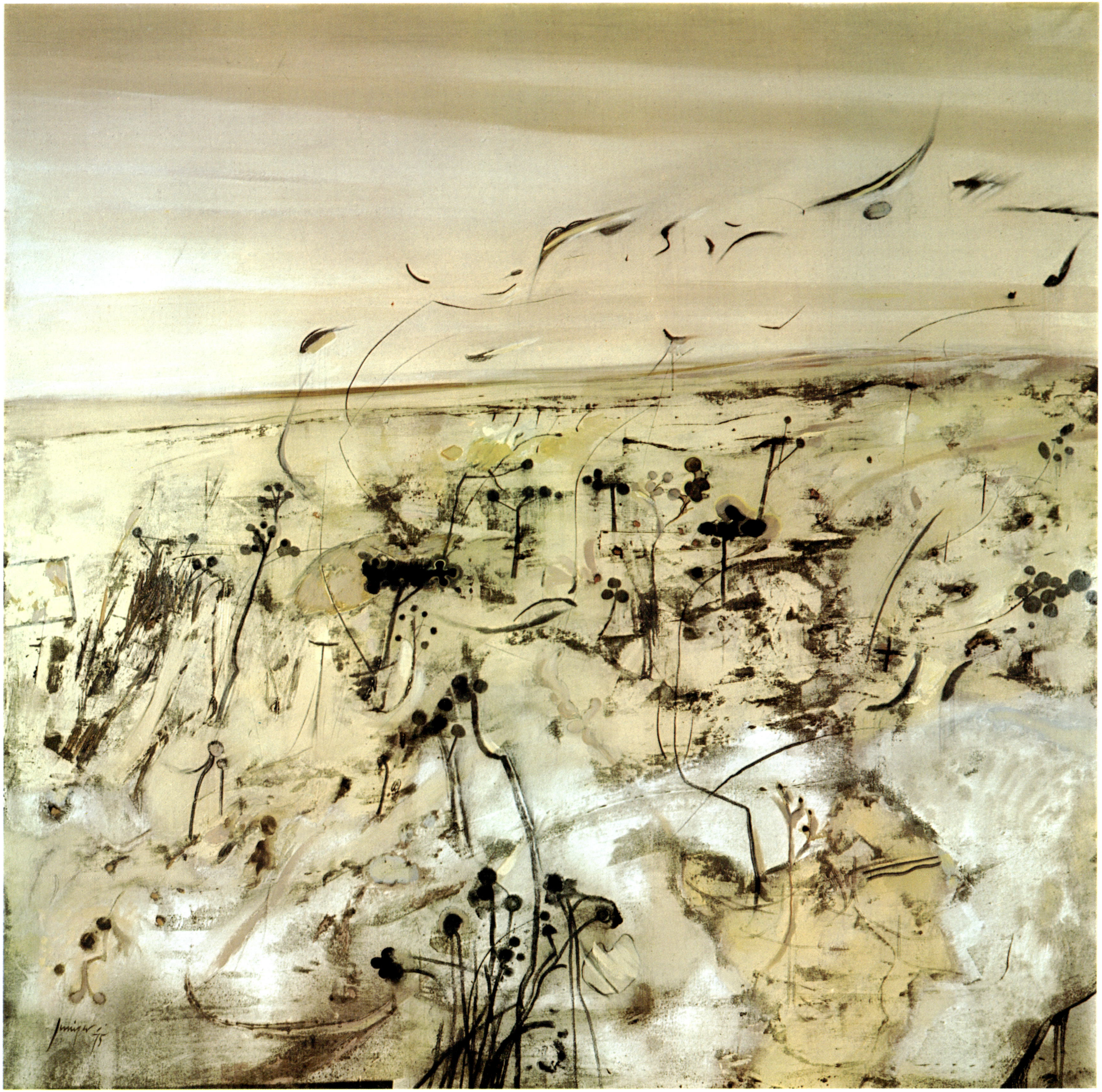

Murchison Sand Plain

Tom Roberts

Thomas William Roberts, born Dorchester, England in 1856. Arrived Melbourne 1869; died Kallista, Victoria 1931.

Tom Roberts was the first Australian artist to come in contact — even if it was hearsay contact — with French Impressionism. He went to London in 1881, and on a walking tour in the South of France and in Spain in 1883, he met two artists, Laureano Barrau and Ramon Casas, who had studied in Paris.

What Roberts, Arthur Streeton, Charles Conder and Frederick McCubbin thought of Impressionism is summed up in the quotation from Gérôme used in the catalogue for the '9 × 5 Exhibition' of 1889, in which the four participated: 'When you draw, form is the important thing; but in painting, the first thing to look for is the general impression of colour'. That form of Impressionism is exemplified in *Evening When the Quiet East Flushes Faintly the Sun's Last Look,* painted a year before the Heidelberg School moved from Box Hill and Mentone to Eaglemont, overlooking the Yarra. (David Davies visited them; his brother, Charles, was the estate agent who managed the property.)

The *theory* of Impressionism was suited to the Australian bush which, not being full of deep shadows, encourages a light palette and is admirably suited to open-air painting. When their '9 × 5 Exhibition' was criticized, Roberts, Streeton and Conder protested to *The Argus:* 'In looking at the works of modern European and American painters, who have in a great measure discarded the studio for their painting ground, and whose aim has been to sacrifice no truth to effect, the spectator may feel a certain want as of finish or arrangement, and here let us leave our mind open, and forget for the moment our own idea of what ought to be in a picture, realise the intention of the artist, then judge if the impression given is true under the conditions represented . . .'

The sketch of Coogee, a location also painted by Conder, Streeton and Lloyd Rees, is more luminous, more compact and exhibits a greater inner sparkle and a greater range of harmonies. It is more climactic than *Bailed Up,* which, despite the dramatic moment, is almost casual, except for the tension created by the log across the road and the rearing head of the horse. The scene looks nostalgic and was based on the tale of a Cobb and Company coach-driver, 'Silent' Bob Bates (there is a portrait of him by Roberts in the Art Gallery of New South Wales) who told Roberts of the hold-up on the Tenterfield Road some twenty years before.

Evening When the Quiet East Flushes Faintly the Sun's Last Look
Oil on canvas; 1887; 50.8 × 76.2 cm.
Acquired: 1944, Felton Bequest.
National Gallery of Victoria.

Holiday Sketch at Coogee
Oil on canvas; April 1888; 40.3 × 55.9 cm.
Acquired: 1954
Art Gallery of New South Wales.

Bailed Up
Oil on canvas; 1895/1927; 134.6 × 182.9 cm.
Acquired: 1933
Art Gallery of New South Wales.

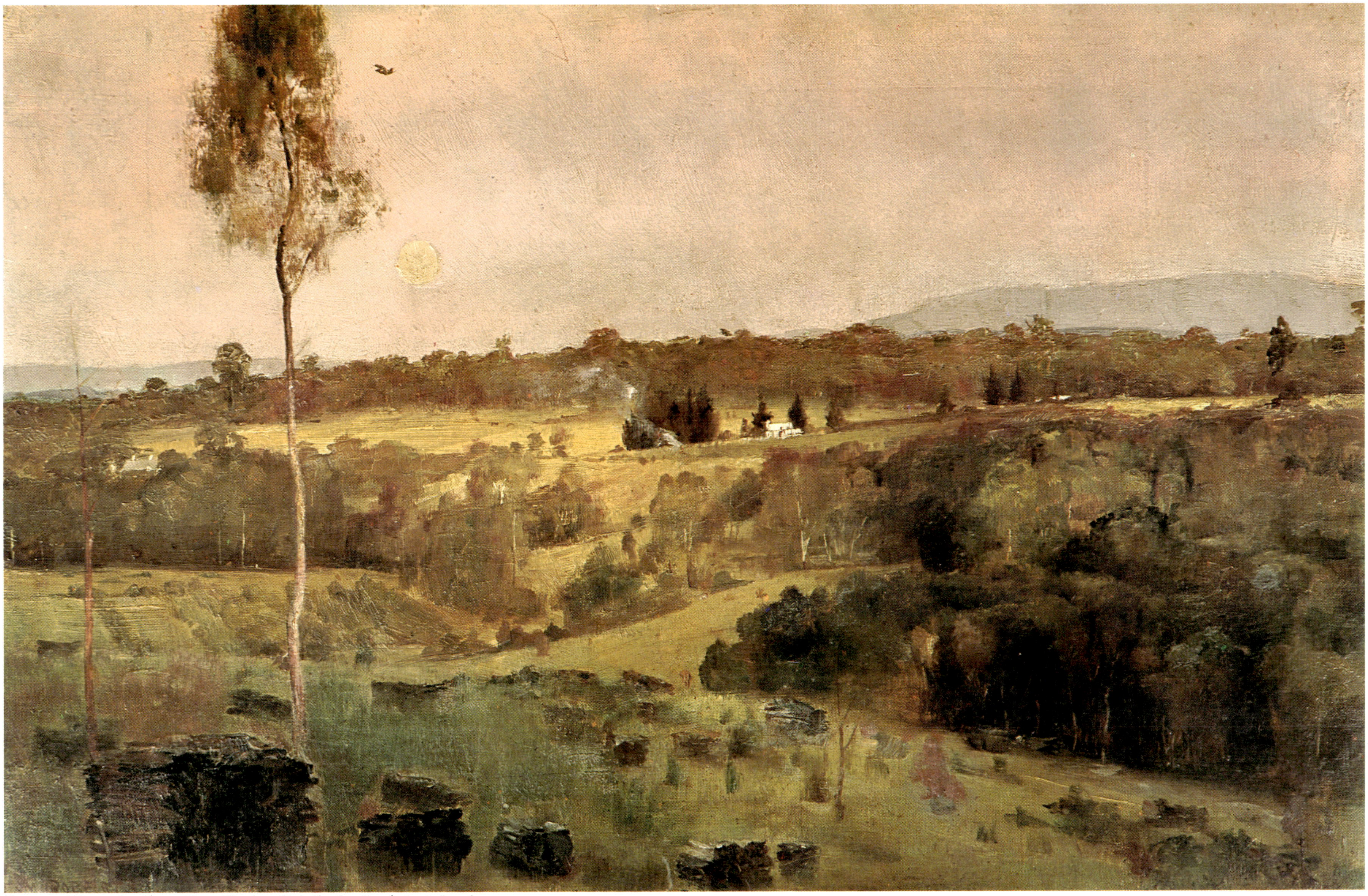

Evening When the Quiet East Flushes Faintly the Sun's Last Look

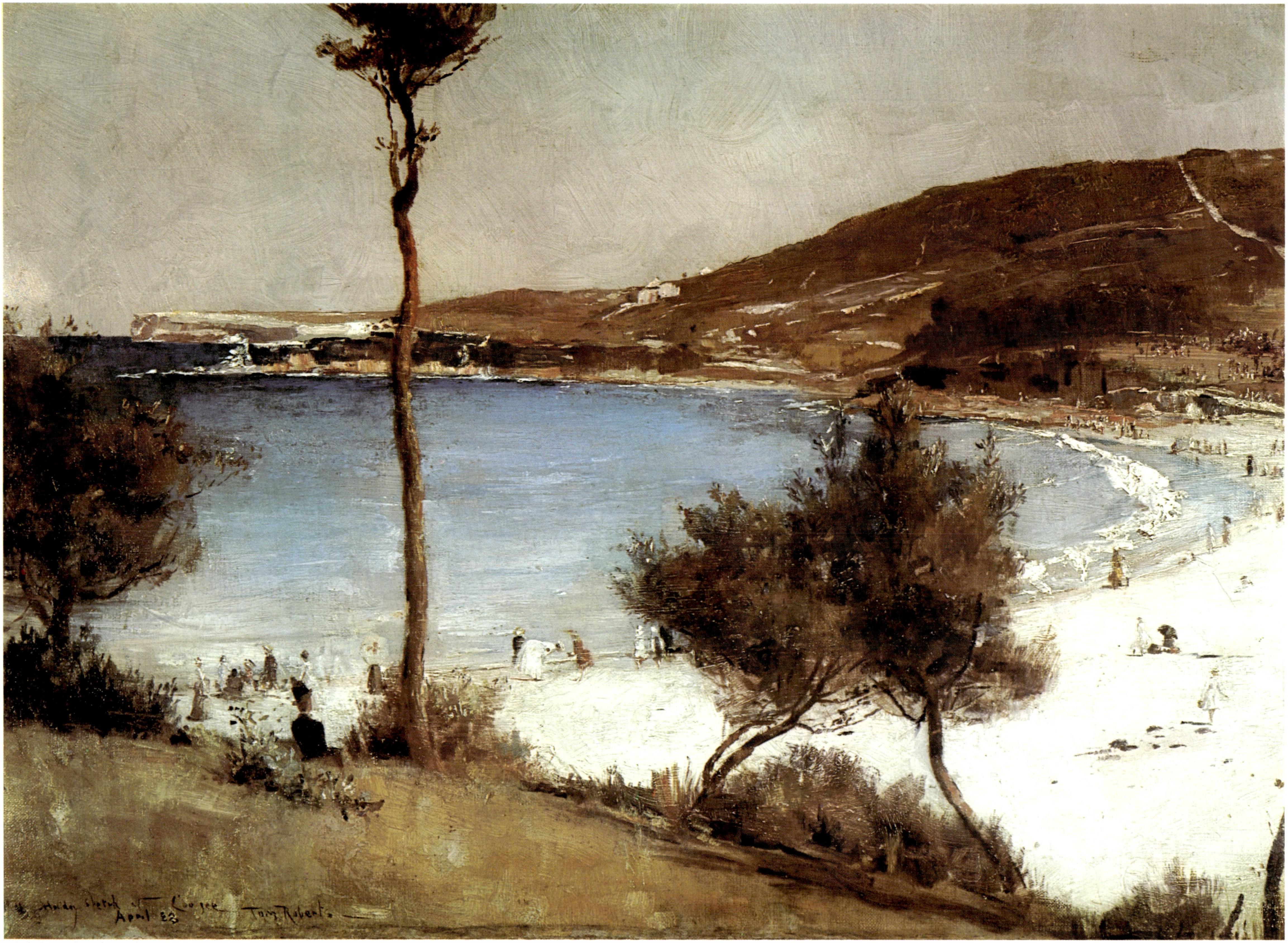

Holiday Sketch at Coogee

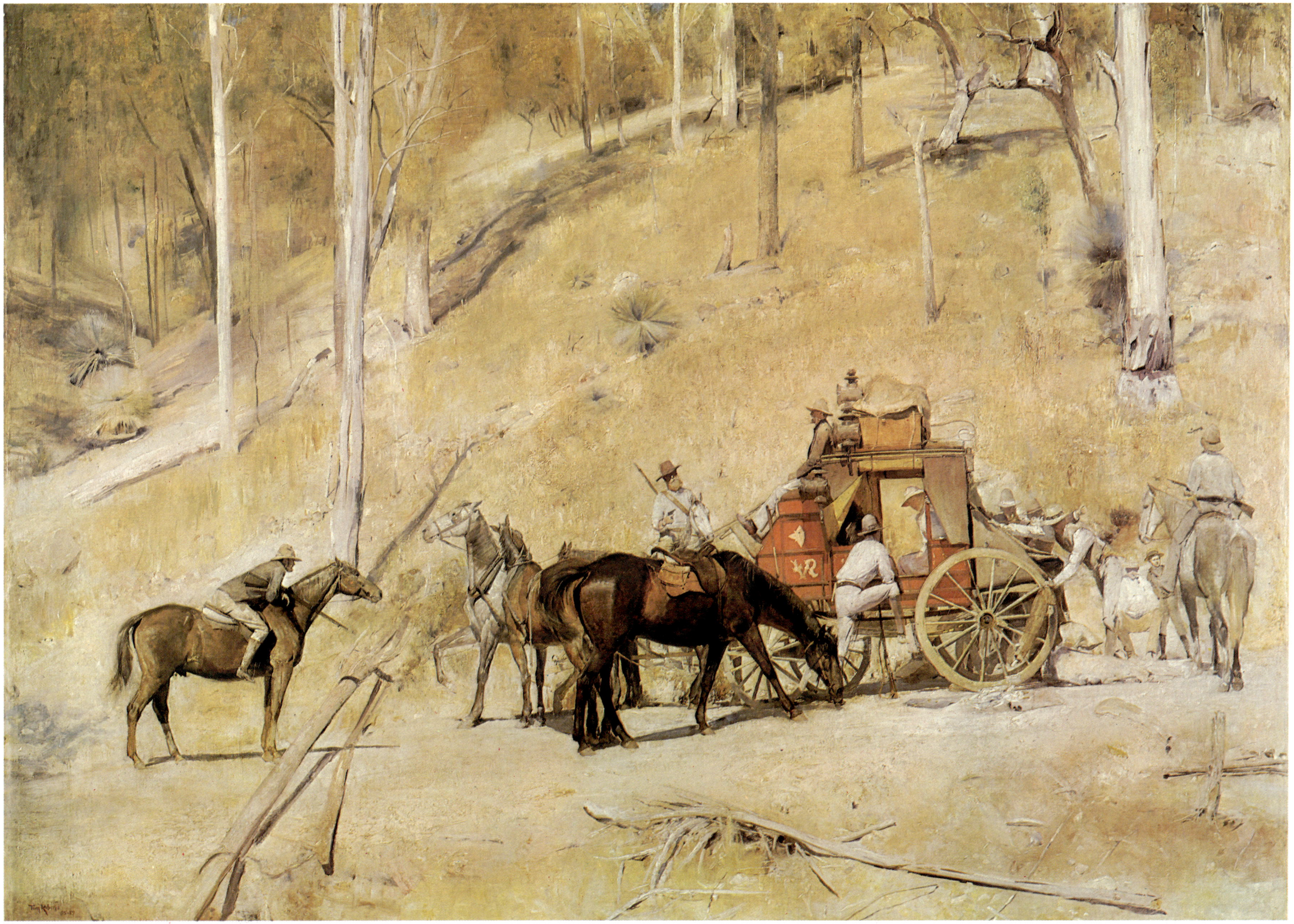

Bailed Up

Charles Blackman

Charles Raymond Blackman, born Sydney in 1928, where he now lives.

Charles Blackman's drawings of boats, bathers, seashores and landscapes have long paid tribute to the dark drawings of Georges Seurat. *Beach Album* indicates Blackman's creative relationship to Seurat and his resolution of a curious contrast in Seurat's approach. For Seurat drew as if to say 'let there be darkness', and painted with such a sparkling, broken Impressionist touch as if to say 'let all be light'. In this intricate and vividly composed combination of drawing and collage, Blackman, much of whose painting is full of dark, illusionistic tonalism and, closely juxtaposed, areas of brilliant light, has used reproductions of a photograph of a beach, Seurat's peasant boy of about 1882, three greyish Seurat reproductions, two details of coloured sketches and a detail from Seurat's *Sunday Afternoon on the Ile de la Grande-Jatte.* It is a series of vignettes balancing colour and darkness, various perspectives and differently scaled human beings; the blacks are bold and the colours are retiring. Where Tom Roberts gives us an immediate view of Coogee Beach, Blackman presents multiple aspects of *a* beach and his art.

For Blackman, the image, canonised by the Antipodean Manifesto of 1959, is the true path to pictorial inventiveness. The Manifesto, signed by Blackman, Arthur and David Boyd, John Brack, Bob Dickerson, Clifton Pugh and Bernard Smith, exalted the image over what was thought to be the pervasive and meaningless elegance of abstract art. Barbara Blackman, the artist's wife, in something of a defence of the Manifesto, stressed that in practice and in partnership, the signatories (except the historian Bernard Smith) had already worked together; Pugh and Blackman had painted in Queensland's Glasshouse Mountains; Pugh and Perceval painted the Hurstbridge district in Victoria; and Pugh, Perceval and Arthur Boyd painted around Williamstown, Victoria. They did not form camps like the Heidelberg artists, but they admired the same landscapes.

Blackman has always been concerned with the transformation of the image by the imagination, the memory of the past and the distance of time. In a catalogue note he wrote: 'To come again to the scene of a time where one has lived before is not to revisit the past. The past begins to change the moment one takes a step away from it. Memories grow up out of what is seen, coloured and shaped by the associations and emotions felt at a time, and the little details of fact and minute wither and are forgotten. Nor is it the same person who returns. One grows new eyes every time one looks at something'.

In *Beach Album*, Blackman is looking simultaneously at his past and then present creative processes. It celebrates the memories of an artist's journey.

Beach Album
Charcoal drawing on paper with collage; 1967; 47.2 × 68.6 cm.
(Signed twice; in charcoal and in ink)
Courtesy of the Rudy Komon Gallery, Sydney.

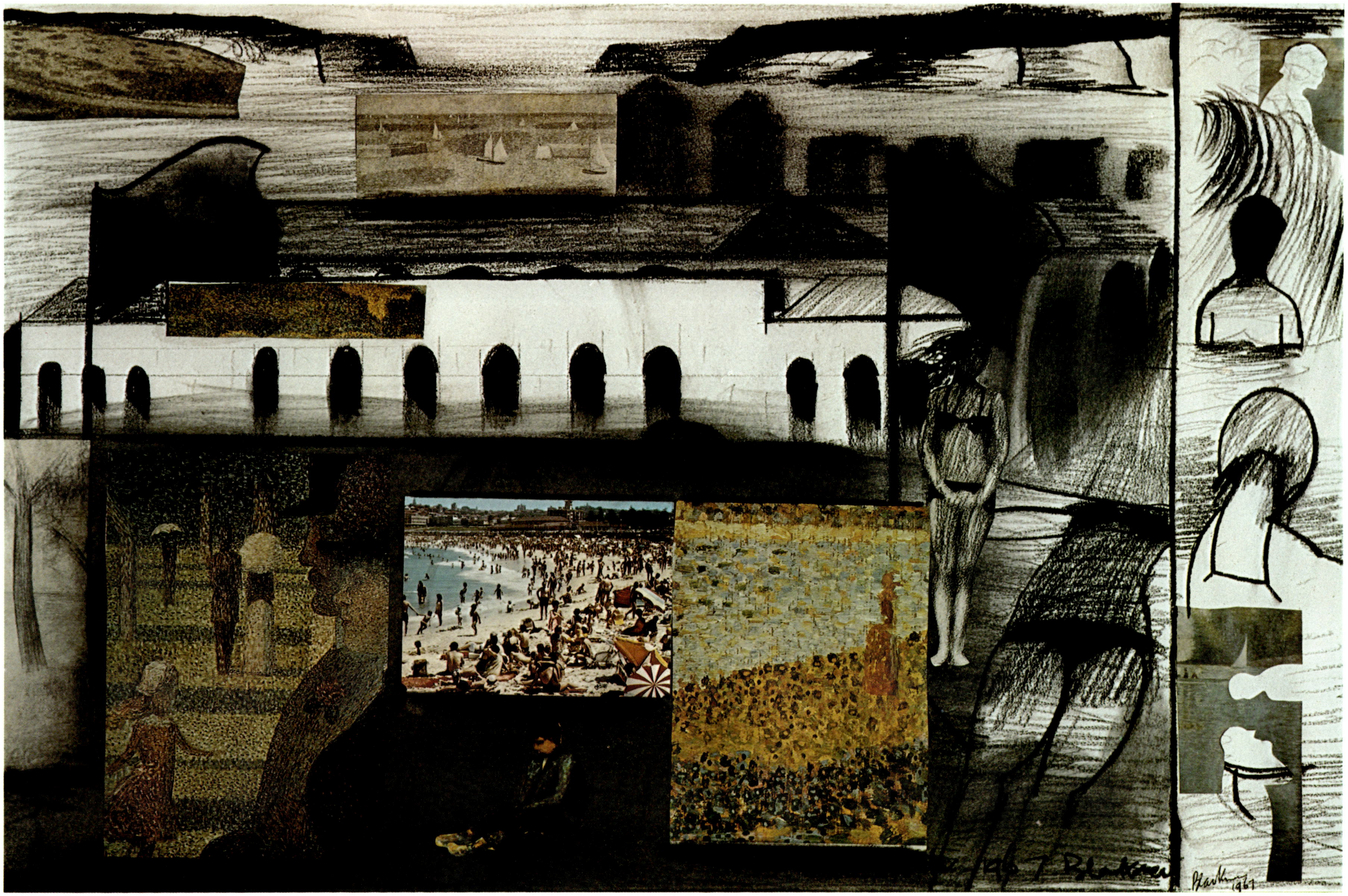

Beach Album

David Davies

David Davies, born Ballarat, Victoria, 1862. In 1897, went to England, where he died in 1939.

If *Golden Summer* is compared with Charles Conder's *Yarding Sheep* one could say that Conder is a born Impressionist dissolving all into a golden haze; Davies sought the shadows and though he was in a Paris sparkling with Impressionism in 1890, his shadows that lurk under logs and trees in *Golden Summer* grew to embrace the whole landscape. Of his later painting Frederick McCubbin could write: 'his work seemed the result of long contemplative brooding over the subdued effects of quiet light' — and, though he is not discussing *A Summer Evening* his description is appropriate: 'The beautiful tonality of this picture, the economy of means with which he has rendered the dried up grass and weeds, the quality of its colour, gives the canvas a beauty that always delights you afresh when you return to look at it'.

For Davies light does not fall on objects as a happy additive as it does with Elioth Gruner; it does not dissolve form as it does with Phillips Fox; whether sunlight or moonlight, the light suffuses the painting that pulsates in such a way that it seems to generate light itself. This is mystical, visionary painting; the spirit of nature is personified. It is a spirit that does not recur in Australian art until the later paintings of Desiderius Orban and Judy Cassab.

In *A Summer Evening,* Davies preserved the heat and glow of the day to counter the cooling light of the moon; the very curve of his simple horizons (later to influence Lloyd Rees) gave his landscapes a strength and swelling volume that contrast with the bleached, blurred, muted and stippled touches of paint. His misty, lyrical nocturnes, still and melting with elusive shadows, his tawny mauves and dusty blue-pinks have been appreciated, perhaps a little to the neglect of the concealed muscularity of his hillsides.

Though Davies painted alongside the Heidelberg artists, he regarded the earth as a symbolic presence rather than something of pure, visual delight. It was Rees, Brett Whiteley and Fred Williams who were to continue the tradition of the earth as biomorphic symbol.

Golden Summer
Oil on canvas; 1888; 60.6 × 91.3 cm.
Acquired: 1937, Felton Bequest.
National Gallery of Victoria.

Templestowe
Oil on canvas laid down on hardboard; 36.5 × 46.4 cm.
Acquired: 1965
Australian National Gallery, Canberra.

A Summer Evening
Oil on canvas, later glued to hard board; c.1896; 71.1 × 91.2 cm.
Acquired: 1896
Art Gallery of New South Wales.

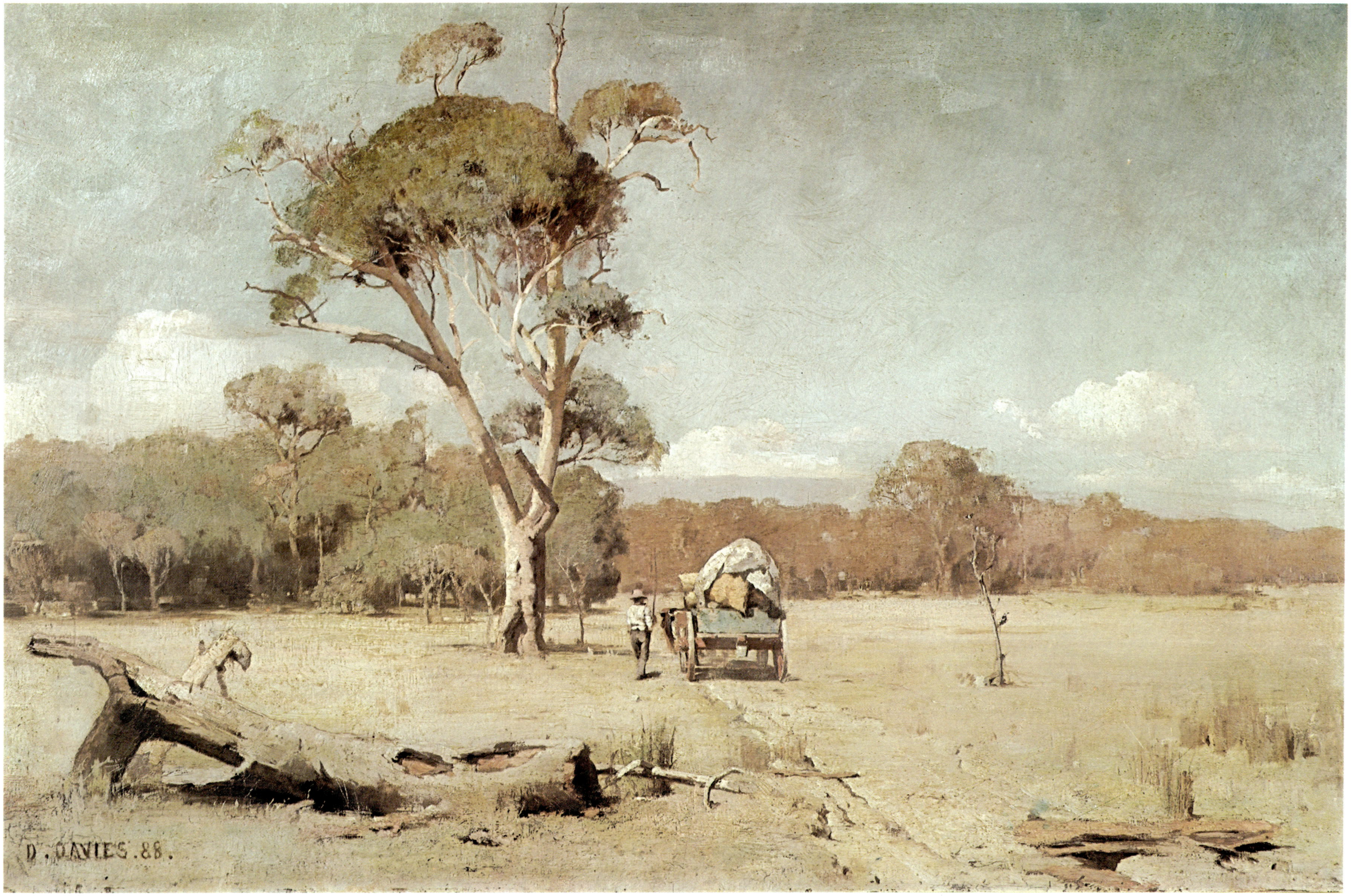

Golden Summer

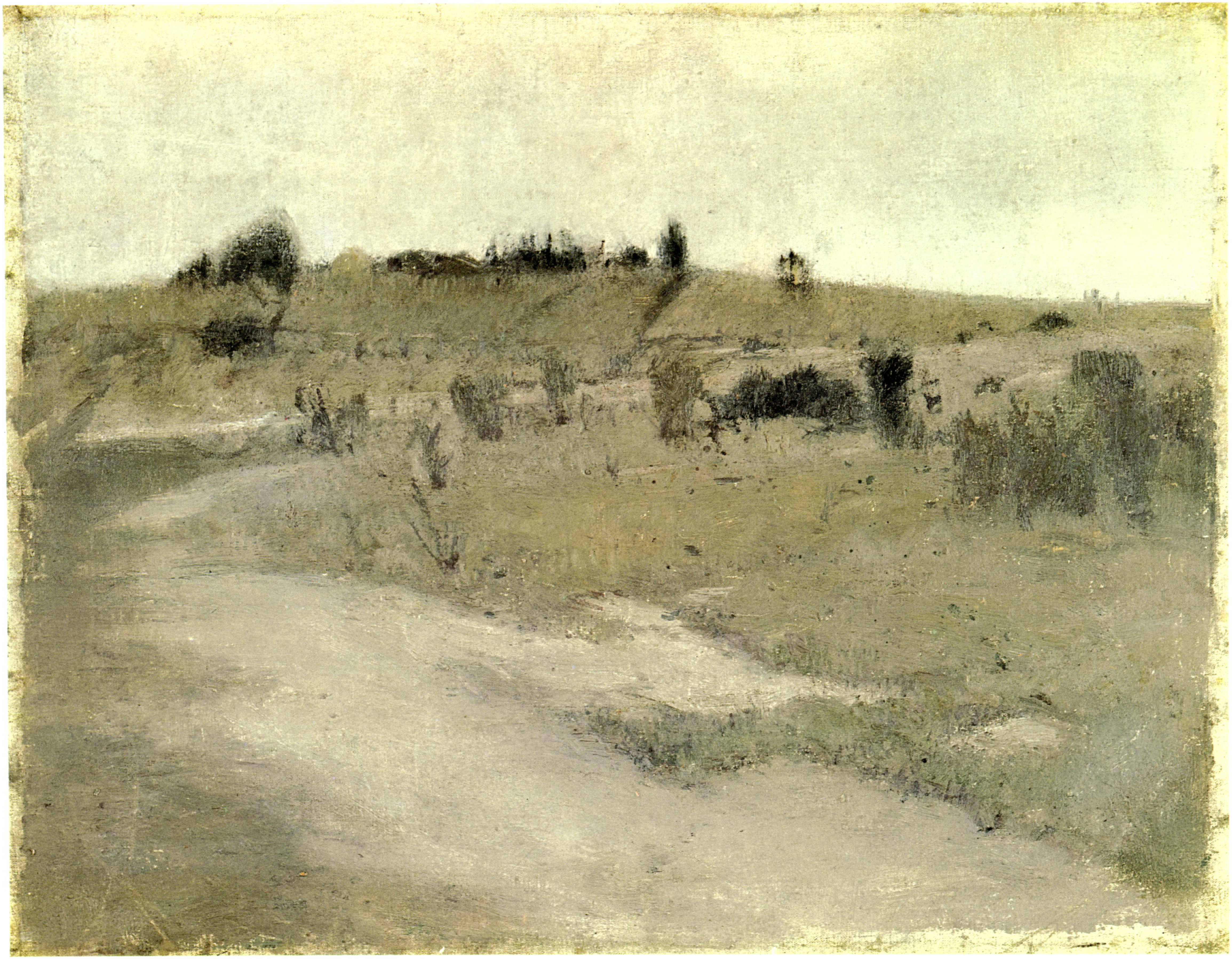

Templestowe

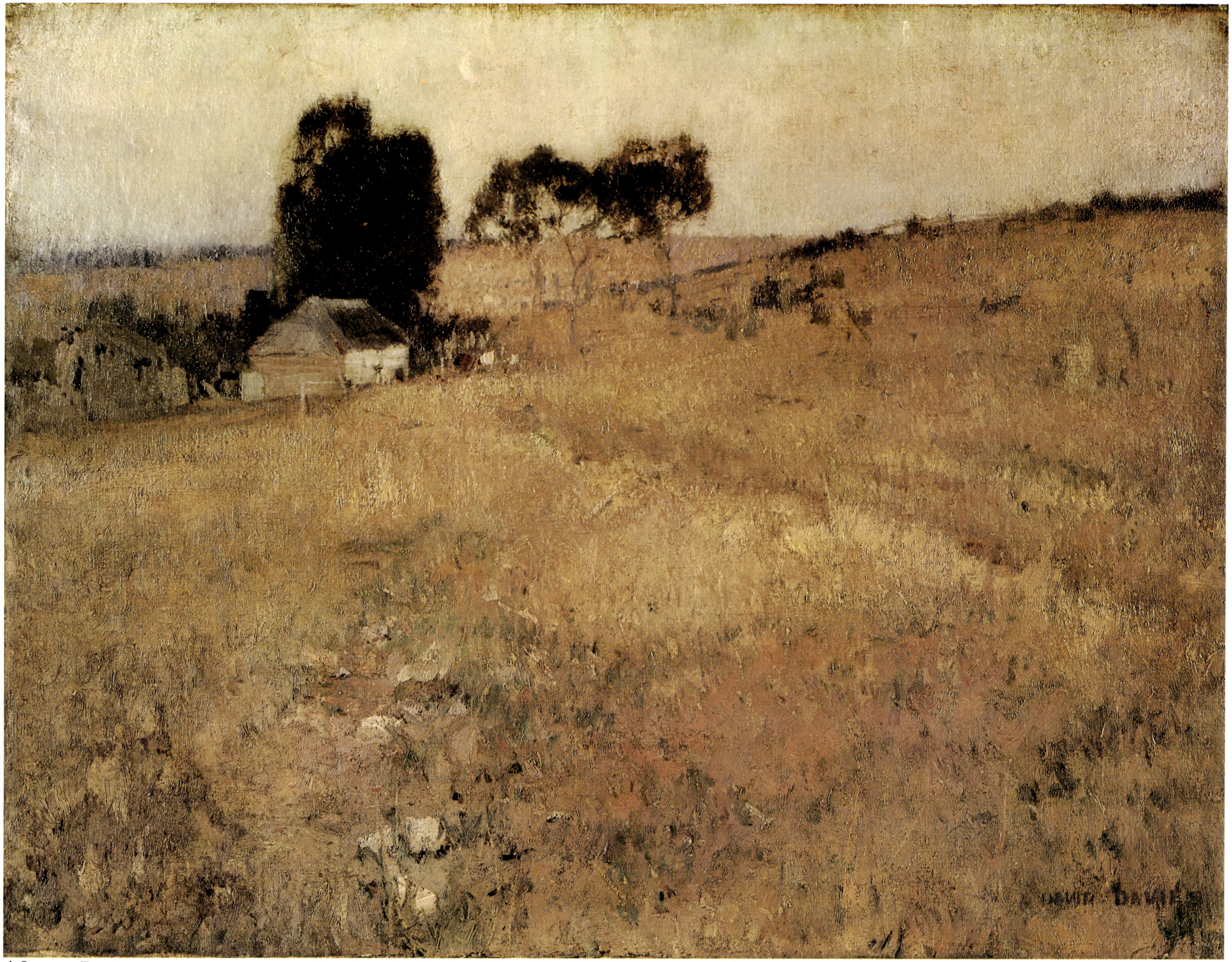

A Summer Evening

E. Phillips Fox

Emanuel Phillips Fox, born in Melbourne 1865, where he died in 1915.

Phillips Fox was steeped in the Impressionism that celebrated the vibrant, unpolluted and caressing air of the countryside where it seemed always to be early Spring, and where people led lives of quiet and relaxed rapture. With David Davies the moon begins to cool the hot, parched and subdued earth; nature seems to be a powerful, barely tamed force falling to sleep. Fox's moon, as it does in another *Moonrise* in the Tasmanian Museum and Art Gallery, showers and blesses the world with sparkling, dewy light. Davies' nocturnal hills are ancient, remote and, despite the subtle tenderness of hues, evoke melancholy. Fox's world is not a Utopia or Arcadia, but a Garden of Eden, though a very homely and hospitable one without a trace of the exotic or symbolic.

Although Fox studied under William Adolphe Bouguereau and Jean Léon Gérôme whom the 9 × 5 Impressionists were to quote in 1889, he was more directly influenced by Impressionism, because at the age of twenty-one he went to Paris, and only returned to Australia in 1892. Not only did Fox have opportunities to study the overall patterns of divisionist strokes of complementary colours, but he was able to hear of Impressionism from the Australian expatriate, John Peter Russell, who practised Impressionism with a fluid lyricism and had Impressionists, like Claude Monet, as his friends.

The Impressionists relished the cheerful, solacing, tranquil and domestic world; they excluded fantastic, imaginary, historical, tragic and nocturnal subjects; why was Fox, then, attracted to the moonlight and the slight haze it gave to his landscapes? Fox's moonscapes were not like those of James Whistler or David Davies: there is nothing gently sad about Fox's nightfall. For him the moon was another source of light and life like the sun. He probably found that much of the landscape of Australia in the blaze of noon lacked nuances of hue and gradations of tone. He did not want to render it in the golden haze of Charles Conder or the slow broad rhythms of Arthur Streeton; he wanted it to sparkle, vibrate and pulsate with painterly touches and the moonlight, rarely painted by Impressionists, allowed him to do so.

Sunrise, sunset and moonrise ring dramatic changes on the appearance of the Australian landscape; in Europe subtle effects of light occur throughout the day so that Monet could paint the hourly variations in a haystack or the facade of Rouen Cathedral with differences as distinct as those Fox saw between noon and moonrise.

It was such chromatic variations that stirred the twenty-six year old Roland Wakelin when he saw them exhibited in Sydney in 1913.

Moonrise, Heidelberg
Oil on canvas; c.1900; 75.8 × 126.5 cm.
Acquired: 1948
National Gallery of Victoria.

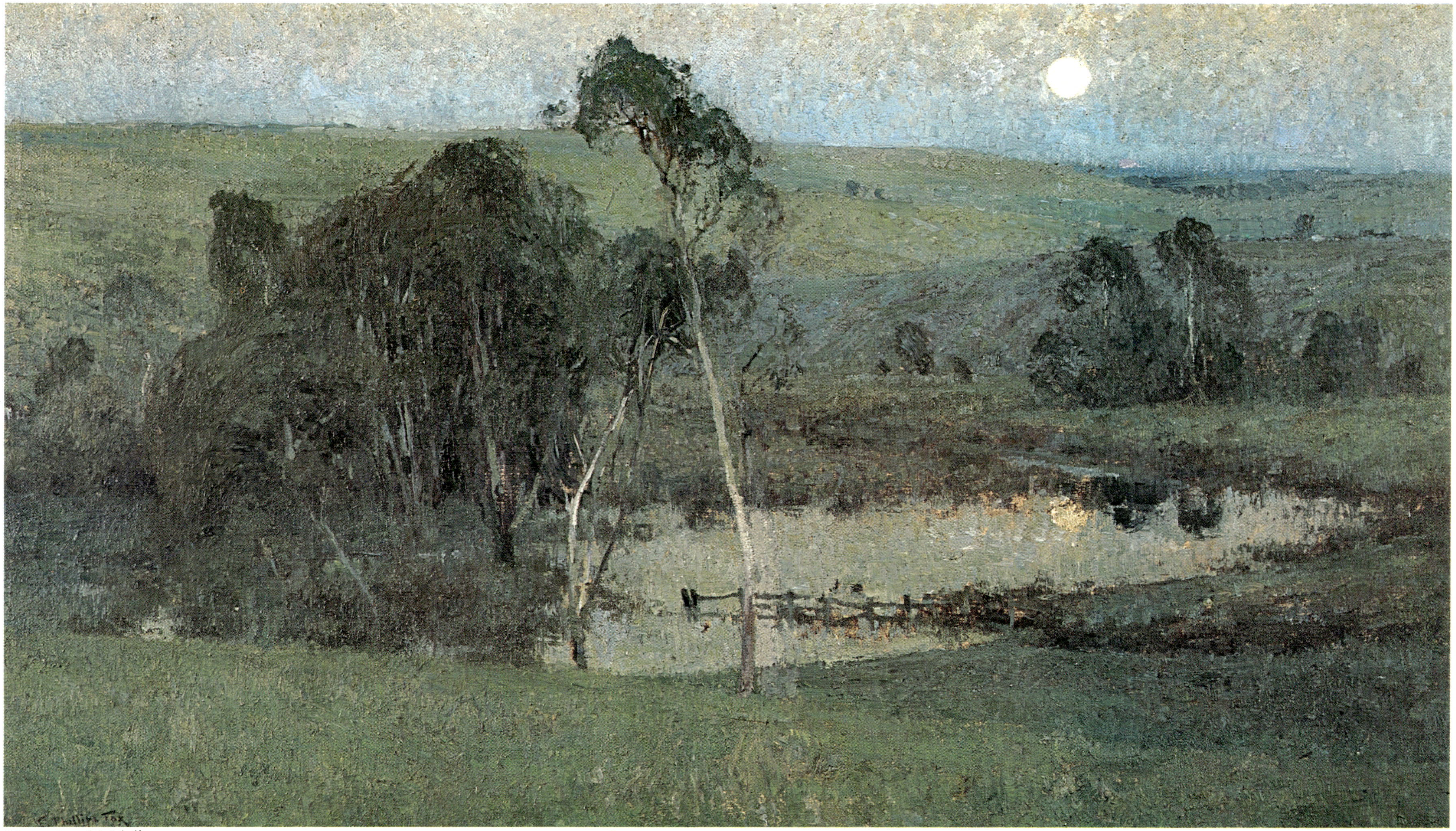

Moonrise, Heidelberg

Blamire Young

William Blamire Young, born Yorkshire, England, 1862. Arrived Katoomba, New South Wales, 1885; died at Montrose, Victoria, 1935.

To the detriment of his contribution to Australian landscape painting, overmuch has been made of Blamire Young's decorative manner; as he wrote several plays there is a tendency to see his work as theatrical backdrops and, as he trained in London with the poster-makers, The Beggarstaff Bros, there is an inclination to treat him as a deployer of decorous forms.

His hills and houses may be enlivened with decorative touches, but they are positive, frontal and uncompromised by their rather sparse adornments.

Blamire Young was self-taught and became interested in painting while mathematics master at Katoomba College in the Blue Mountains. He went to England and trained with the Beggarstaff Bros (actually brothers-in-law, Sir William Nicholson and James Pryde) who made of the poster a direct and flat image. James Pryde, whose paintings of melancholy buildings influenced *Rats' Castle*, said, 'We decided that a silhouette treatment was the best'.

The name, Beggarstaff Bros had been seen in an old stable on a stack of fodder and suited the desire for a down-to-earth title: in these three watercolours by Blamire Young, there is no Impressionist sparkle, no lushness and no sense of domestic enjoyment; the world is harsh, dry and worn. Julian Ashton prized his work, and both artists, as Ashton's *Cumberland Street* attests, like the detached and undramatic.

The poster enabled Young to eschew the illustrative and to adopt a broadsweep and frontality that, along with his textural effects gained by using unorthodox techniques, makes him a forerunner of modernism.

Compared with Donald Friend's *Brisbane River,* a glance back at Romantic spontaneity, *Rats' Castle* is impressively formalised: the background hills display a Cézannesque elevation before Cézanne was known in Australia and the emphatic and inventive use of the silhouetted, dark shapes, lead from Japanoiserie to Post-Impressionism.

Rats' Castle, Hobart
Watercolour on paper; 42.6 × 54.6 cm.
Acquired: 1923
Art Gallery of New South Wales.

Dry Weather
Watercolour on paper; c.1912; 56 × 76.8 cm.
Acquired: 1912
Art Gallery of New South Wales.

Winter's Grey Mantle
Watercolour on paper; 37.8 × 50.8 cm.
Acquired: 1912, Felton Bequest.
National Gallery of Victoria.

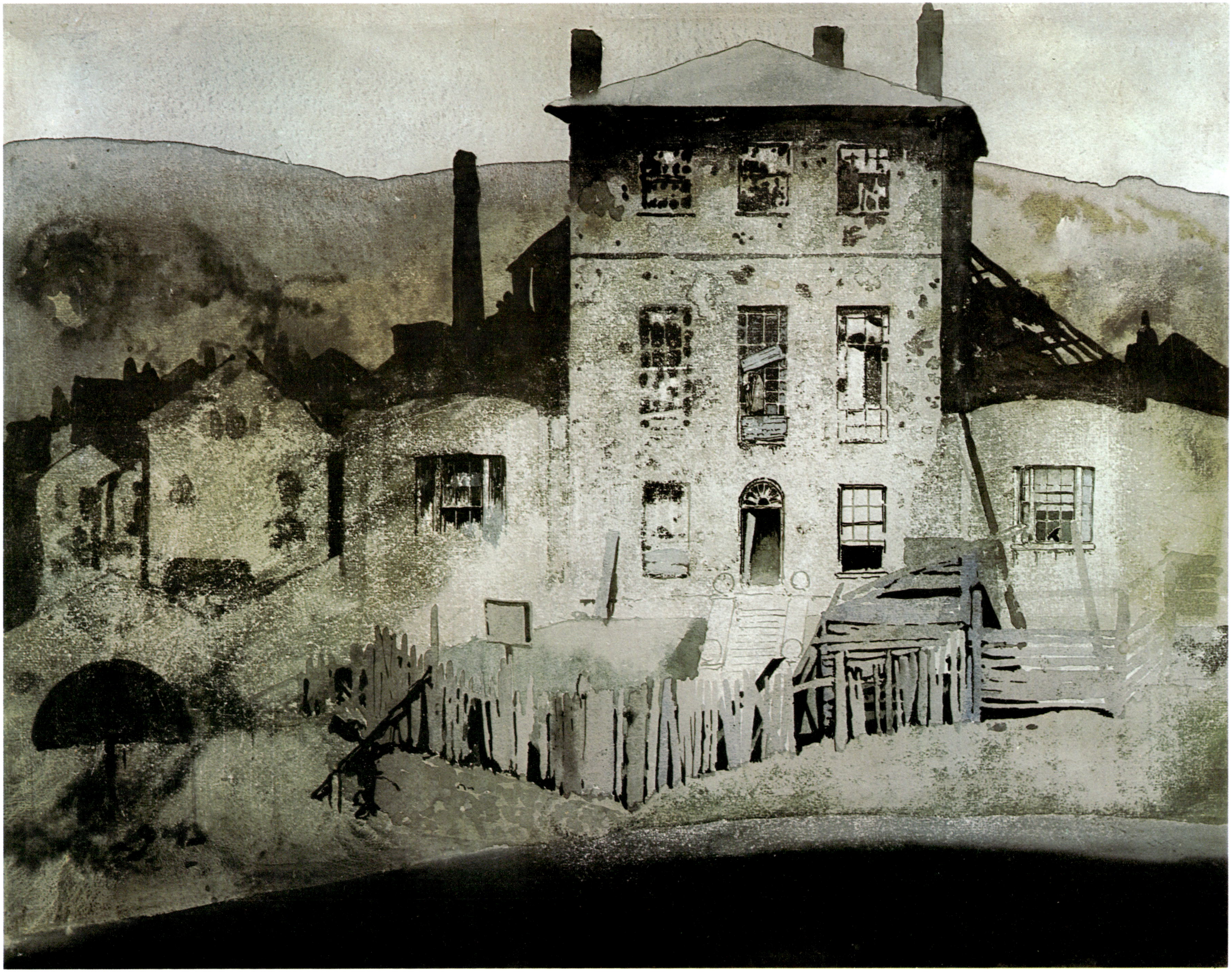

Rats' Castle, Hobart

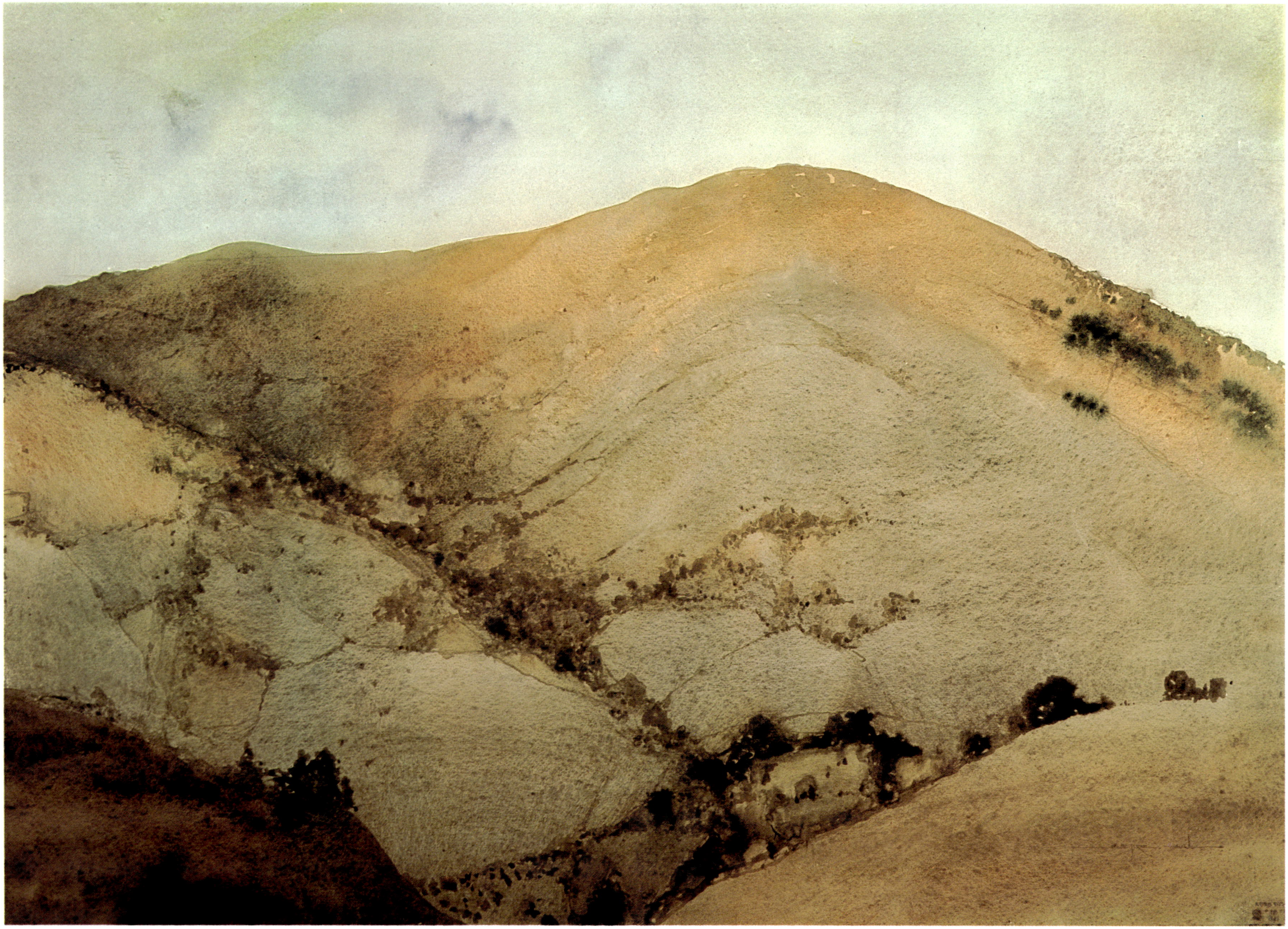

Dry Weather

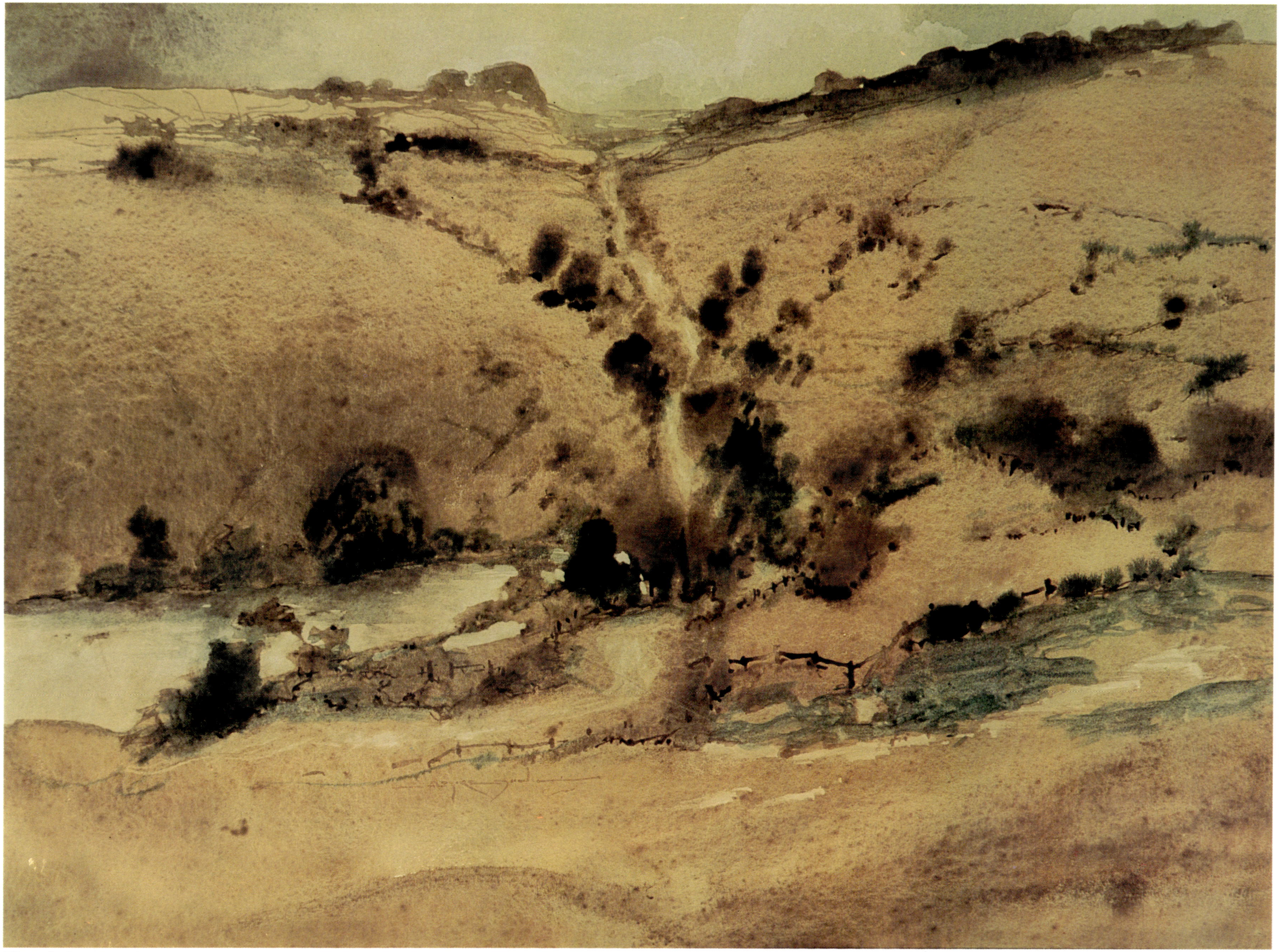

Winter's Grey Mantle

Donald Friend

Donald Stuart Leslie Friend, born Sydney, 1915; now lives in Bali.

It was almost predictable that John Olsen, when writing of Donald Friend, would emphasise his expressionist fervour: 'Friend is a remarkably vital technician. He is at the height of delight when wading in coloured puddles of ink, slashing a line with the rasp-like pen'; but Friend is also a brilliantly suave and witty draughtsman whose more expressive Neo-Romanticism was most tellingly effective during the war. He first met Russell Drysdale in Albury in 1942 when Drysdale was living away from Sydney; in 1943 Drysdale was to paint the sheer loneliness of *Albury Station* and Friend, a related work, *Brisbane River*, in 1944. (Friend was to record his war-time experiences in the book, *Gunner's Diary* 1943.) After the war his work became more delicate, fastidious, and entertaining in the best sense for he objected to the idea that only the profound could be art.

With lively and graceful decoration he depicted the transitory and exotic: in Ceylon, Africa and Bali, he treated moods and mores with a light, satirical and vital touch. His life was almost as restless as his pen and his wayward washes of ink and watercolour, for in 1949 he went to Hill End (others might treat the old gold town as Romantic and portentous, but Friend saw it as a frolic), 1950 to Sydney, 1951 to Florence, again to Hill End in 1952, to Ceylon in 1958 for six years, to Paddington, Sydney in 1964 and, heaven at last, to Bali in 1967.

Brisbane River has none of the simple frontality of Blamire Young's *Rats' Castle* with which it has kinships; but Friend's wash drawing is no 'interesting ruin', for there is a slight note of anxiety and restrained frenzy in the broken pen strokes and the untidy accumulation of effects. The few touches of grey gouache in the sky, on the pylons and in the water add to the unrest and the suggestion of foreboding. Where Blamire Young is the cool recorder, Friend exhibits a quiet desperation. Dobell imbues his *Opera House* with aspiration, but Friend is Dickensian in this rare example of despair. The anonymous buildings loom across the river and the torn sky predicts doom; Friend has caught a wartime mood of alienation and rejection; his tattered skies threaten; Dobell's surge with praise.

Brisbane River
Tinted pen and wash drawing with watercolour on paper; 1944; 44.0 × 58.5 cm.
Acquired: 1944
Art Gallery of New South Wales.

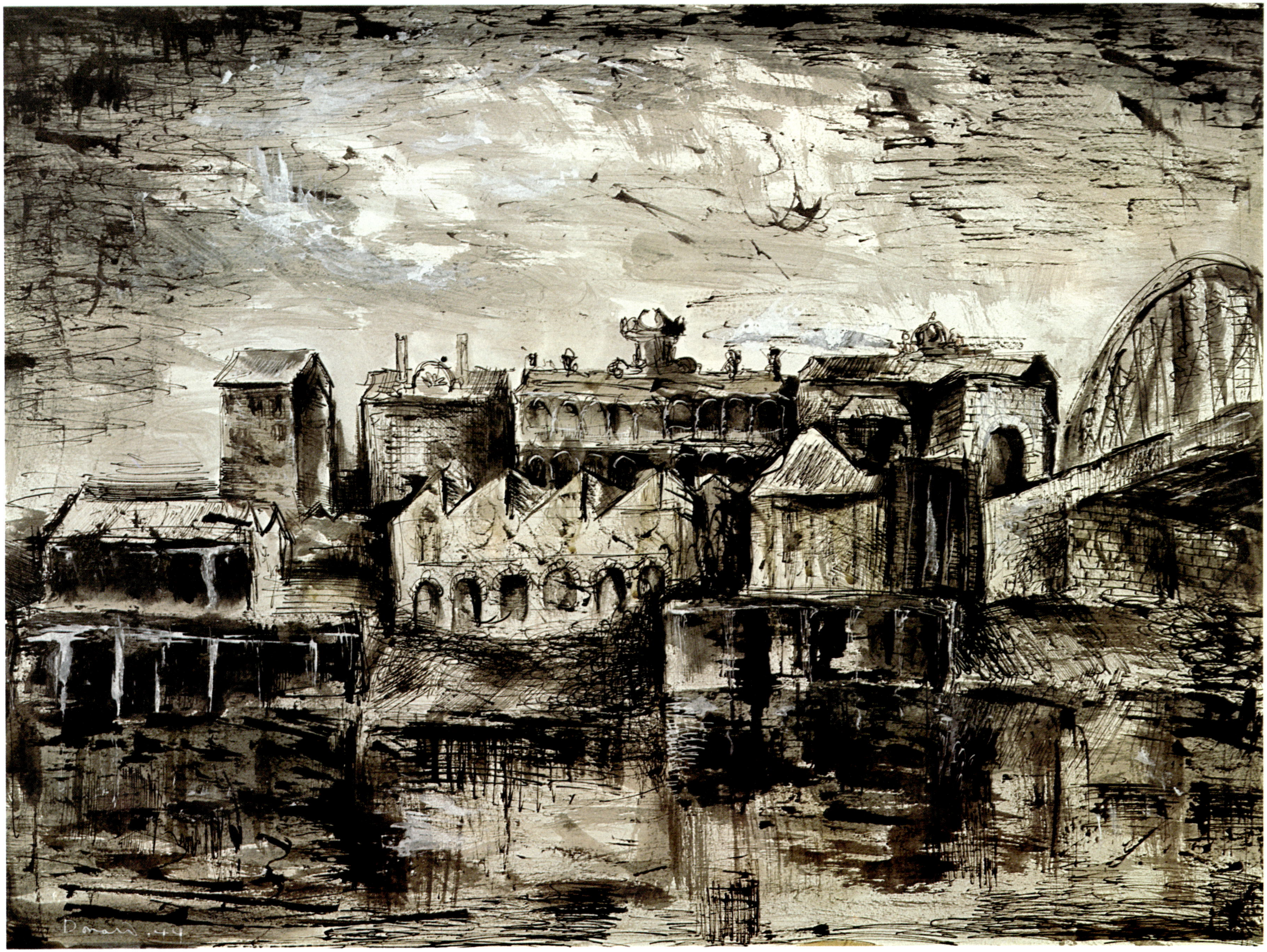

Brisbane River

Charles Conder

Charles Edward Conder, born in London, 1868. Arrived in Sydney in 1883; returned to England in 1890; died near Windsor, England, 1909.

Charles Conder, who was painting with the Australian Impressionists at Eaglemont Farm in 1888, was an Impressionist by hearsay and could rapidly absorb what he needed from the work and opinions of others, but he never really espoused Impressionist techniques. He employed a loose, decorative brushstroke, a practice that was expanded in the fans and screens he painted in London where he became quite famous. He also became a firm friend of Henri de Toulouse-Lautrec and took him to see Oscar Wilde in prison.

Conder was but twenty when he painted at Eaglemont Farm and twenty-two when he painted these three works: *Under a Southern Sun* is reminiscent of Arthur Streeton but is more decorative and less concerned with the exact rendition of light; indeed, Conder painted Coogee Beach from the same spot as Tom Roberts, but Conder is more wilful and less factual, for, well before he went to Paris and London, Conder suffused the world in a green or golden haze.

David Davies' *Golden Summer* was painted two years before Conder's *Yarding Sheep;* Davies' painting is firmly structured; trees, dray and shadows locate the scene firmly, but Conder melts his scene into a golden thought in a golden shade. Nothing could be more Utopian, but perhaps his paintings were less Utopian than we now think because Dugald Macoll, a critic writing of an exhibition of Australian art at the Grafton Gallery, London, said: 'There is no Australian art. There are a number of young men who would like to be artists . . . The difference between manufacturing art in so newly manufactured a country and growing it in the richer deposits of the Old World is proved very neatly by the presence in this collection of two works by Mr Charles Conder, who was in Australia for a few years in extreme youth, but who was lucky enough to escape. We know what he has done since; it would be hard to find the faintest trace of his remarkable gift in the two pictures here . . .'

Today Conder's Australian works are preferred.

A comparison of *Sandringham* with Tom Roberts' and Charles Blackman's beach compositions indicates how spontaneous, casual and decoratively vivacious Conder is; and a comparison of *Under a Southern Sun* with paintings by John Glover and Hans Heysen reveals how Conder could fuse the decorative and the authentic.

Sandringham
Oil on cedar panel; 1890; 12 × 21.5 cm.
Acquired: 1973
Australian National Gallery, Canberra.

Under a Southern Sun
Oil on canvas; 1890; 71.5 × 35.5 cm.
Bequest of Mary F. Meyer in memory of her husband, Dr Felix H. Meyer, 1975.
Australian National Gallery, Canberra.

Yarding Sheep
Oil on canvas; 1890; 36.2 × 55.8 cm.
Presented 1944 under the terms of the Will of the late Mrs E.E. Keep.
National Gallery of Victoria.

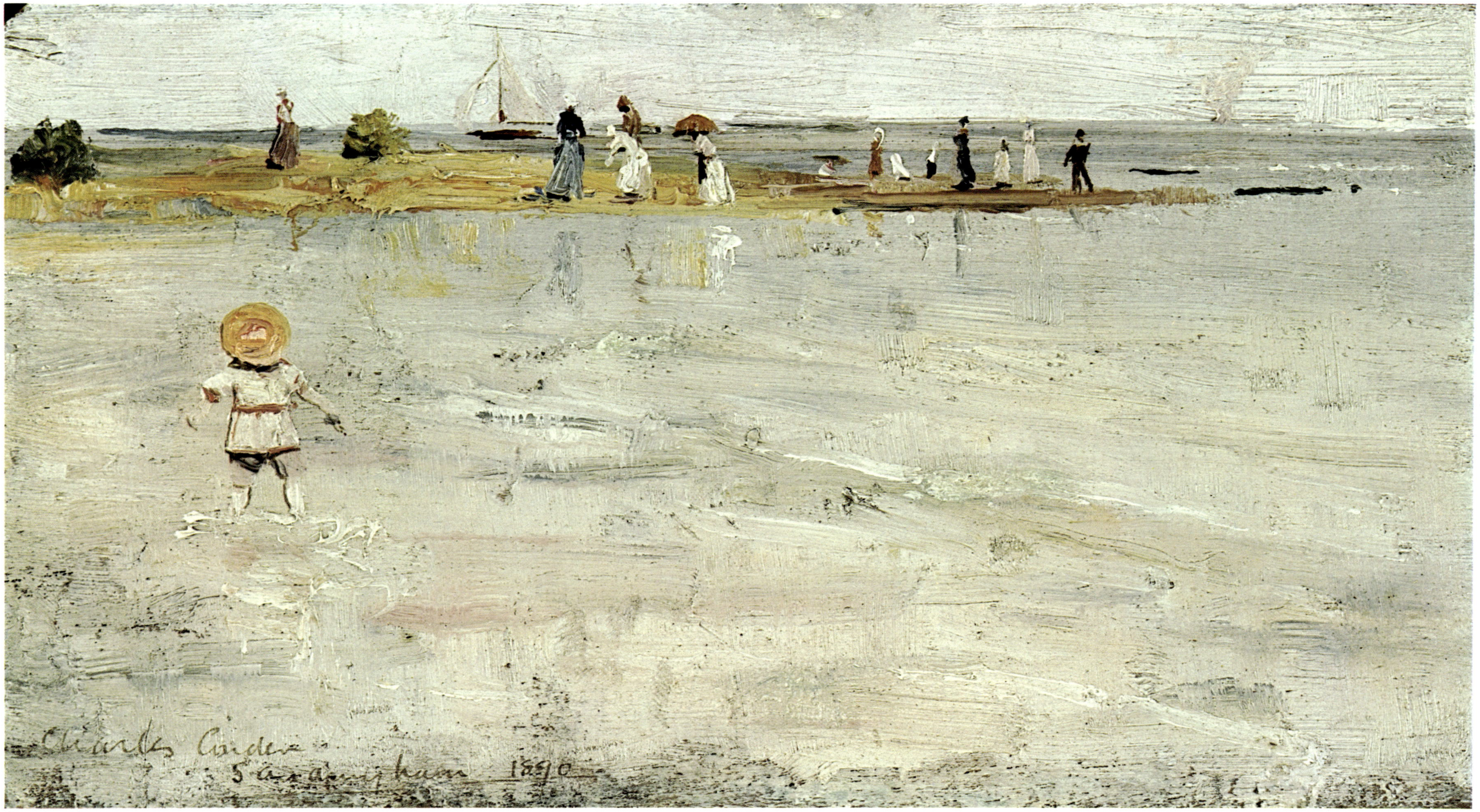

Sandringham

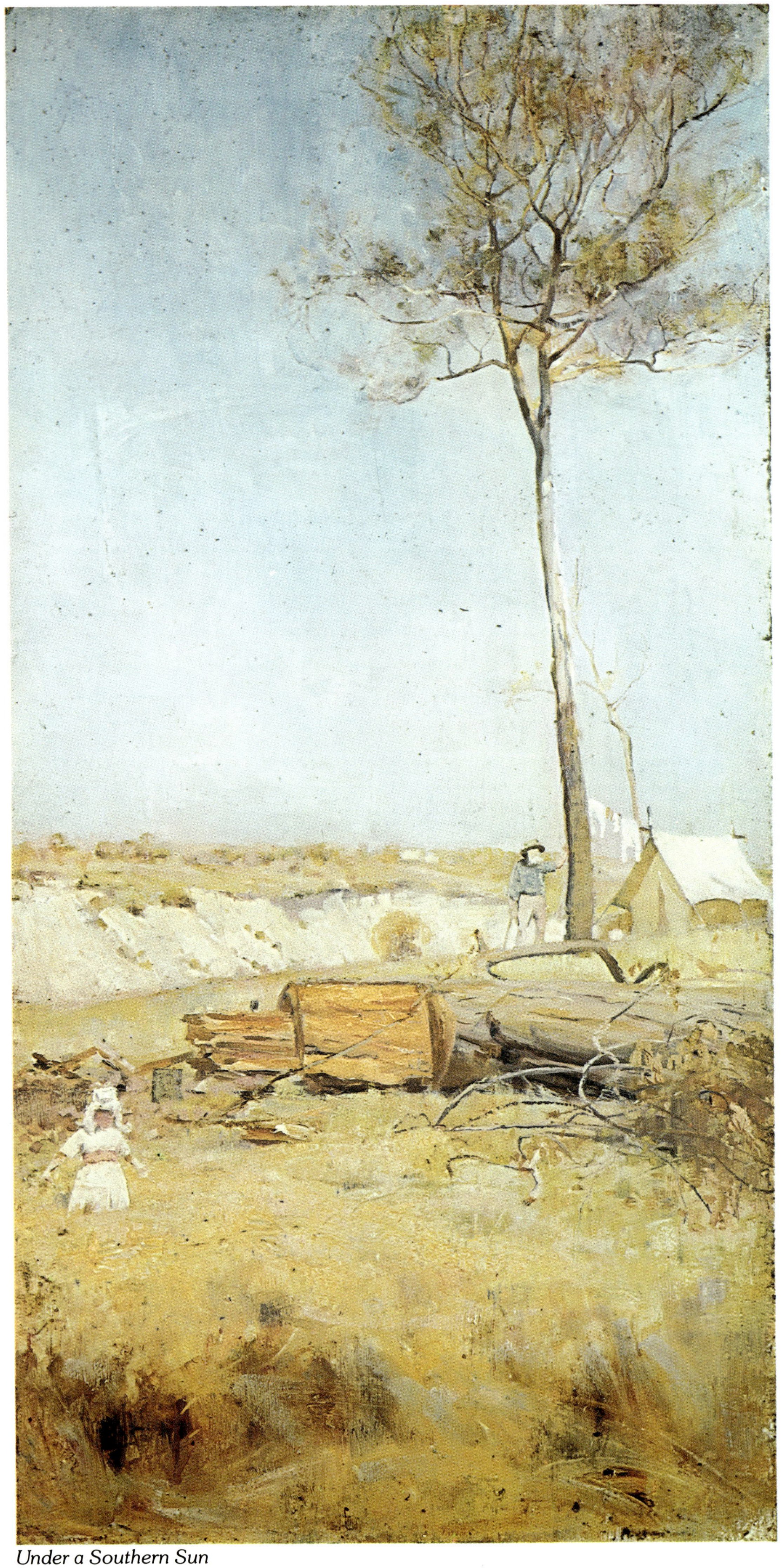

Under a Southern Sun

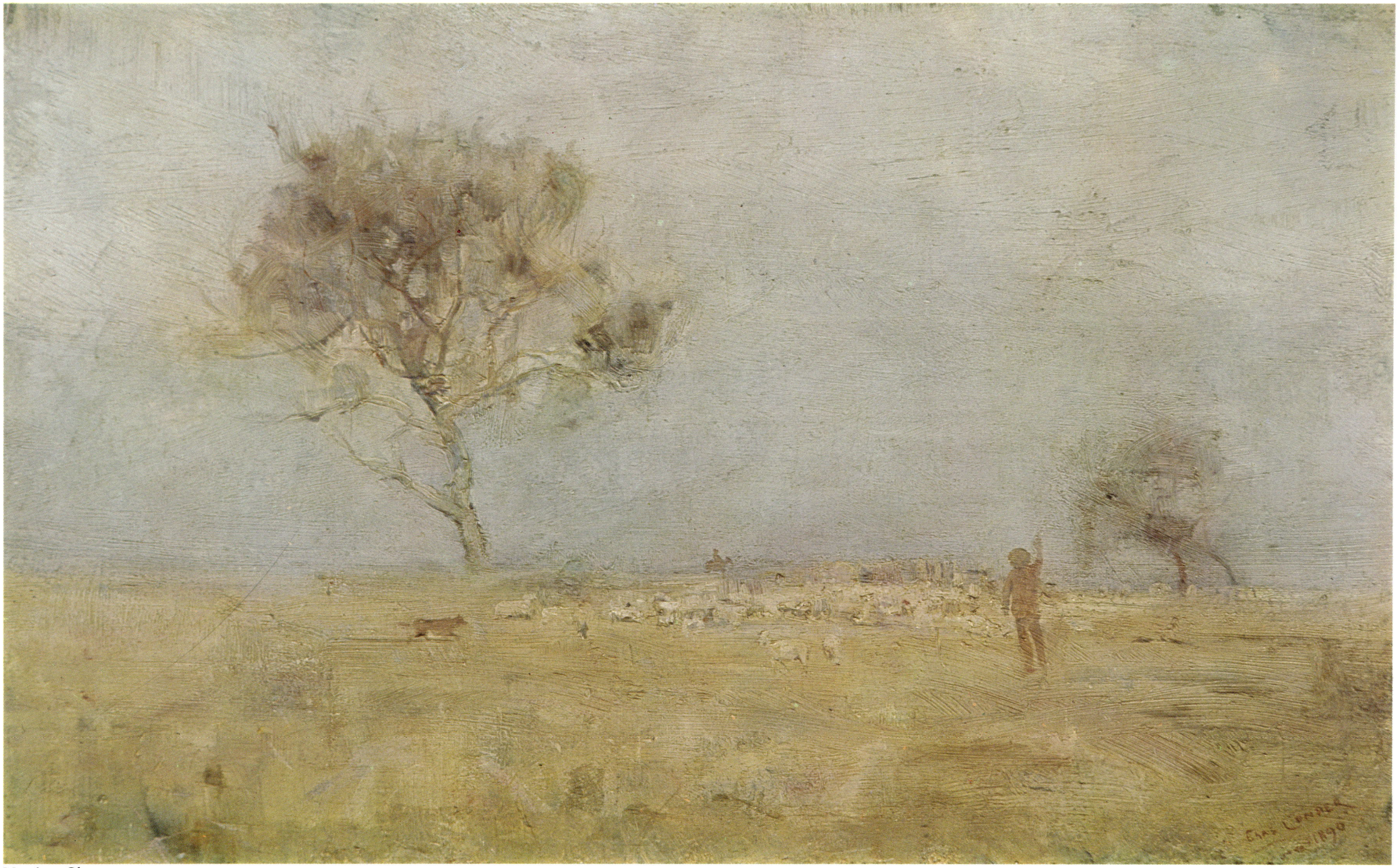

Yarding Sheep

Walter Withers

Walter Herbert Withers, born at Handsworth, Staffordshire, 1854. Arrived in Australia 1882; died at Eltham, Victoria 1914.

Walter Withers, who had one of the lightest touches of the Australian Impressionists, almost missed becoming a member of the Heidelberg School. Having arrived in Melbourne in 1883, he left for England and Paris in June 1887, met Phillips Fox in Paris, and returned to Australia in 1888. It was not until after his immersion in French Impressionism that he met Arthur Streeton and Charles Conder, whom he joined, with Tom Roberts, at Eaglemont Camp in 1889. Then, thoroughly converted to landscape painting — he painted little else — he set up a camp at Charterisville in 1890 which he leased to others. The result was that he and David Davies lived longer in the Heidelberg area than any other artists.

Withers oscillated between two moods, one subtle, dry, bleached and often still or subdued by storm clouds, reminiscent of David Davies; the other, light and fresh. In the former style, he won the Wynne Prize for landscape with *The Storm* in 1897 (and again in 1900 with *Still Autumn*). The latter style is described by Frederick McCubbin: 'He loved the green, fresh landscape — the approaching shower of rain — the dreamy, soft atmosphere of winter . . . That sunlight has lost its fierce power of burning hillside and plain, and the absence of the hot wind, drying and withering all things green and fresh, is seen in the delightful tenderness and freshness of the landscape. This sunlight is gracious and friendly'.

Because of Withers' fastidiousness about his personal belongings, Tom Roberts nicknamed him 'the orderly colonel', but Withers was the only Heidelberg painter who regularly preferred a slight disorder in his landscape. He not only wanted to depict pulsation and atmospheric vibration, but also the illusion of the movement of storm-driven clouds and foliage tossed by light breezes.

Breezy Day Near Geelong
Oil on canvas; 25.7 × 51.1 cm.
Acquired: 1958
National Gallery of Victoria.

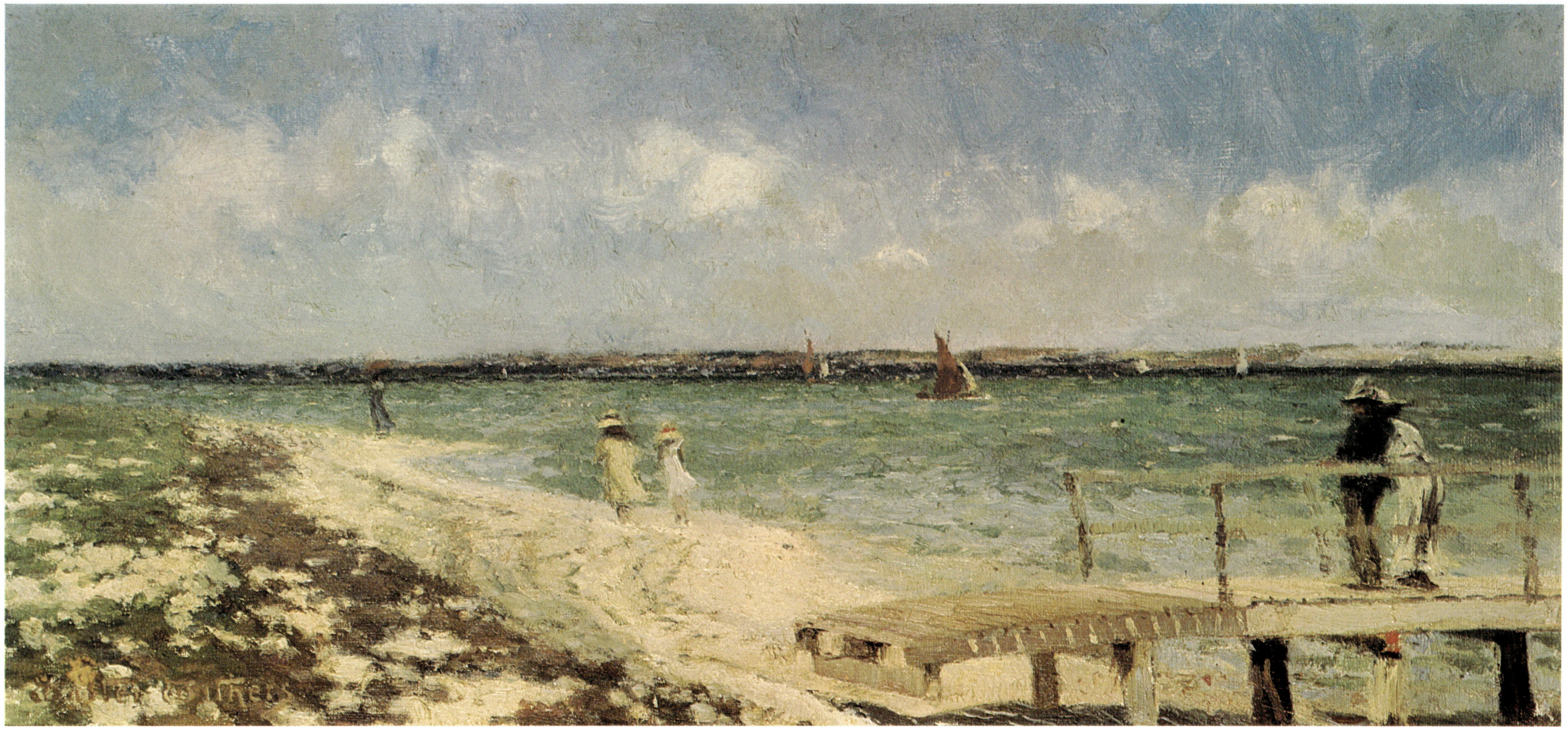

Breezy Day Near Geelong

Ray Crooke

Ray Austin Crooke, born Auburn, Victoria 1922; lived for a long period in Queensland; lives in Sydney.

When Ray Crooke exhibited in 1964 at The Commonwealth Institute, Sir Daryl Lindsay wrote in the catalogue introduction that his works 'had a certain affinity with some of our early Nineteenth Century topographical artists who paid great attention to detail. He did not seem to be concerned with composition or effects of light so much as taking a slice of bush or a piece of pastoral country and describing it literally with infinite care in rather dry paint'.

Crooke has an eye for the naturally composed landscape; his placement of trees and rocks and folds in hills has no suggestion of classes in composition but has a reality that is almost physical. When he does 'compose' by observing the world of palms and natives, or barns and shearing sheds in bright sunlight from the window of a darkened room, he renders the view with natural casualness, but there is always an unexpected shape or fall of light. Gauguin-like views of the lush, tropical world, paradoxically painted with a surface drier than Gauguin's, are the result of his stay on Thursday Island and Cape York during the war and his later return to northern Queensland.

He has also been attracted by the dry grasslands with their sparse trees inland from the tropical coast. The bleached hills and valleys of thick grass frequently roll away from a straggling fence or a scatter of thin, frontal trees, but what dominates is the sense of an infinite, tawny landscape. The painterly touch and vast sweep of the terrain may be prompted by the Heidelberg School but *Cape York Landscape* is untamed; it is no Arcadia, but looks as worn, ancient and remote as a David Davies; the dappled blonde grasses, the dry folding and eroded hills, and the juts of whitish rock offer none of the exhilaration of an Arthur Streeton. It is no lush *Valley of the Tweed* nor does it possess the grandeur that Hans Heysen can conjure from a common quarry; yet Ray Crooke remains something of a factual romantic; he does record the topography but not as impartially as Australia's early artists.

Cape York Landscape
Oil on canvas; 1964; 71.5 × 96.5 cm.
Courtesy of Miss Pamela Bell.

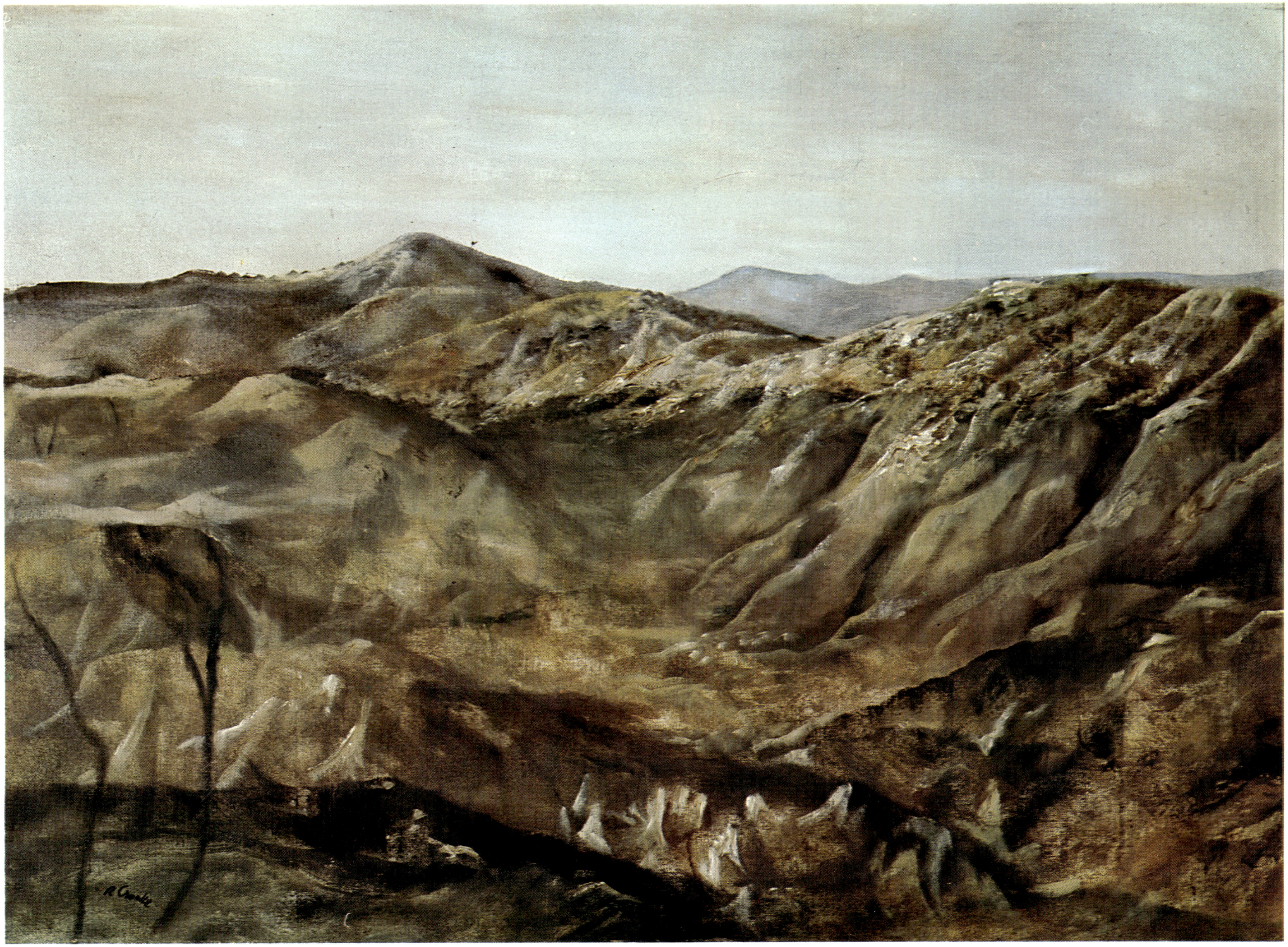

Arthur Streeton

Sir Arthur Ernest Streeton, born at Mount Duneed, near Geelong, Victoria, 1867; died at Olinda, Victoria, 1943.

Arthur Streeton persuaded Australians that theirs was a vast, golden, tawny landscape, its leisurely rivers and equally leisurely vistas, blessed with an eternally blue sky that, in turn, blessed the land with azure shadows. He was able to make a reality of the Utopian dreams of others. 'I fancy,' he wrote, 'canvases all glowing and moving in the happy light and others bright, decorative and chalky and expressive of the hot, trying winds and the slow immense summer. It is IMMENSE, and droughts and cracks in the earth and the creeks all baked mud'.

Though John Olsen was writing of *Circular Quay* in the Art Gallery of New South Wales, what he said is pertinent to the one in Canberra: 'It is interesting to compare *Still Glides the Stream and Shall Forever Glide* with *Circular Quay*. In the former, the artist has attempted to condense form into curved, rhythmic patterns, keeping light to a fairly muted value. In *Circular Quay,* the dancing calligraphy plunges deeply and dramatically into the picture plane, the brush moves with hasty, joyous delight . . .'

Still Glides the Stream and Shall Forever Glide depicts the Yarra River at Eaglemont and was painted just before Streeton left Heidelberg; first titled *An Australian Gloaming,* Streeton retitled it from a line in 'After-Thought', the concluding sonnet of thirty-four that comprise William Wordsworth's 'The River Duddon' that flowed through country beloved by John Glover:

'as I cast my eyes,
I see what was, and is, and will abide;
Still glides the stream and shall forever glide;
The Form remains, The Function never dies;'

Streeton subdued his sense of the transitoriness of life; man is nowhere to be seen amid these beautifully casual rhythms, but a suggestion of a symbolic hope is conveyed in the distant, golden hills.

In *Fire's On, Lapstone Tunnel,* the death of a miner, which so moved Streeton, has been reduced to a painterly notation. From Glenbrook in the Blue Mountains, Streeton wrote to Frederick McCubbin in 1891, of the scene: 'There is a cutting through the vast hill of bright sandstone; the walls of rock run high up and are crowned by gums bronze-green . . . and behind is the deep blue azure heaven, where a crow sails along like a dot with its melancholy, hopeless cry . . . the ganger cries, "Fire, Fire's On"; all the men drop their tools and scatter . . . they raise the rock and lift him onto the stretcher, fold his arms over his chest, and slowly six of them carry him past me. Oh, how full of dread is the grey mysterious expression of death — 'tis like a whirlpool for the eyes'.

Among Streeton's many achievements was his use of the landscape as a repository of the feelings; he could imbue it with the emotions without losing any of his immediacy and sharpness of observation. His landscapes trace stages and development of the feelings; *Still Glides the Stream and Shall Forever Glide* glides through the life of man from rough, loosely painted foreground, to meandering streams and folded hills and, finally, in the words he wrote to Tom Roberts 'the great gold plains'.

Circular Quay
Oil on canvas; 17.73 × 46.2 cm.
Gift of H.S. Irvin, 1958.
Australian National Gallery, Canberra.
Reproduction by kind permission of Mr Oliver Streeton.

Still Glides the Stream and Shall Forever Glide
Oil on canvas; 1890; 82.0 × 153.0 cm.
Acquired: 1890
Art Gallery of New South Wales.
Reproduction by kind permission of Mr Oliver Streeton.

Fire's On, Lapstone Tunnel
Oil on canvas; 1891; 183.8 × 122.5 cm.
Acquired: 1893
Art Gallery of New South Wales.
Reproduction by kind permission of Mr Oliver Streeton.

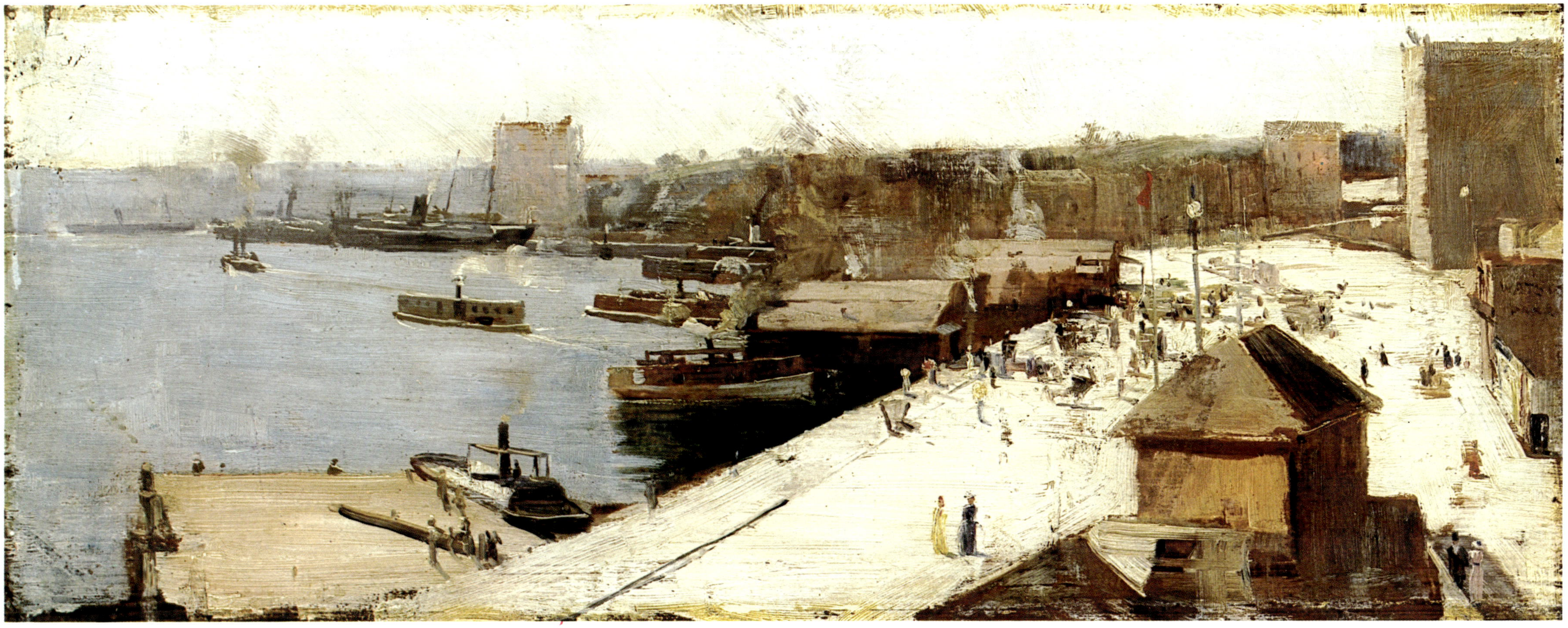

Circular Quay

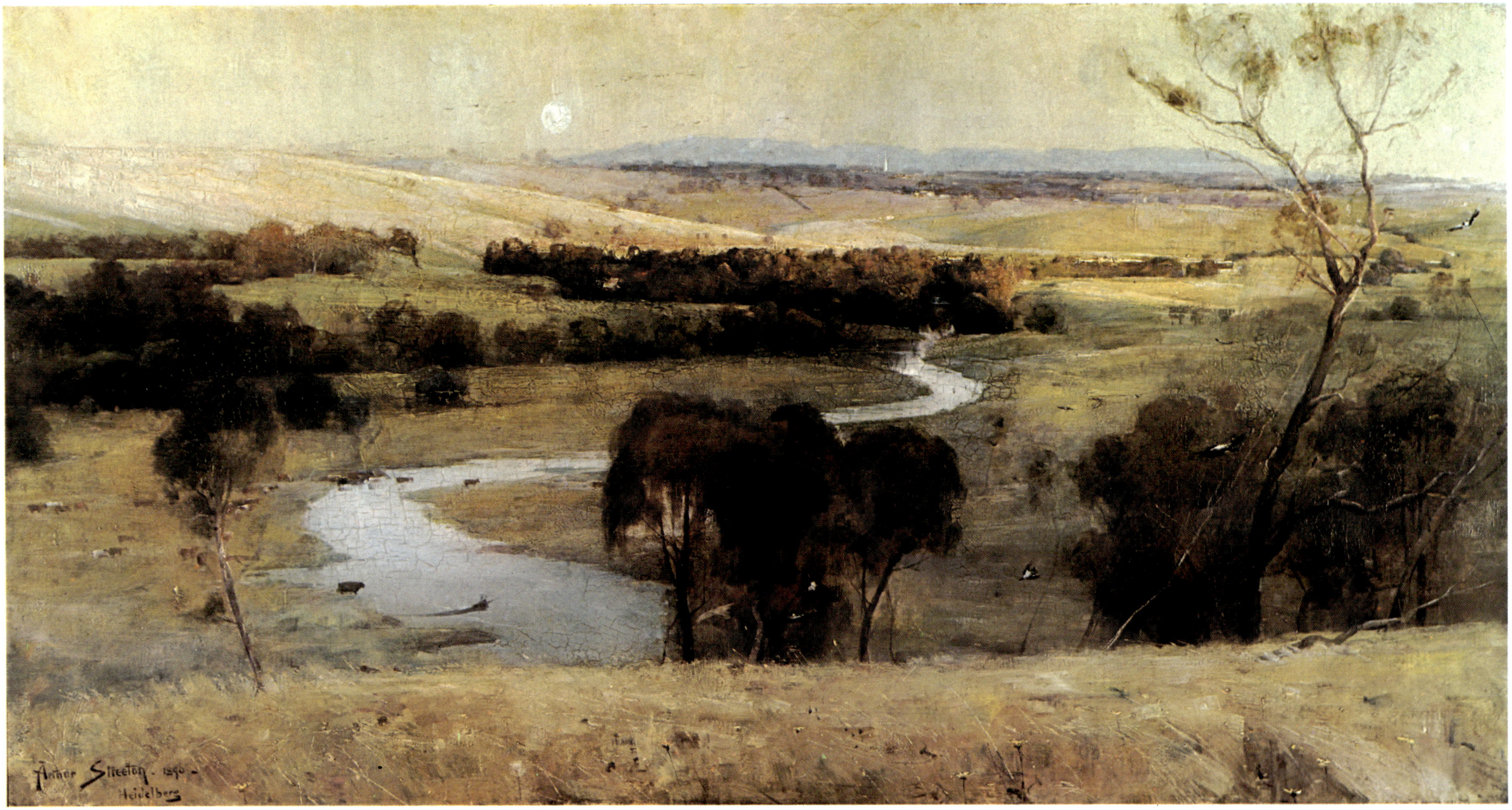

Still Glides the Stream and Shall Forever Glide

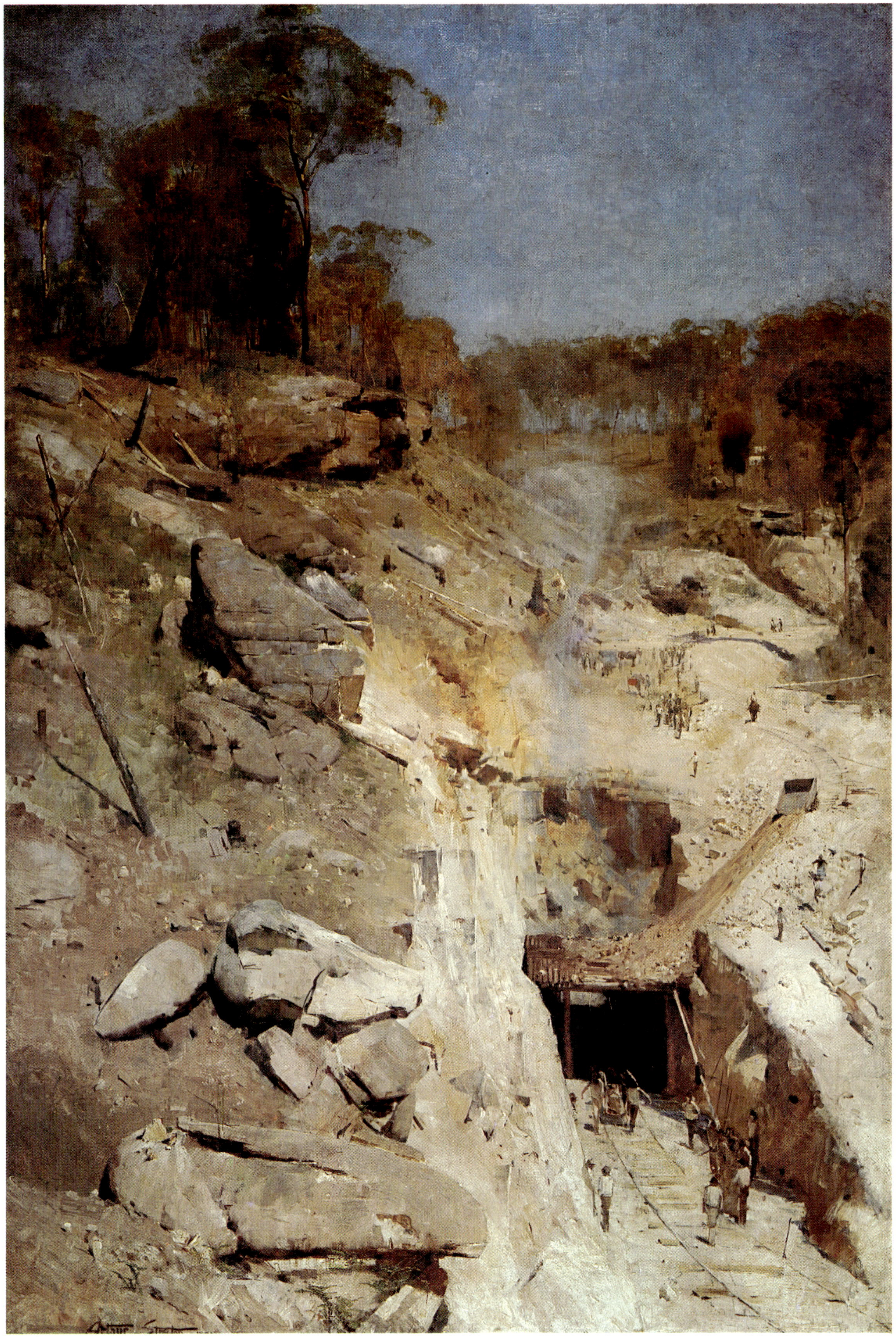

Fire's On, Lapstone Tunnel

Bryan Westwood

Bryan Westwood, born in Lima, Peru, 1930. Arrived in Australia to attend school in 1940; lives in Sydney.

Centennial Park
Oil on canvas; 1972; 76 × 101 cm.
Courtesy of Mrs Caroline Hagan

His broad sweep of yellowed grass and harmonious recession of the vista might have kinships with the Heidelberg School but Bryan Westwood is no Impressionist because his paintings are not built from light; the sun is absorbed by the grass and the trees; light falls upon the signpost but it is not reflected. To sparkle, to vibrate, to catch fleeting changes in dappled shadows or in the gradual sweep of sunshine across a field are not Westwood's aims. The result is that his paintings, whether of fields, walls and cliffs, have a quiet poetic evenness that is not found in a recent group of painters called variously New Realists, Photorealists, Radical Realists and Sharp Focus Realists. Westwood has introduced a new form of realism, but it is not as uncanny as Jeffrey Smart's, as anecdotal as Julian Ashton's, as ordered as Rah Fizelle's or as romantic as Blamire Young's and Donald Friend's. He is not concerned with simulating textures in the manner of Sali Herman.

Westwood's paintings are very formal and very conscious of composition; their geometry is precise and calculated; nothing is indeterminate. Consequently his work should resemble Rah Fizelle's but does not because Westwood creates, by the very size of areas and the subtle juxtaposition of hues, dream-like poetic moods. In *Centennial Park* the signpost and fence, the edge of the trees and the path are firmly plotted; the acute-angle shape between the trees is repeated where fence meets post and, inverted, with the shape of the grass; but these formal elements are subordinate to the visionary mood, the key to which is the pale figure in the distance. The whole of the park seems to be his dream and the painting's sharp observations are like those clear images that appear in dreams along with the vague and suggested.

What he does have in common with the Heidelberg School and Ray Crooke, one of its very distant cousins, is the belief that man is not alienated from the landscape, or urbanscape, and, in turn, that he has not rendered city or country inhospitable.

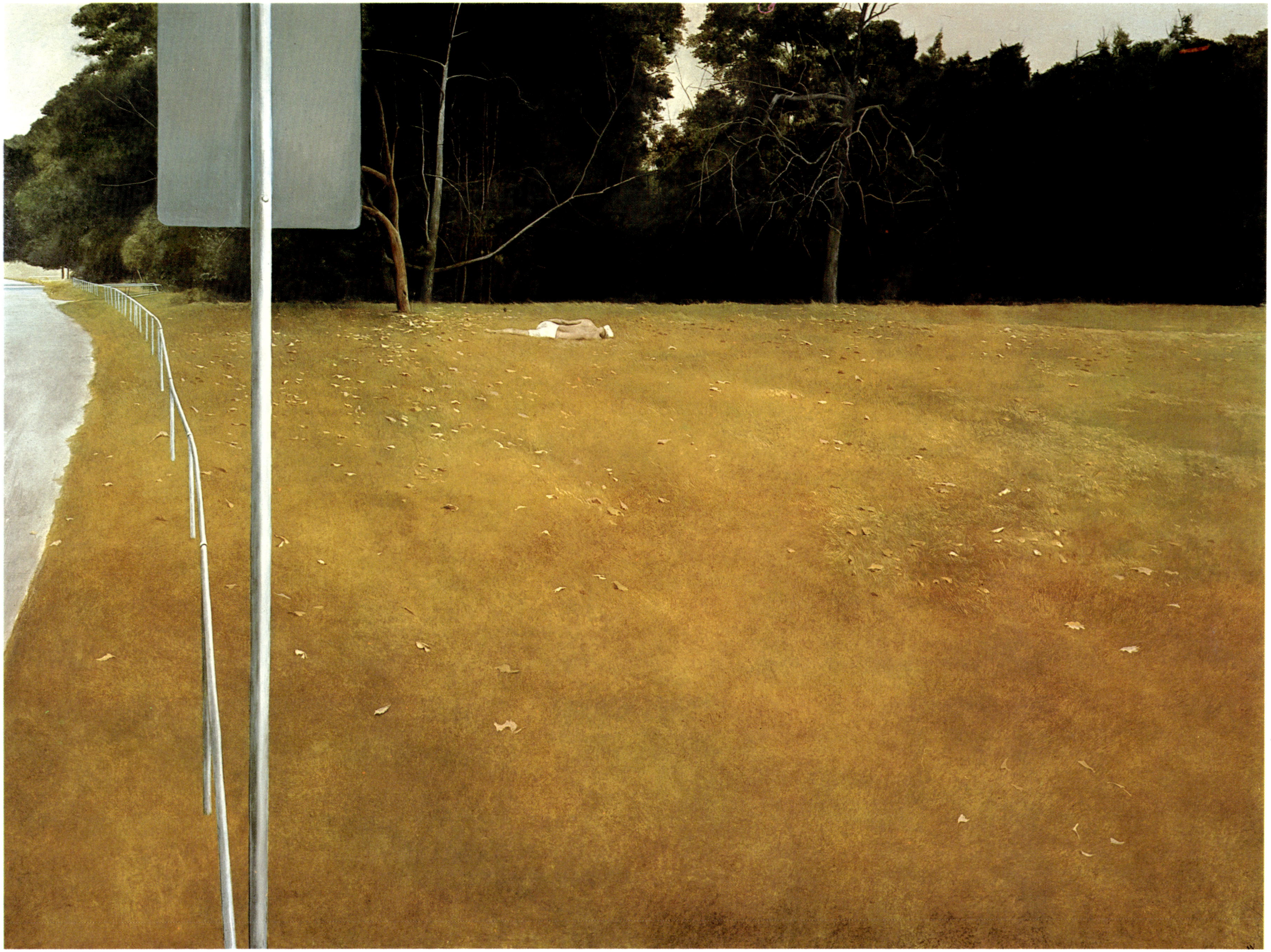

Centennial Park

Frederick McCubbin

Frederick McCubbin, born West Melbourne 1855; died South Yarra, Victoria, 1917.

Frederick McCubbin, who painted at Box Hill with Tom Roberts and Arthur Streeton, has long been considered the artist of the melancholy bush within whose grey-green enclosure of close foliage pioneers are down in their luck, their children are lost and their friends receive a bush burial. That there were more facets to his work than the elegiac is amply demonstrated by *Winter Sunlight* and *View towards Melbourne from the Yarra.* He did want to ennoble the grief and trials of the bushman in a manner not attempted by others of the Heidelberg School; he continued the early genre and anecdotal interests of Conrad Martens and S.T. Gill into the Impressionist period, but it was not until 1907 that he was confirmed in Impressionist techniques which did not suit his former subject matter and were not attuned to the teachings of Eugen von Guerard whose classes he attended at the National Gallery School, Melbourne, from 1876.

The early painting, *Old Stables,* where the gloomy, enclosed space is opened by the flight of a single bird, reminds one of the simile that life is like the flight of a bird from darkness to darkness, and indicates McCubbin's predilection for the symbolic. Consequently most of his work was not concerned with expansive vistas, but with a screen of trees, subtle shadows and a stilled, quiet, contemplative atmosphere. The subdued pulsation of his surfaces was paralleled in David Davies.

McCubbin did reconcile genre painting with a low-keyed Impressionism, but he wanted to make the human presence of psychological importance; Julian Ashton assured him that it was just as historical to record life around one as to seek subjects from the past, and, it seems, saved him from Victorian anecdotalism.

However, it was McCubbin's sojourn in London in 1907 that drove out figures and replaced them with Arcadian scenes, alive with flecks of high-keyed paint often applied with the palette knife, as in *Winter Sunlight*. He wrote from London: 'Turner — divine like pearls — dreams of colour, no theatrical effects, but mist and cloud, sea and land, drenched, as they actually are, in light'. *View towards Melbourne from the Yarra* is the most felicitous blend of Turner and Heidelberg painting in Australian landscape art; the rainbow gently suggests that the earth is being born anew, but lest symbolism intrude unduly the cows are indifferent. His countryside was no longer drenched in shadow and meaning; it was domesticated and lively and peopled by happy folk and happy fowls. It was still the landscape of the ordinary man but life was casual; the 'chook' is no bird of destiny. It is a long way from *Old Stables.*

Old Stables
Oil on canvas; c.1880-85; 45.8 × 61 cm.
Acquired: 1932, Felton Bequest.
National Gallery of Victoria.

Winter Sunlight
Oil on canvas; 1908; 58.0 × 76.2 cm.
Acquired: 1960
Art Gallery of South Australia.

View towards Melbourne from the Yarra
Oil on canvas; 1913; 92.5 × 182 cm.
Acquired: 1973
Australian National Gallery, Canberra.

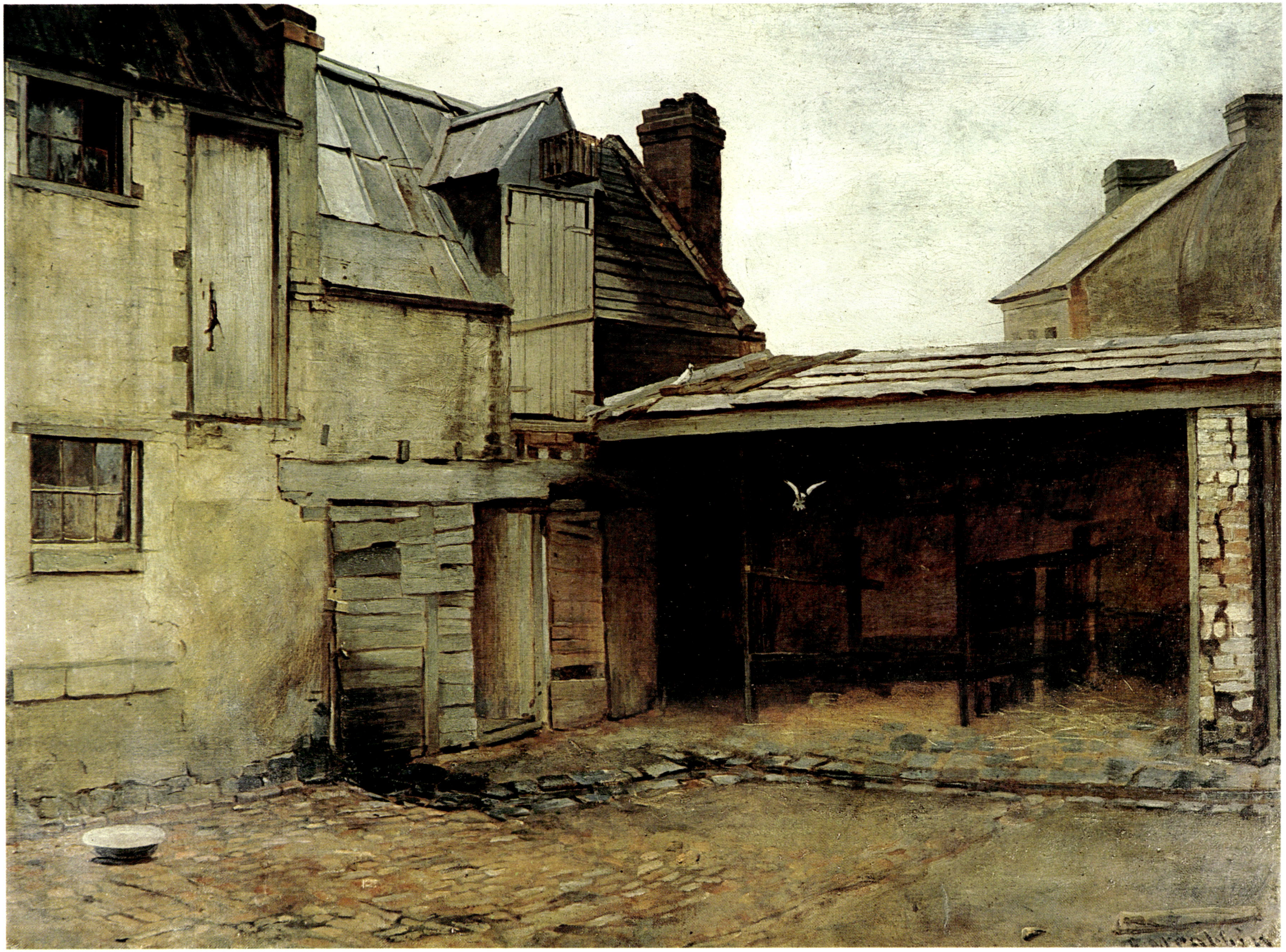

Old Stables

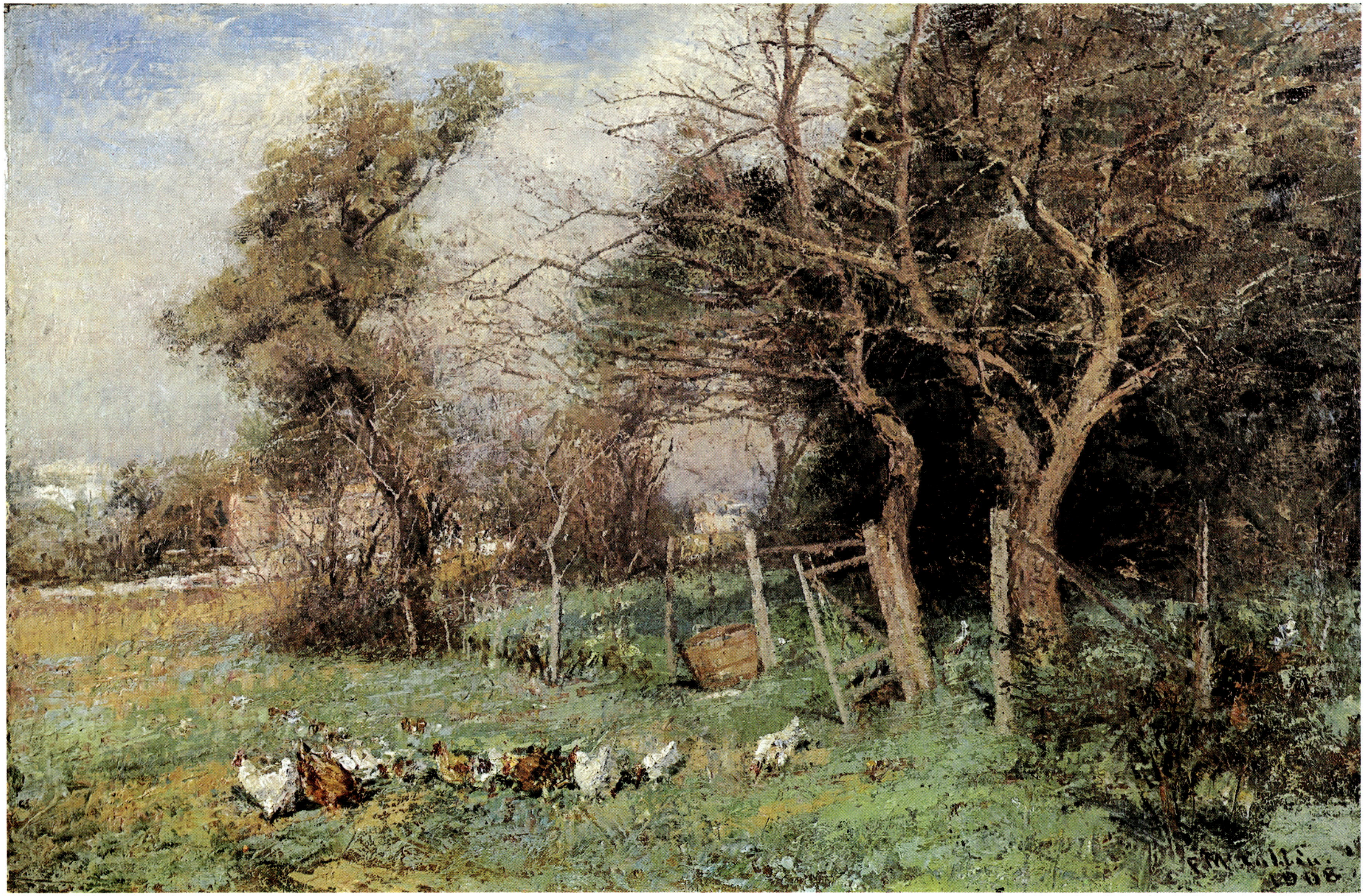

Winter Sunlight

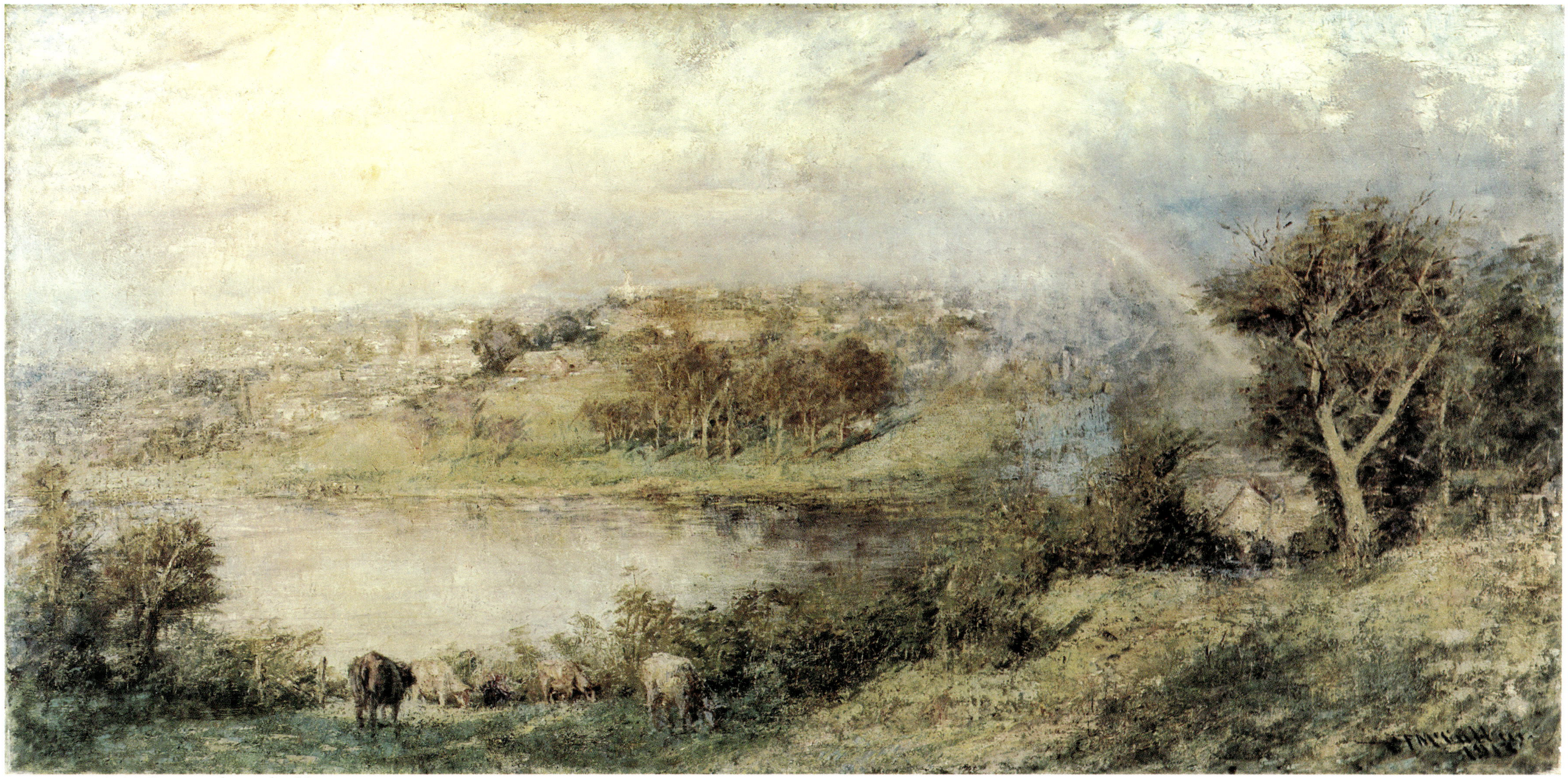

View towards Melbourne from the Yarra

Sydney Long

Sydney 'Sid' Long, born Goulburn, New South Wales, 1878; died in London, 1955.

Sydney Long was one of those rather rare painters who was not over-concerned about developing a consistent and recognisable style; nor did he feel that a failure to fulfil one's aspirations meant artistic defeat. He could paint a native as flute-player in an *art-nouveau* landscape decorated with magpies; a file of flamingos following Pan, all in *art-nouveau* rhythms, across an idealised landscape; broadly swept and quite realistic landscapes in the manner of Arthur Streeton, albeit with large decorative areas; closely observed scenes like Argyle Street and Argyle Cut (near Cumberland Street that Julian Ashton, his teacher, painted) and scenes of Devon and Constable's Country.

Long felt that the Australian landscape was open to fresh interpretations and wrote in 1905: 'The exhibitions have consequently reflected not the primitive landscape of the country, but bits of seascape, scraps of orchards and blossom that might be anywhere, not forgetting the eternal view of the Harbour. There seems to be as much difficulty in getting the artists further afield as settling the man on the land . . . This Australian feeling is not to be got by sticking in a gum tree. Even the universal recipe of the inevitable swagman, given us by some of the critics, will not always answer. If the delicate relation of the colour values is not there, all the swagmen and cows in Australia will not make it Australian'.

However, Long did win the Wynne Prize for landscape — in those days *very* Australian — in 1938 and 1940.

Long was critical of his own activities but he was living in a period when Heysen and Streeton may have felt tempted to disown their followers.

Certainly the delicate nuances and harmoniously subtle gradations are present in *Feeding Chickens at Richmond;* trees and grass may owe something to Streeton, but the dashing strokes at both sides are his own and indicate that Long was a rare Impressionist who appreciated the summariness of peripheral vision. His dream of an Australian painting was not one of grandeur but of casual fleeting notation. Compare the tiny white bird to the left of the girl with McCubbin's; Long's painting is full of exhilarating charm.

Feeding Chickens at Richmond
Oil on canvas; c.1896; 57.5 × 77.4 cm.
Acquired: 1963
Australian National Gallery, Canberra.

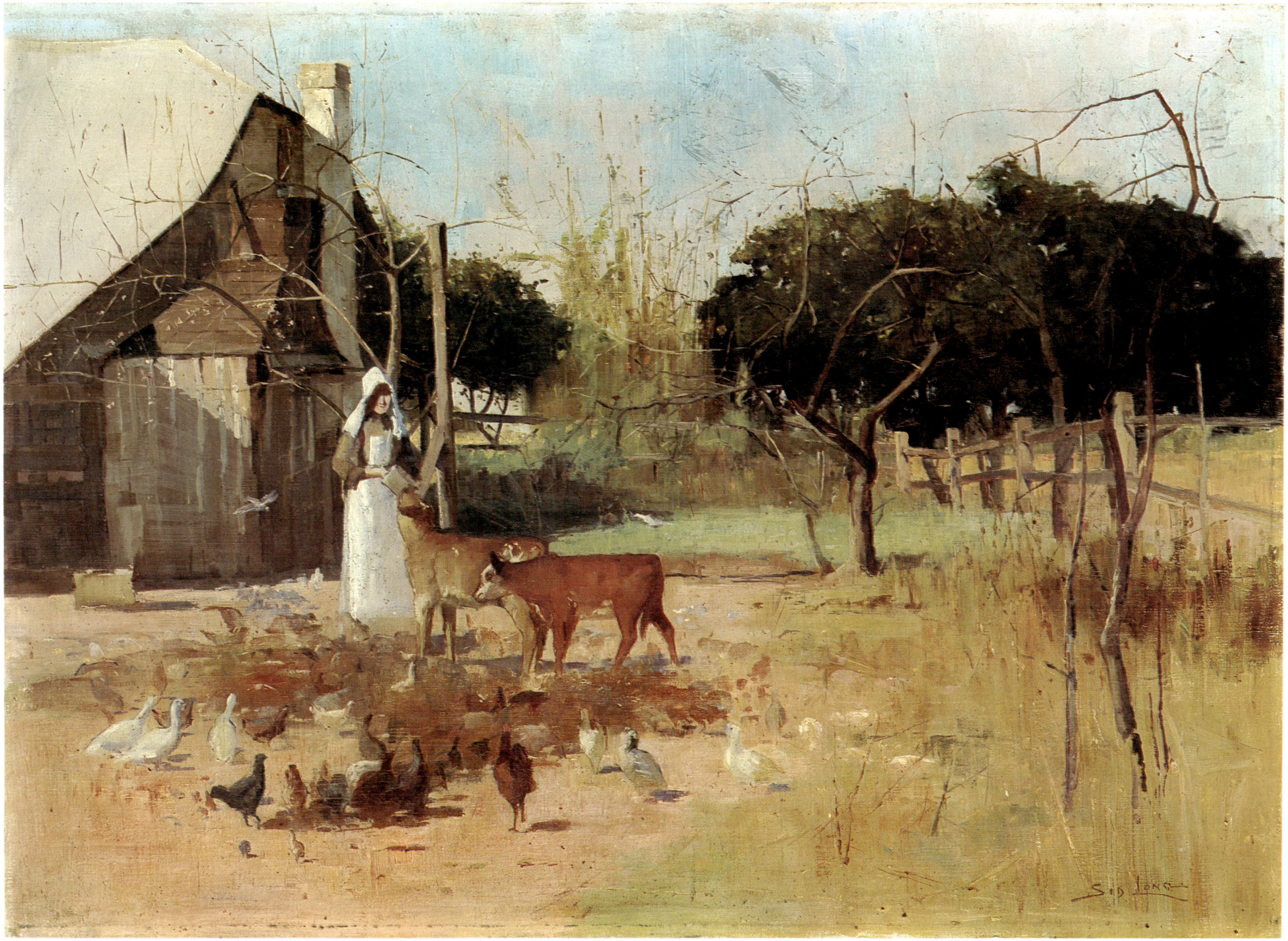

Feeding Chickens at Richmond

Hans Heysen

Sir Hans Heysen, born Hamburg, Germany, 1877. Arrived in Adelaide 1883; died at Hahndorf, South Australia, 1968

As with Arthur Streeton, followers have obscured the contribution of Hans Heysen; one of the penalties of his fame, (and the fame included winning the Wynne Prize for landscape painting eight times between 1904 and 1932) wrote Robert Campbell is 'that he has had like Streeton, a host of imitators who, lacking the master's knowledge and amazing technical ability, have debased the integrity of his vision with a multiplicity of works in the same vein', for Hans Heysen has been falsely associated with stalwart gums, rosily lit by the dawn or shrouded in soft mist. His aim was to combine the massiveness of the Barbizon school with the intimacy of fleshy pinks revealed by peeling bark and sunlit ochres and aquamarines. Heysen brought Buvelot's worship of the Barbizon painters down to earth. He wrote to Lionel Lindsay, 'It is just this feeling of exhilaration and love for sunlight that I miss in the Barbizon Painters — but it seems almost a sacrilege to say one misses anything in the works of these fine and sincere men'.

Sincerity was Heysen's motivation; a bent tree in *Sunshine and Shadow* — and it is only with Sidney Nolan, William Salmon and Fred Williams that we encounter such a frieze and palisade of trees — does not disguise its dependence on Corot, for, in 1920, Heysen was writing to Lindsay of 'a tree that Father Corot would have loved and watched'.

Heysen saw the tree as individual presence, but also as essential pictorial structure; *The Quarry* is constructed with the same bony firmness as the bare hills of the Flinders Ranges; 'I also think is absolutely essential to have a definite plan of attack before beginning each watercolour,' he wrote. 'To "muddle" around in the hope of getting something in watercolour must lead to chaos and *mud*, and yet how often do we see this indecision and its consequences'.

Some Heidelberg painters seemed to be undecided and tentative to him; too preoccupied with dissolving form, for, as in *The Hill of the Creeping Shadow, Flinders Ranges,* he wanted, 'Fine big simple forms against clear transparent skies — and a sense of spaciousness everywhere'.

Only Nolan and Drysdale have achieved such spaciousness and only they and Heysen have seen the desert as Heysen did: 'I have seen it on calm days of crystalline purity when the eye could trace, as it were, to the end of the world, bringing with it that wonderful sense of infinity that a land of moist atmosphere could never give'.

The Quarry
Watercolour on paper; 1922; 48.2 × 64.8 cm.
Acquired: 1922
Art Gallery of New South Wales.
Reproduction by kind permission of Mr David Heysen.

The Hill of the Creeping Shadow, Flinders Ranges
Oil on canvas; 1929; 66.0 × 92.0 cm.
Acquired: 1929
Art Gallery of New South Wales.
Reproduction by kind permission of Mr David Heysen.

Sunshine and Shadow
Oil on canvas; 1904-5; 176.5 × 114.3 cm.
Acquired: 1906, Felton Bequest.
National Gallery of Victoria.
Reproduction by kind permission of Mr David Heysen.

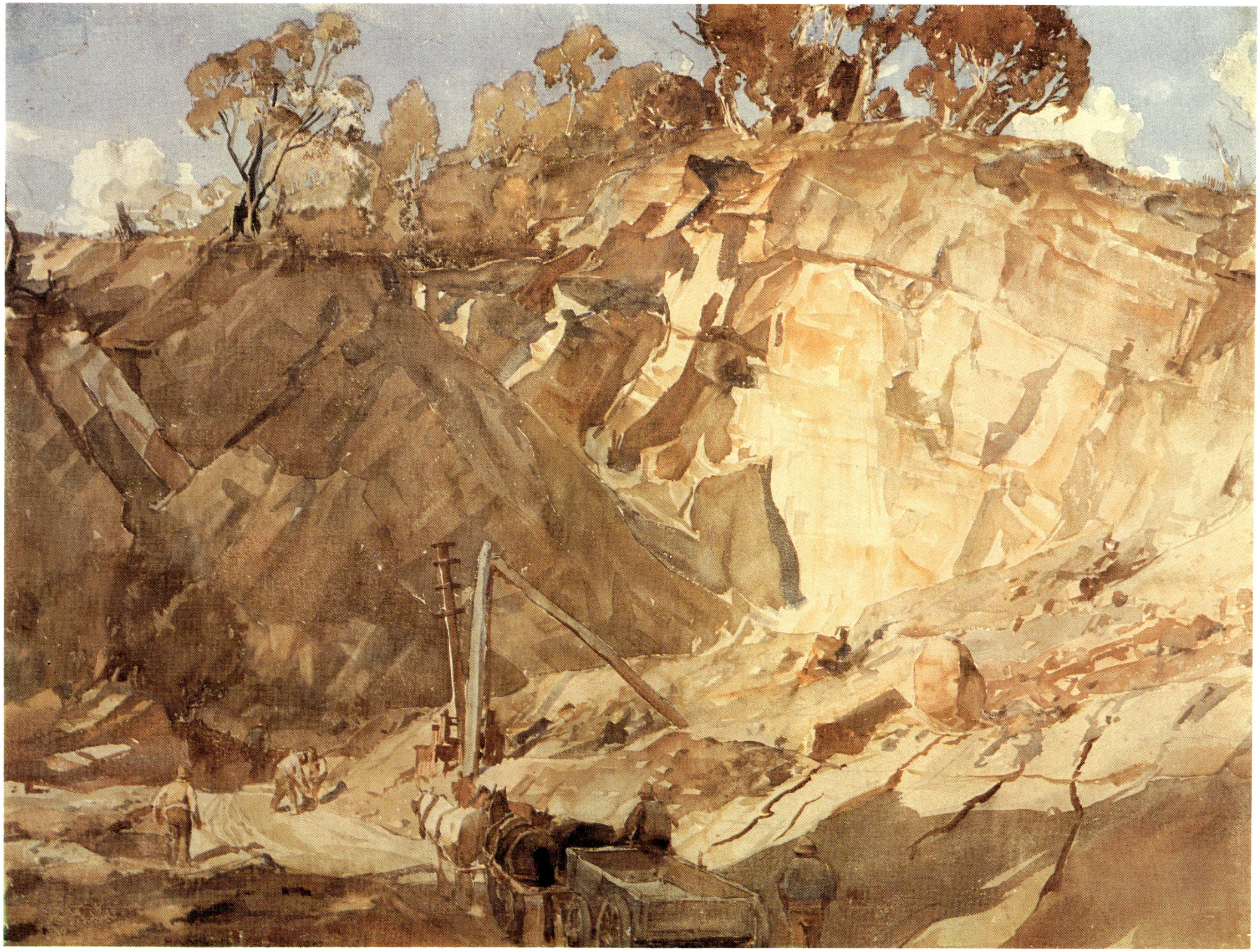

The Quarry

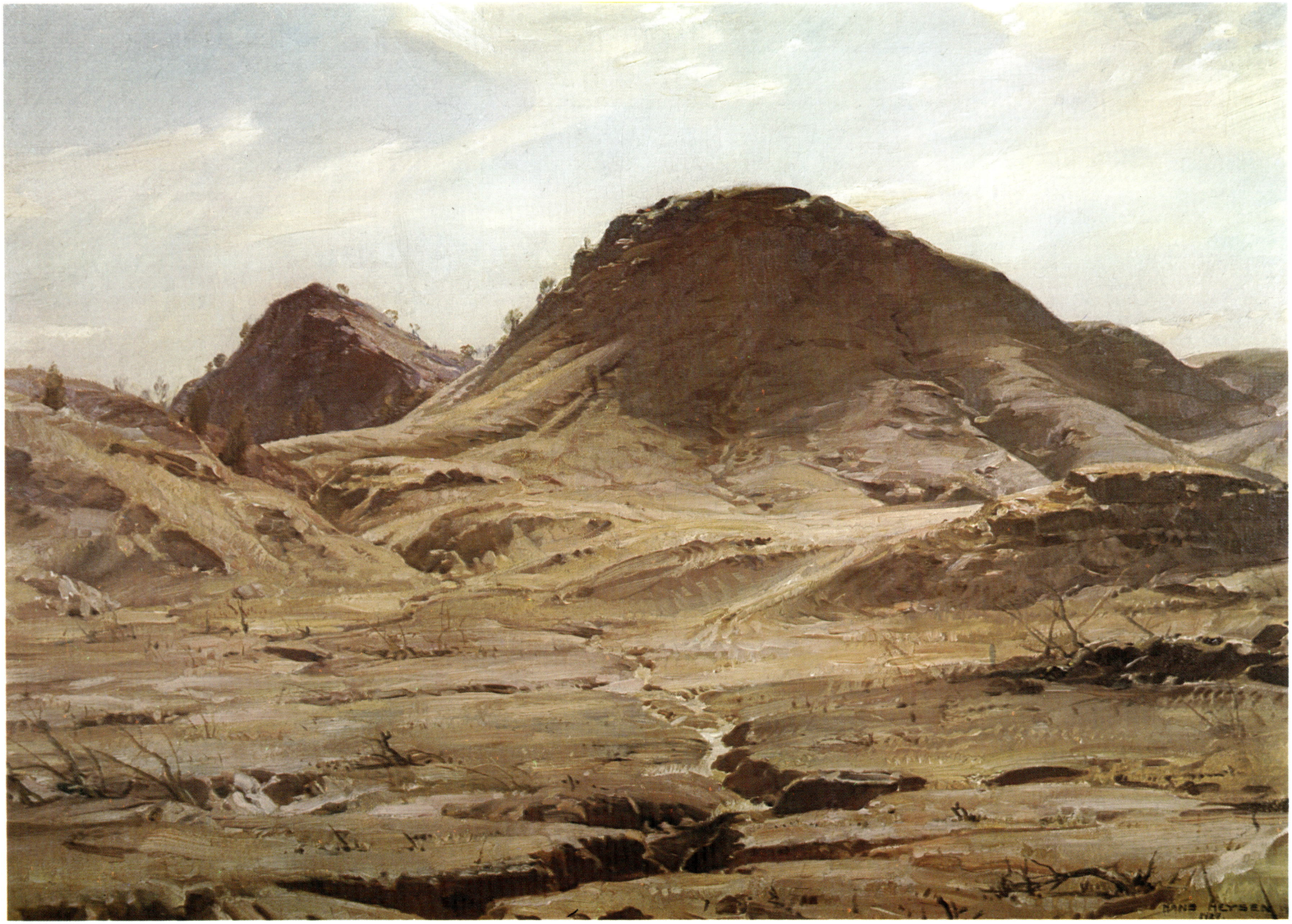

The Hill of the Creeping Shadow, Flinders Ranges

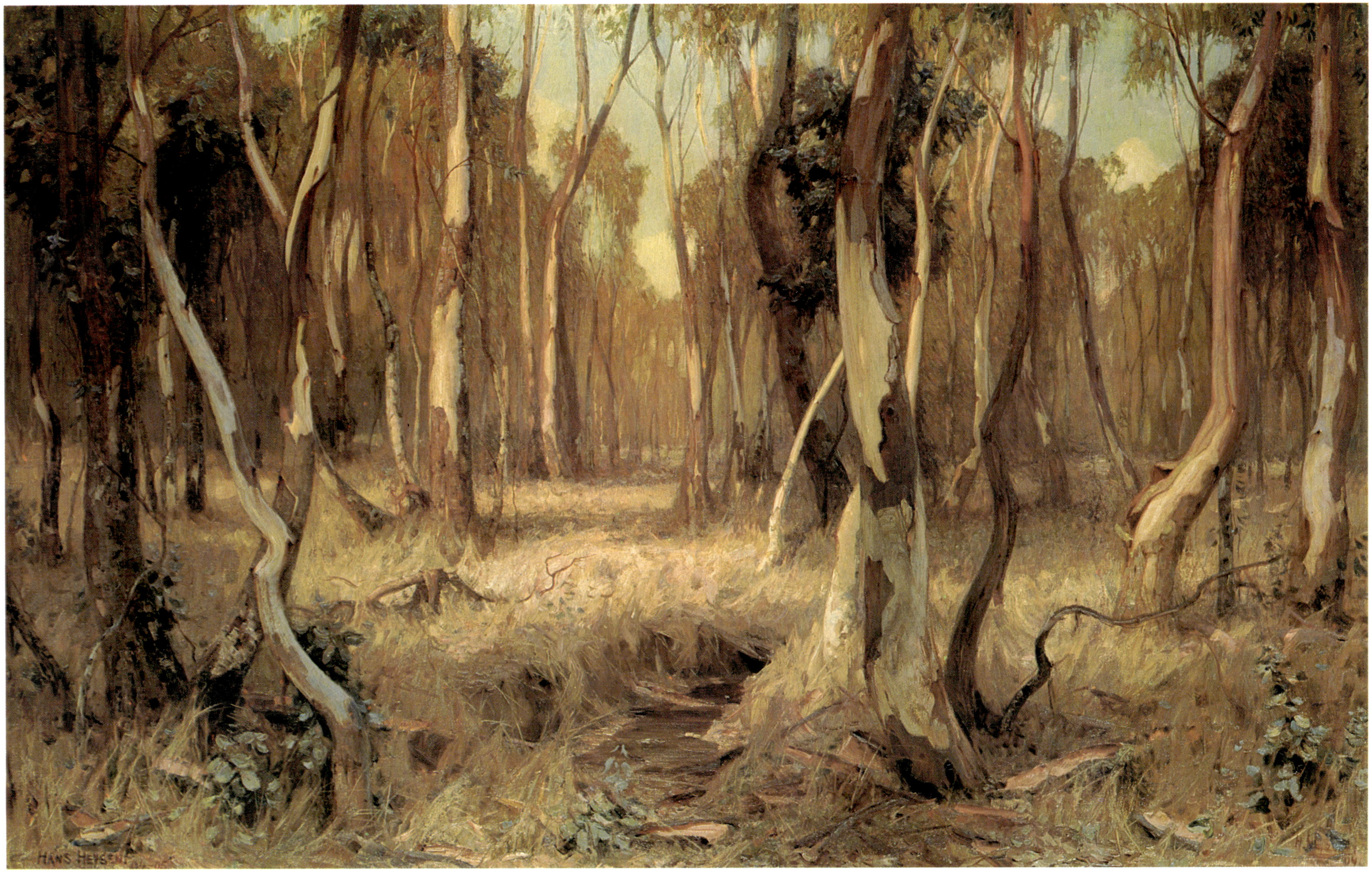

Sunshine and Shadow

Eric Smith

Eric John Smith, born in Melbourne, 1919; lives in Sydney.

Falling Bark with which Eric Smith won the Wynne Prize for landscape painting (he won again in 1974) is a close view of the impenetrable bush. Frederick McCubbin and Sidney Nolan have at times been concerned with the facade of the forest that will scarcely allow the permeation of light; it seeps through, spent, divided and weakened. Smith's solution is to let the limbs of the gums create a loose design across a tawny background, soft, tremulous and fleeting, that resembles a pattern of light seen out of focus. From this, rather than being imposed upon it, arise the branches and falling bark. Broken outlines allow the trunks and branches to fuse partially with the background.

It is as if a tree in a mist-laden Hans Heysen were seen at close quarters, but Eric Smith is not seeking grandeur and permanence, for all partakes of John Olsen's 'flux'. The bark falls, the pale, fleshy limbs of the tree are momentarily revealed, the background shifts and shivers, the limbs trace a delicate, transitory pattern. A galah flashes into sight.

Eric Smith was closely associated with John Olsen and his notion of the landscape as encompassing flux, for in 1956 Smith, Olsen, John Passmore, Robert Klippel and William Rose formed Direction 1 which signalled a new abstraction rather inaccurately described as Abstract Expressionism, but certainly avoiding the formalities of geometrical abstraction. Never a pure abstractionist, Smith was concerned with placing images of flowers, trees, Christ and elements of still-life in a background that was on the plane of the foreground. He often accomplished this by scumbling a thick surface over a richly coloured under-painting which showed through in broken patches. This preoccupation with narrowing the distance between image and ground results in a rather mystical, visionary view of the bush; mystical in the sense of seeing the universe in a grain of sand or piece of bark. The minutiae of the bush epitomises the forest of gum trees.

Falling Bark
Oil on canvas; 1972; 183 × 244.3 cm.
Acquired: 1972
Art Gallery of New South Wales.

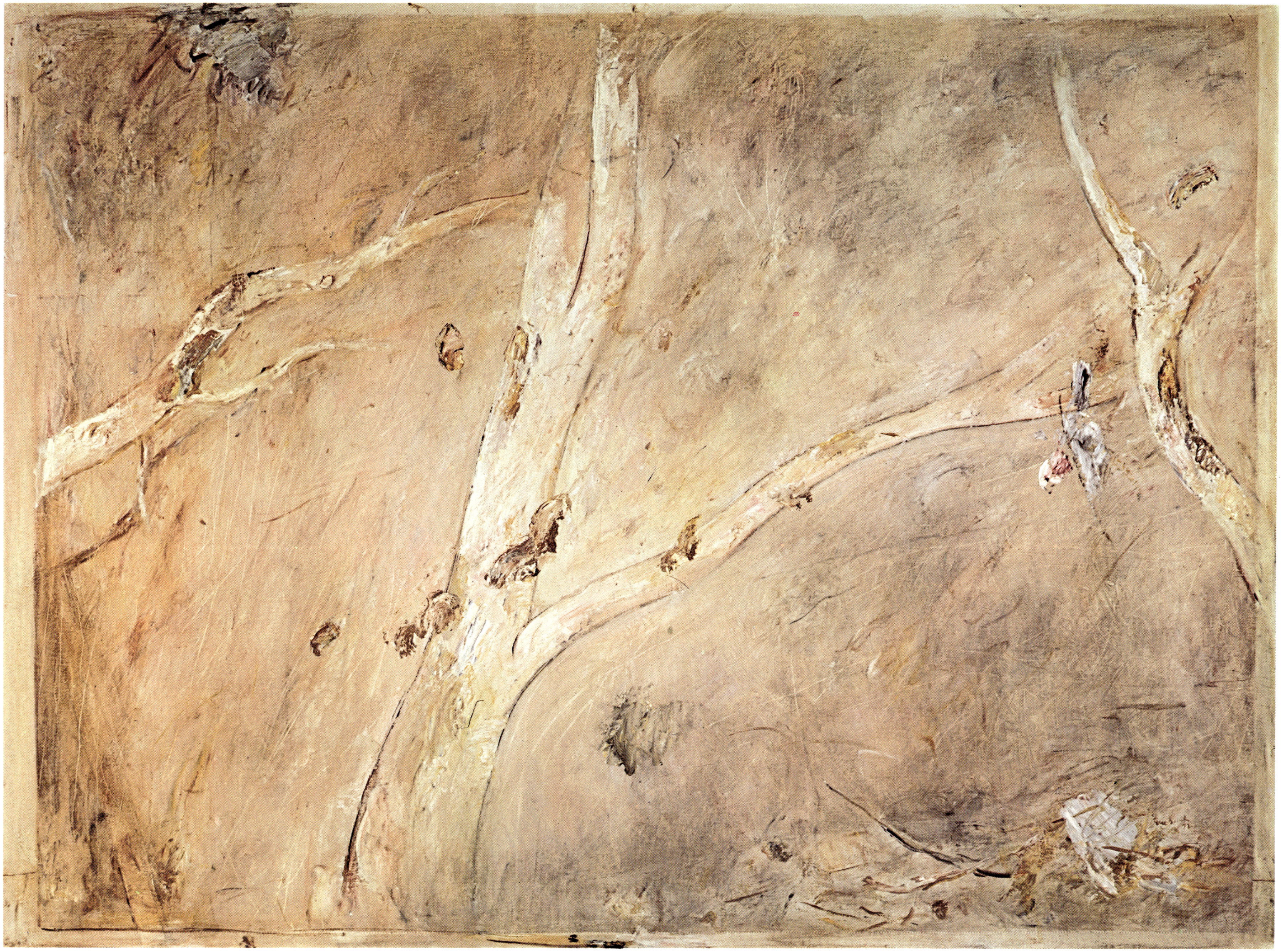

Falling Bark

Elioth Gruner

Elioth Gruner, born Gisborne, New Zealand, 1882. Arrived in Australia, 1883; died in Sydney, 1939.

Elioth Gruner first achieved fame through catching, with lively verisimilitude, the raking, oblique light of early morning on fence, foliage or sloping hillside. Such practice led to his being called the last of the Australian Impressionists, but he did not compose through dappled areas or juxtaposed brush-strokes of complementary colours; indeed, his flecks of light seem added, like snow-flakes, to a solid structure.

It is misleading to say that he forsook Impressionist techniques for a greater interest in embracing vistas after his trip to Europe in 1923. Two years earlier he painted, without his habitual inflections of paint and accents of light, the broad expanse of the Tweed Valley. A typical landscape had been commissioned by the Trustees of the Art Gallery of New South Wales in 1919; Gruner discovered this vast panorama near Murwillumbah and painted it over four months in the open air. With it he won the Wynne Prize for landscape in 1921 — a prize he won six times between 1916 and 1937.

Bellingen Pastoral reveals the true force in Gruner's work; like Heysen, he admired Arthur Streeton's command of broad, rhythmical, rolling and sweeping landscape and it was Streeton's expansive grasp and interpenetration of slow, leisurely curves of river, rock and ridge that were to be continued by Lloyd Rees. Gruner, however, was more detached than Streeton, Heysen and Rees; he did not want to infuse his meadows, slopes and tree-clad hills with emotion. He followed the advice that William Orpen had given in London when criticising the Australian exhibition there in 1923; less detail, drier paint and pastel surfaces. *Bellingen Pastoral* and the quieter, more intimate and very modest *Spring at Bathurst* reveal how Gruner abandoned flecks of Impressionist paint, careful tonal gradations and fastidious touches for simpler spaces that were to influence painters like Dorrit Black and Douglas Dundas.

Gruner so reduced romantic overtones that it was not until Jeffrey Smart, Bryan Westwood, Rah Fizelle and William Salmon, that a similar mood recurred in the depiction of Australian landscape. Gruner's dry understatement has been a constant tradition in Australian art from Gill, Young and Julian Ashton to Nolan and, at times, Fred Williams.

The Valley of the Tweed
Oil on canvas; 1921; 142.2 × 172.7 cm.
Acquired: 1921, having been commissioned by The Trustees of the Art Gallery of New South Wales.
Reproduction by kind permission of the Perpetual Trustee Company Limited.

Bellingen Pastoral
Oil on canvas; 1937; 63.8 × 76.2 cm.
Acquired: 1940, Felton Bequest.
National Gallery of Victoria.

Spring at Bathurst
Oil on canvas; 50.6 × 61.0 cm.
Acquired: 1935, Felton Bequest.
National Gallery of Victoria.

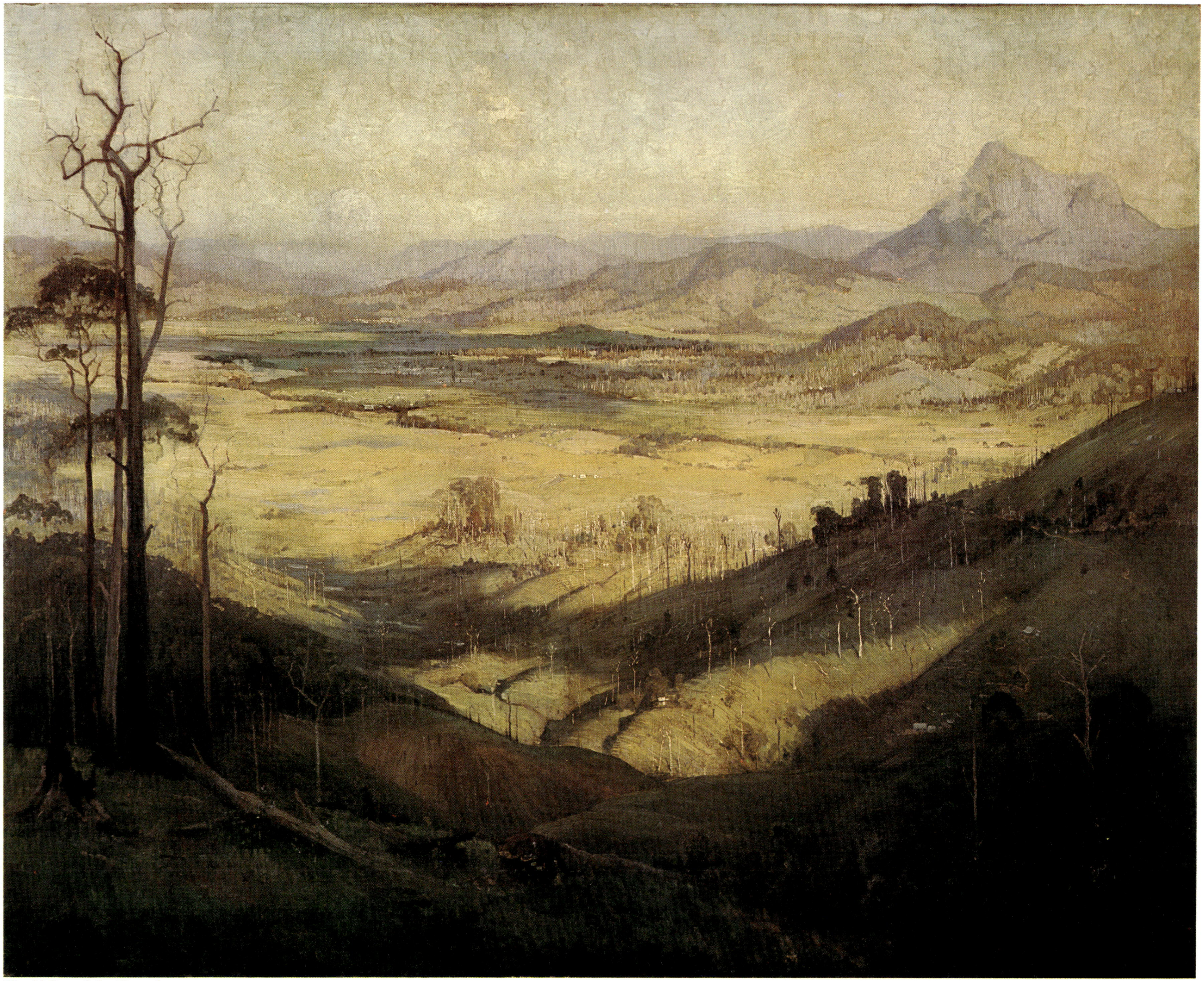

The Valley of the Tweed

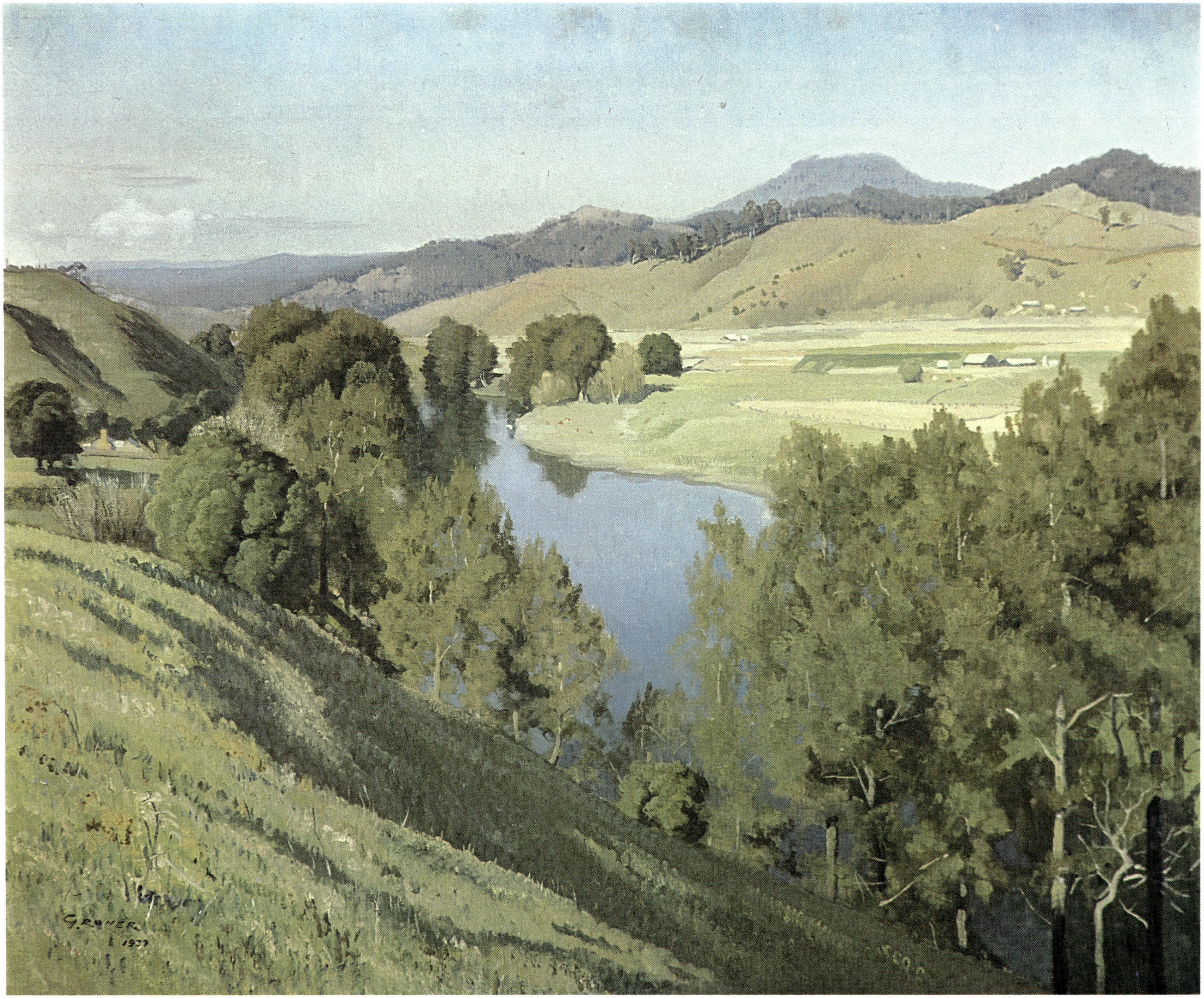

Bellingen Pastoral

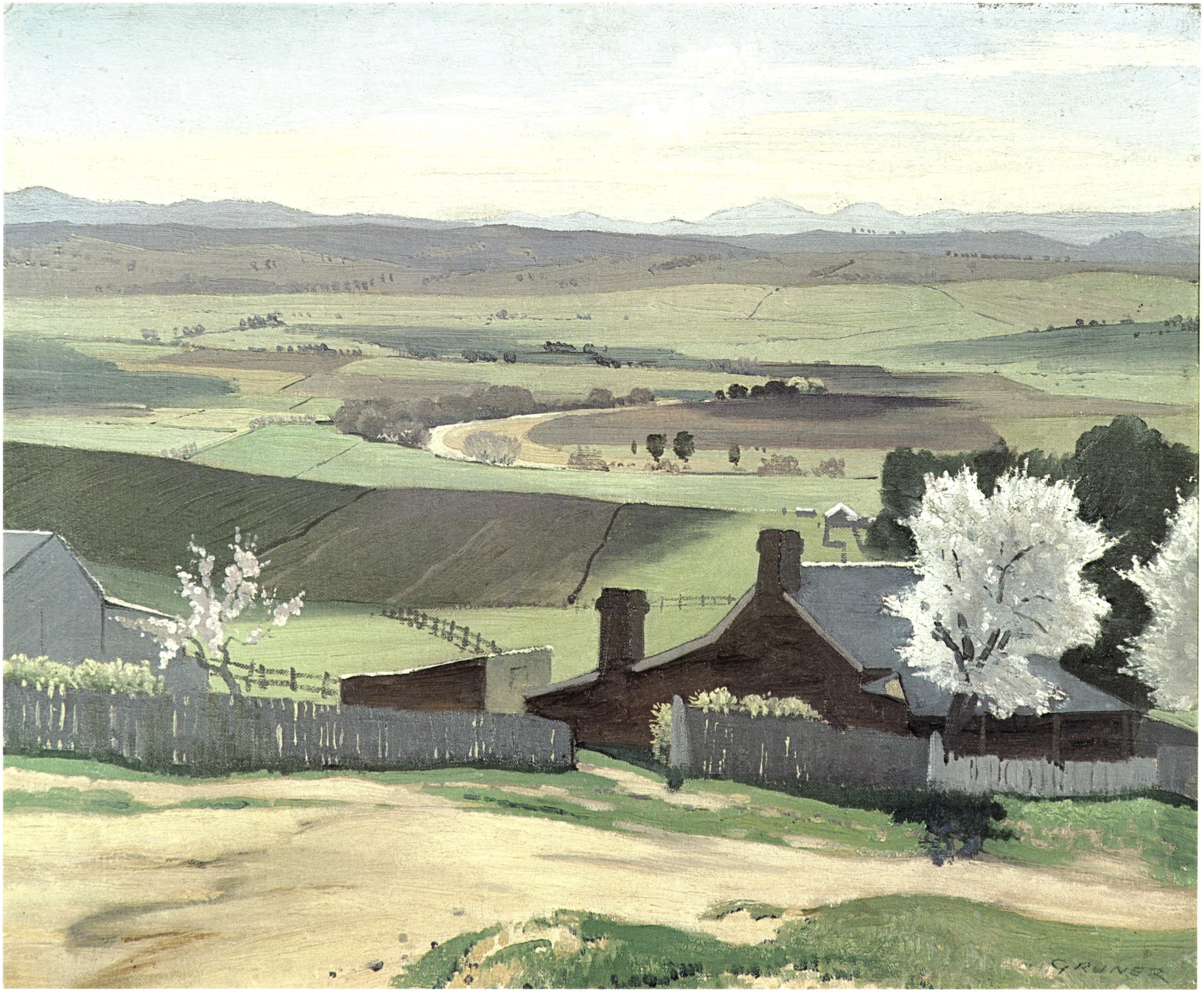

Spring at Bathurst

Brett Whiteley

Brett Whiteley, born in Sydney, 1939; lives in Sydney

Baudelaire's Drive is an ambiguous title; there is the drive and dedication that directed Baudelaire, poet and critic, or the drive through the territory of the Baudelairian imagination with its fusion of fantastic, hyperbolic and realistic images.

Visual and literary ambiguities have continually fascinated Brett Whiteley; he relishes the antithesis between good and evil and a multiple reading of forms. In his first one-man show in London in March 1962, a series of paintings and collages teemed with sensual shapes that could be read as hill or buttock, breast or mountain, and clefts in body and landscape. These eroticised landscapes in succulent creamy whites, subdued brick-reds and golden ochres were enlivened by his inventive line, at times casual and tentative, at times purposeful in its trajectory.

As John Olsen noted, such shapes nod in the direction of Lloyd Rees, but Whiteley so piles his bulging forms pell-mell that they leave little room for air, relaxation or easy rhythms.

In *Bauderlaire's Drive* the mood is relaxed, the tumult stilled and the muscular wrestling of forms concluded. It is an apostrophe to the evening's pervasive peace. 'For a long time,' Whiteley said, 'I tried in the Baudelairian sense to bring the two things (good and evil) together . . . to try to reconcile them. I thought it was immoral to paint a picture which was about the good forces without making reference to vice and the attraction of evil. Now I don't do that'.

One of twelve paintings on the theme of the river and exhibited in 1975, *Baudelaire's Drive* is a deep blue nocturnal landscape traversed by a river that swells and contracts with biomorphic ease and flows through incidental images of multiple associations: a bird nests on a branch levitated in the evening shadows; another leaves an undulating line behind it; enclosed, bejewelled gardens and curvilinear clouds are afloat and a curious sharp green tree rises on the river bank. This is no calm stream out of Arthur Streeton nor a majestic river from Nolan's domain; it could flow from the Anna Livia chapter in James Joyce's 'Finnegans Wake' where Finnegan's dream is full of associations with names of the world's rivers. 'It all but husheth the lethest zswound. Oronoko! What's your trouble . . . Can't hear the waters of. The chittering waters of. Flitting bats, field mice bawk talk. Ho!'

Yes, Ho!, for requests for logical explanations of *Baudelaire's Drive* beg the question of Brett Whiteley's intentions.

Baudelaire's Drive
Oil on canvas; 1975; 229 × 190 cm.
Courtesy of the Kym Bonython Gallery, Sydney.

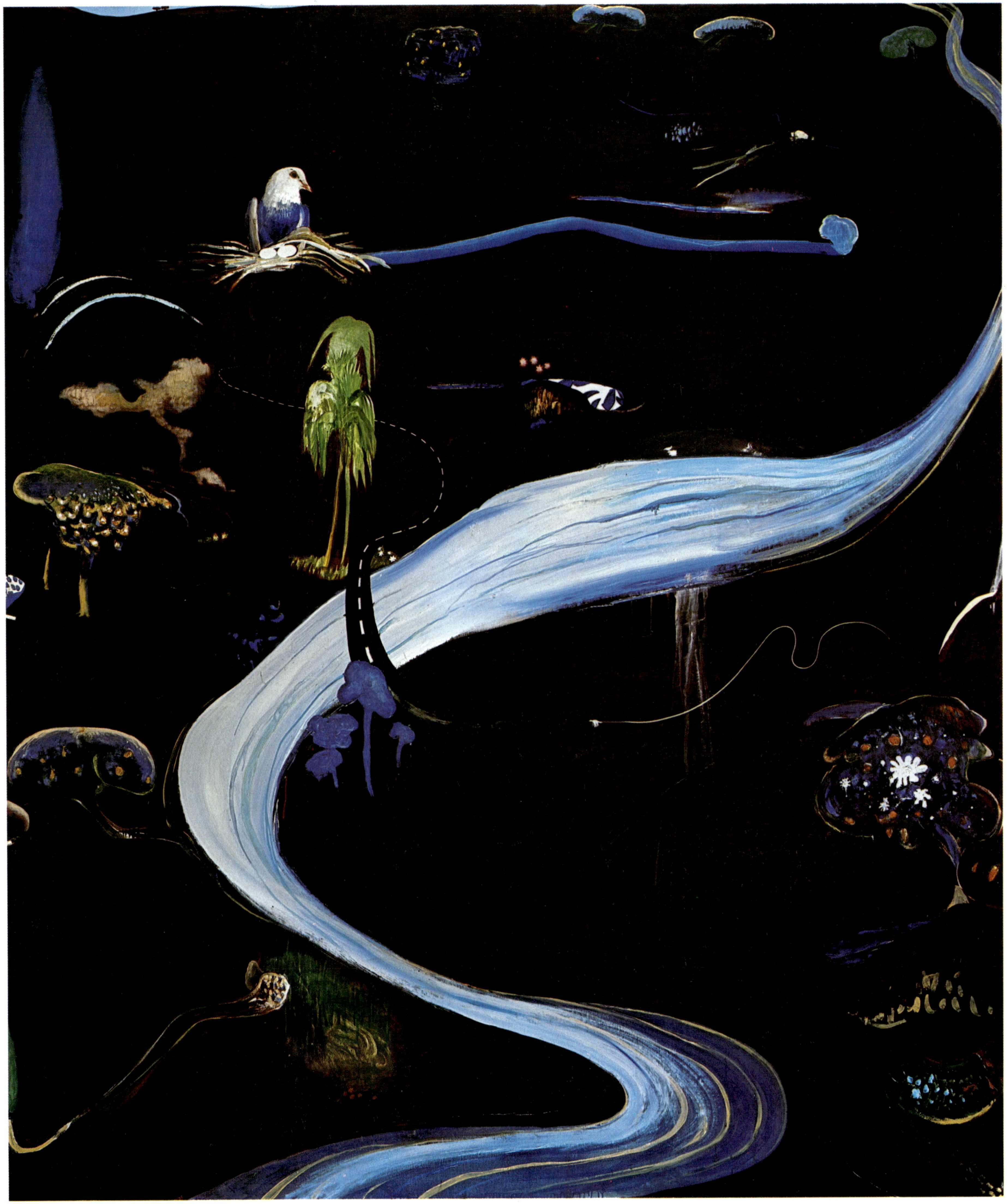

Baudelaire's Drive

Lloyd Rees

Lloyd Frederic Rees, born Brisbane, 1895. Arrived in Sydney in 1917, where he now lives.

With Roland Wakelin, David Strachan and Desiderius Orban, Lloyd Rees is a Neo-Romantic whose works are full of associations, suggestions and veiled meanings; nostalgia is tinged with melancholy; elegiac notes are enlivened with felicitous touches and behind the dreaming vision one senses the power of nature.

The Road to Berry, its green bleaching to pale bone hues, swells and curves with a bodily grace and energy; the surface is like ivory flesh, smooth and pulsating. It was these rhythms rather than the antiquity of the wan hills that attracted Brett Whiteley, and led John Olsen to write, 'He has become a patriach to painters of the middle and younger generations, an influence acknowledged by the youthful Brett Whiteley who has perhaps turned Rees' pre-Freudian biomorphic forms into the abstract erotic'.

Rees reintroduced an anti-Impressionist palette and a linearity into Australian landscape painting; although he may scumble a mountain or cliff with torn shreds of greyed white, he paints as if he wished to restore the monumental massiveness of crag and rugged terrain that the Impressionists had dissolved into a delightful shimmer of colour. His suggestions of antiquity do not permit incidents; none of Sali Herman's stray dogs, strolling cats or pots of geraniums on window sills are permitted in Rees' work; it is full of spectral emanations of places and times long ago and whimsy has no role.

Only Conrad Martens has studied the foreshores of Sydney Harbour with such care, but in Rees' work the sun rarely shines and no shafts of light interrupt the basic rhythms of shoreline and scarp, flooded beach and hill. Occasionally he also shares Martens' topographical concern: the carefully delineated houses that dominate the centre of *The Harbour from McMahon's Point* in a daring compositional risk, won him the Wynne Prize for landscape in 1950.

Like Orban in his old age, Rees too has lightened his palette in his; both men, far from becoming Impressionistic, have pursued a golden and opalescent mysticism where form waxes and wanes. In *The Morning Tide* the pale blues and wan ochres, the barely discernible pinks and creamy ivories sweep and sway, swirl and waver around an unknown centre. Surprisingly there is a person present, ghostly like the monk by the seashore in Caspar David Friedrich; there is a sense of the miraculous forces that release creation.

The Road to Berry
Oil on canvas; 1948; 34.6 × 42.2 cm.
Acquired: 1948
Art Gallery of New South Wales.

The Harbour from McMahon's Point
Oil on canvas; 1950; 77.1 × 99.0 cm.
Acquired: 1950.
Art Gallery of New South Wales.

The Morning Tide
(Formerly *The Southern Sea, Gerringong*)
Oil on canvas; 1971; 89.6 × 109.7 cm.
Acquired: 1973
The University of Sydney.

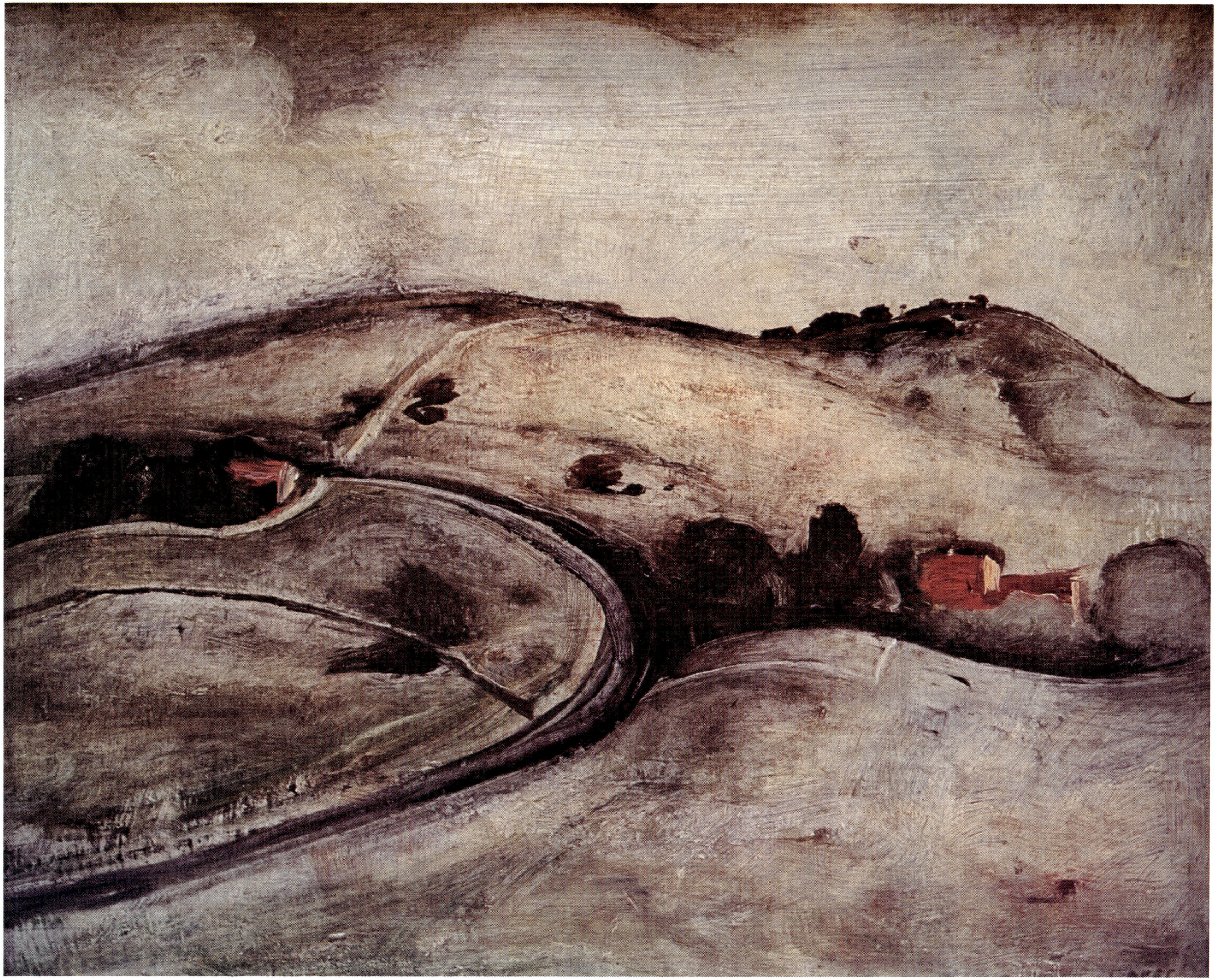

The Road to Berry

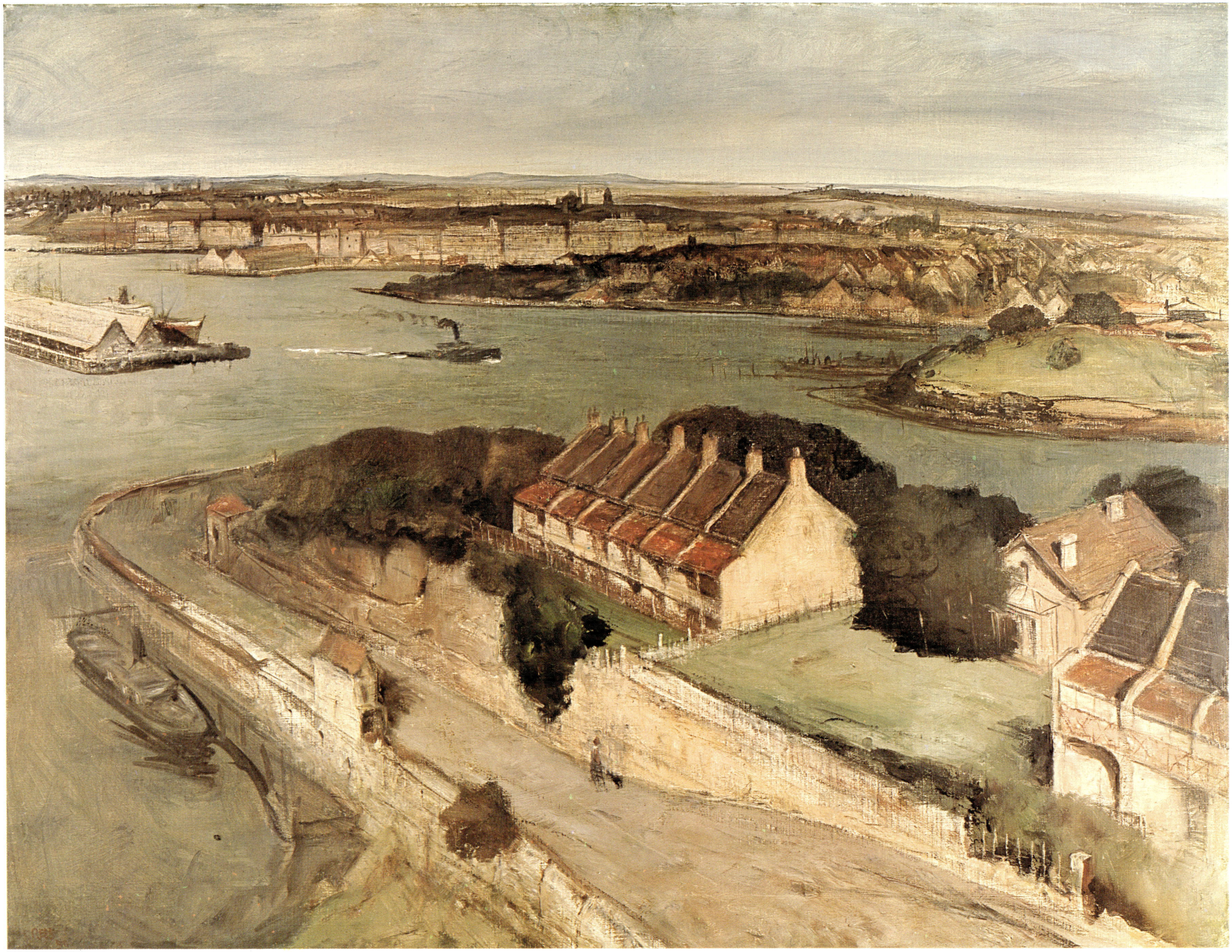

The Harbour from McMahon's Point

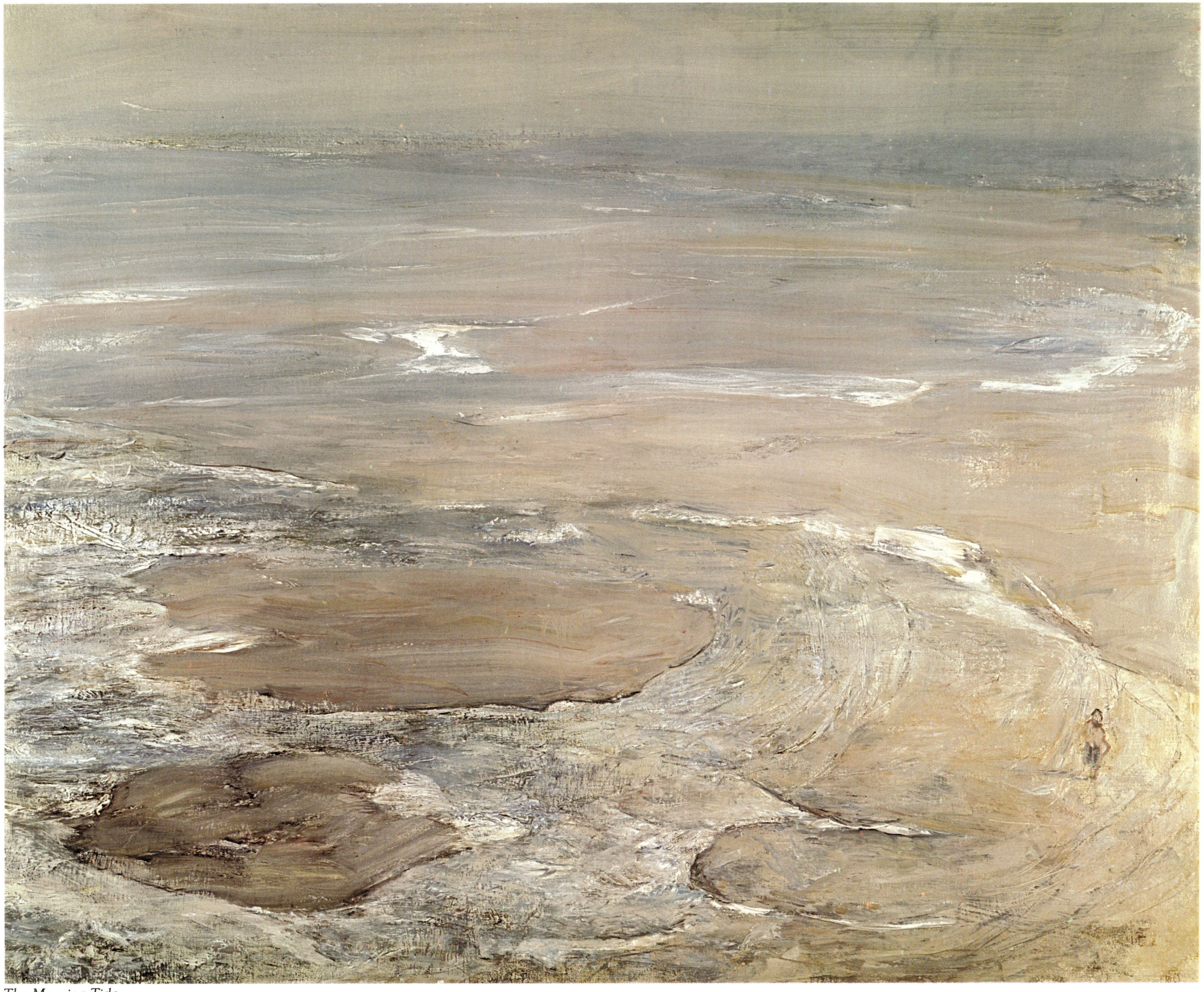

The Morning Tide

David Strachan

David Edgar Strachan, born Salisbury, England, 1919. Arrived in Australia, 1921. Died in a motor accident, Victoria, 1970.

David Strachan sought a sober simplicity in landscape, still-life and portrait painting; he esteemed quietness, the unpretentious and the untheatrical. An even light gave his work a sense of timelessness and associated houses, trees, gulleys, roads and fences in democratic harmony.

In the post-war Romanticism, the former gold-mining town of Hill End in New South Wales became a new gold mine for Sydney artists like Russell Drysdale, Donald Friend, David Strachan and the critic and painter, Paul Haefliger and his wife Jean Bellette. Drysdale, who painted a portrait of Donald Friend dominating the golden-brown township, found it Romantic and Rembrandtian; Donald Friend saw it largely as confectionery: lolly-pink hills and houses of white icing. For David Strachan, it was a nostalgic return to the peace of the bush and to the tradition of Corotesque landscape painting which he knew so well from his long sojourns in Europe. He also had a constant reminder in André Derain's golden-brown tribute to Corot in the Art Gallery of New South Wales.

It was not just simplicity of treatment that engaged Strachan; he liked the evidence of age on the objects and buildings of everyday use. For him the grey paling fence, the humble houses, a single post and the eroded brown and ochre foreground gulley are imbued with enduring virtues. He shares with Julian Ashton a fondness for the commonplace and a dislike of anything suggesting conspicuous consumption. Yet, he was no timid artist; however natural and easeful *Landscape, Hill End* may seem, it is full of the art that conceals art and it is daring enough to make an excavation the centre of a landscape as Hans Heysen did with his quarry.

Landscape, Hill End
Oil on canvas; 1961; 65.4 × 81.3 cm.
Acquired: 1962
Art Gallery of New South Wales.

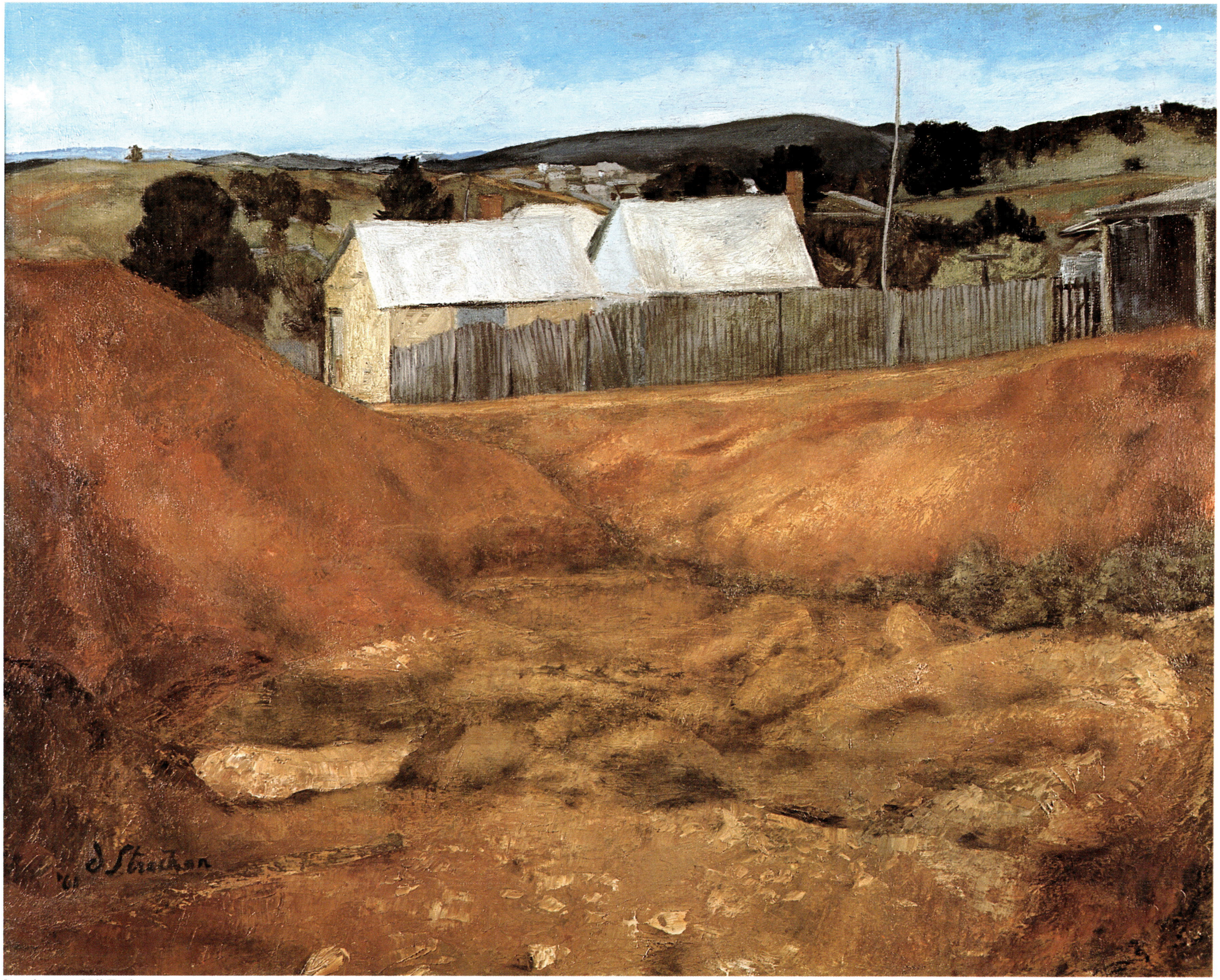

Landscape, Hill End

Roland Wakelin

Roland Shakespeare Wakelin, born Greytown, New Zealand, 1887. Arrived in Australia, 1912; died in Sydney, 1971.

Roland Wakelin began his career of celebrating the Australian landscape as an Impressionist under the stimulus of E. Phillips Fox whose exhibition he saw the year after his arrival in Australia. Wakelin writes of the genesis of *The Fruit Seller at Farm Cove:* 'At the end of 1914 I took the sketch I had made at Pearl Bay the year before and painted a new version, using only alizarin crimson, French blue, and cadmium yellow with white, and applying the colours in small dabs in imitation of the Impressionist method of simulating the vibration of light. Encouraged by the success of this experiment, I set to work on a four-foot by three-foot canvas of *The Fruit Seller at Farm Cove*'.

In fact, Wakelin did not seem content to compose paintings from dabs of paint which he organised and orchestrated with painstaking deliberation; he seems distrustful of their structural function and in *The Fruit Seller at Farm Cove* he emphasized the wall and the curve of the canvas awning. He was to move to a broader, looser treatment by what now looks almost like an accident, though it was the beginning of the modern movement in Australia. For about one year, 1919, under the influence of Roy de Maistre, he made colour music paintings based upon a supposed analogy between the colours of the spectrum and the notes in the musical scale; little did de Maistre and Wakelin realize that some six years earlier, two Americans — Morgan Russell and Stanton MacDonald Wright — had developed a similar painting, called Synchromism, in Paris.

Wakelin's and de Maistre's joint exhibition met with jeers and even Julian Ashton, the artists' champion, protested. But it produced some sparkling, broadly executed works in complementary colours like *Synchromy in Orange Major,* whose subject was also painted by de Maistre.

However, Roland Wakelin was seeking a more pervasive vitality and when he saw a van Gogh exhibition in London in 1923, one of his directions became clear. He wrote: 'It burst upon me like an explosion . . . It was a revelation; none of the few prints we had seen in Sydney could reproduce the vitality in the paint itself'.

He had also seen a Gauguin exhibition and his work became thinner in pigment and broader in treatment. The tone deepened; vast grey clouds were fretted with gold; the fields were sour green-gold or warm yellow; Constable's shadows fell in vast areas across unified landscapes that he sometimes painted in the company of Lloyd Rees; but whether it was a stall at Farm Cove, sails on boats at Double Bay, or the weighty force of Richmond Bridge, Wakelin wanted a positive structure, luminous in light and not composed by it.

The Fruit Seller at Farm Cove
Oil on canvas, laid down on hardboard; 1915; 91.5 × 116.5 cm.
Acquired: 1960
Australian National Gallery, Canberra.

Synchromy in Orange Major
Oil on pulpboard; 1919; 30.5 × 40.65 cm.
Collection of Mr Mervyn Horton, Sydney.

Richmond Landscape, Tasmania
(Also titled *Richmond Bridge, Tasmania*)
Oil on pulpboard; 1944-45; 62.8 × 75.0 cm.
Acquired: 1945
Art Gallery of New South Wales.

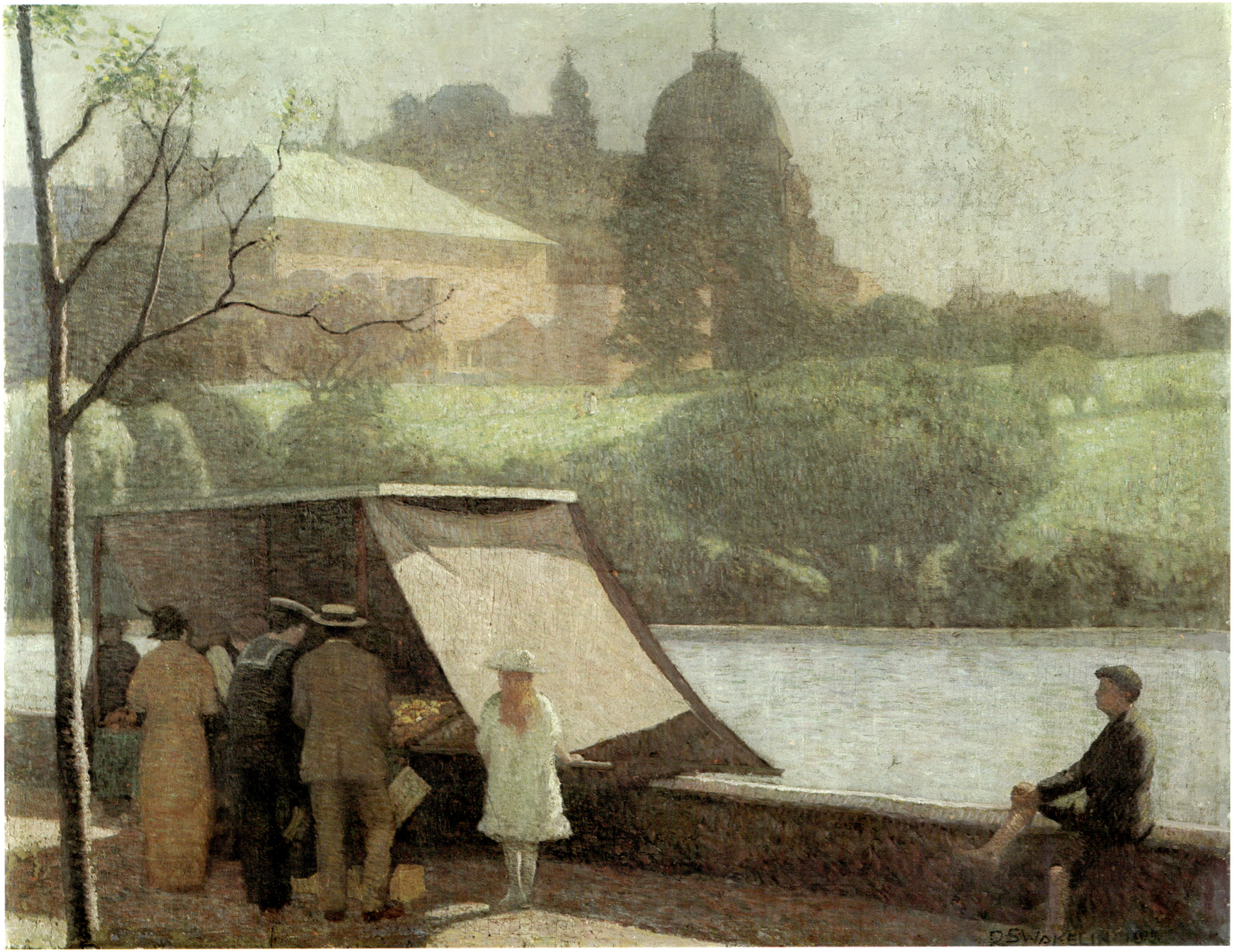

The Fruit Seller at Farm Cove

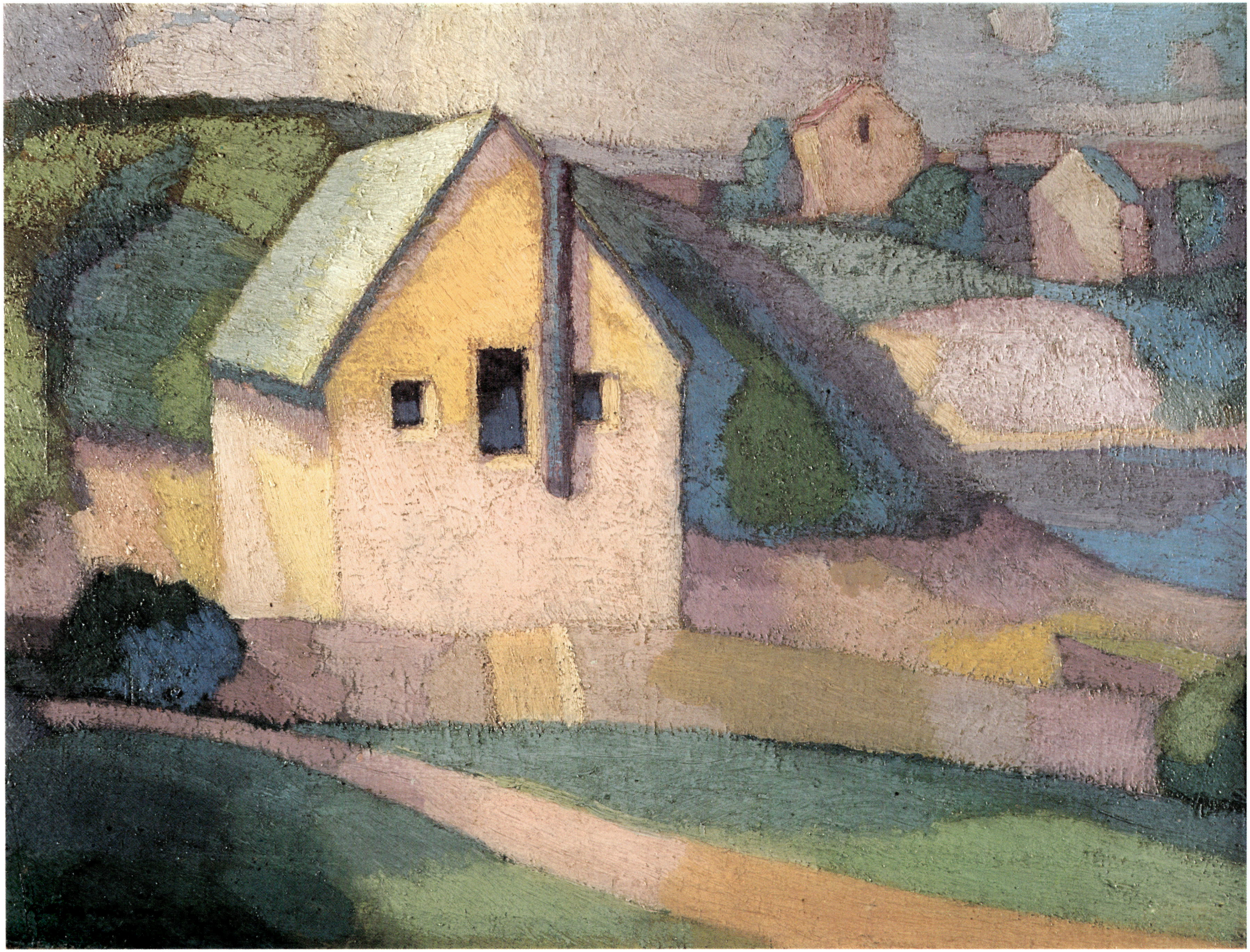

Synchromy in Orange Major

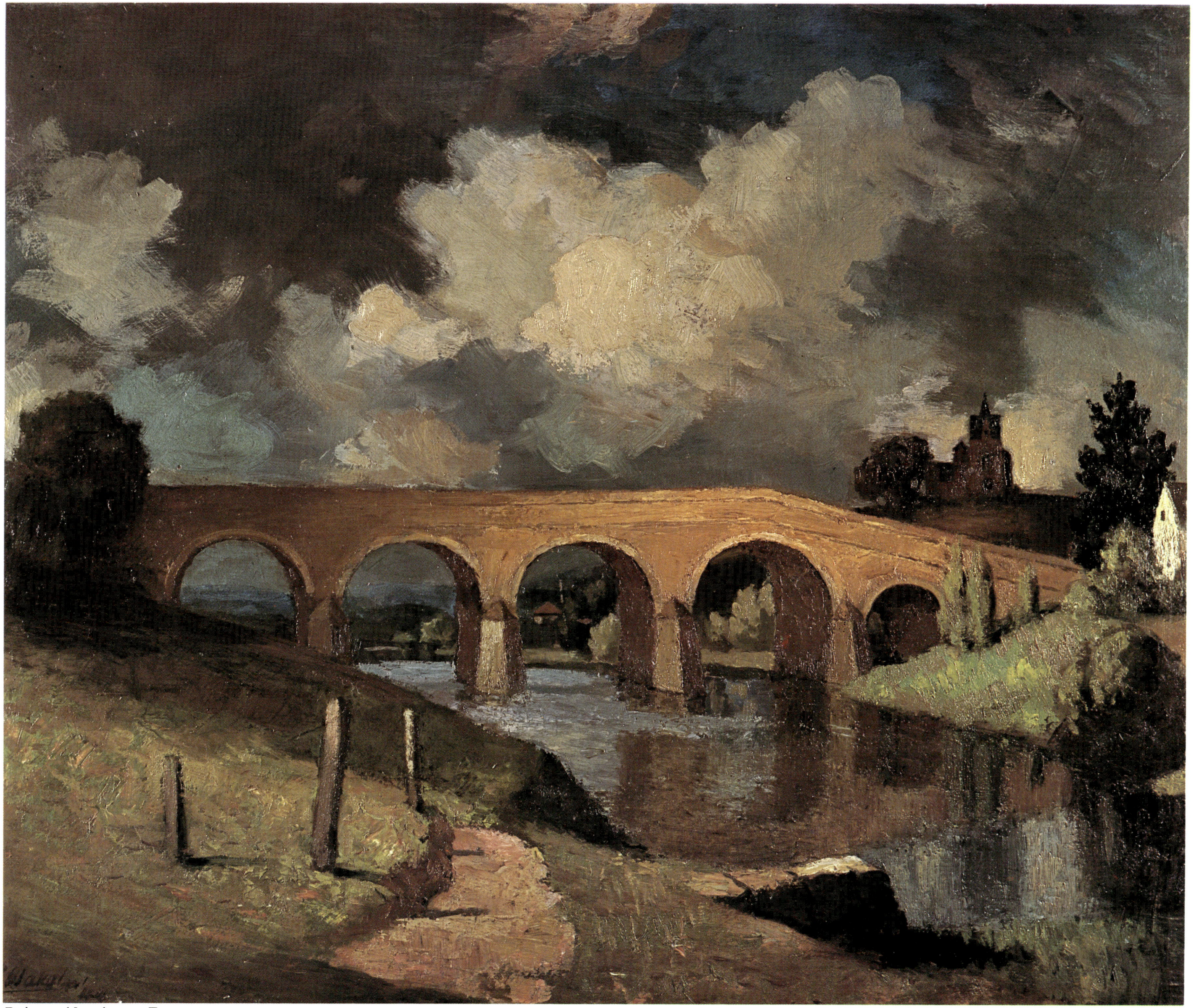

Richmond Landscape, Tasmania

Rah Fizelle

Rah Fizelle, born Goulburn, New South Wales, 1891; died in Sydney, 1964

Rah Fizelle studied at the Julian Ashton art school from 1921-26 but became increasingly interested in the crisp composition of Cubism, especially after Grace Crowley, a fellow pioneer in *avant-garde* painting, returned from Paris where she had studied at L'Academie Lhote in 1927 and 1928.

To a moderately Cubist painter like Fizelle, Julian Ashton's *Old Sydney, Cumberland Street* of 1901 may have looked a little loose, somewhat indulgent, a little too dependent on human interest and too decked out with fowls and sheets in the wind. That is the way orthodox Cubists used to talk of what seemed to them rather unintegrated paintings, not far removed from illustration. So be it.

One thing Fizelle did have in common with Ashton was a rather dry, subdued colour and an avoidance of painterly flourishes. It was not until 1950 that André Lhote's 1939 *Treatise on Landscape Painting* was translated into English, but its views, using as commendable examples, Pablo Picasso, Georges Braque, Robert Delaunay, Orthon Frieze, Fernand Léger, Paul Cézanne and Jacques Villon, had been in the air since 1910. The first chapter, entitled, 'The Decline of the Composed Landscape', was a trumpet blast against art considered too illustrative and over-concerned with anecdotal additives. Fizelle's *Elizabeth Bay* is a splendid example of what such clarion calls could produce. Fizelle himself could almost have written Lhote's views: 'It is necessary to repeat: the picture, whatever the requirements of the subject may be, must remain faithful to its own structure, to its fundamental two-dimensions' and 'First, the surface must be organised rhythmically . . . so as to give it a plastic interest with a series of clear, well-articulated signs which will bring out their respective values by their interactions'.

The repetitive rhythms of the block of flats are continued in diminishing strength elsewhere in the painting; what is signified is clear and positive: no mysterious shadows, no softening chiaroscuro, no melting moments; crisp articulation constructs the painting; two dimensionality is emphasized, though we are allowed a gentle curve and a peep at the Harbour.

Despite the recommendations, Rah Fizelle does present the scene as a way of life.

Elizabeth Bay
Oil on canvas laid down on hardboard; c.1927; 45.0 × 38.0 cm.
Acquired: 1971
Australian National Gallery, Canberra.

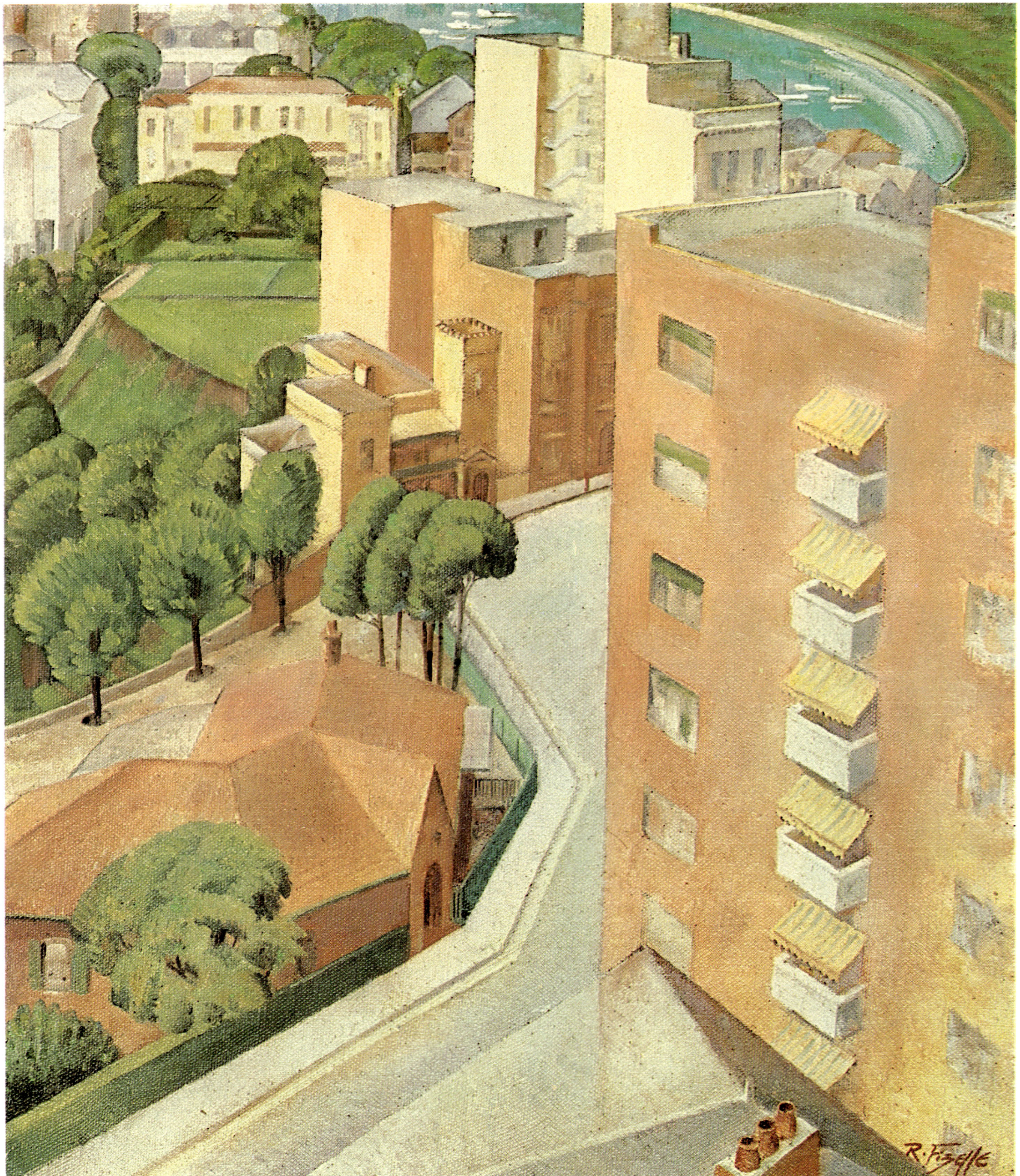

Elizabeth Bay

Godfrey Miller

Godfrey Clive Miller, born Wellington, New Zealand, 1893. Arrived in Melbourne, 1929; then settled in Sydney where he died in 1964.

Godfrey Miller was always something of a recluse, but a gregarious one with selected friends. He first painted at Warrandyte in Victoria. Perhaps it was an interest in infrastructure that led him to take a degree in architecture at Wellington University, New Zealand; perhaps such training prompted his interest in the tensions of thin ink lines against out-of-kilter squares and diamonds of graduated colour. He was fascinated by the tensions of ties and beams in the peaked roofs of churches and longed to experience how a painting was made: it was good, he said, 'to get as much craft into the hands as possible'.

About 1954 he moved to Sydney's Paddington where houses, as Herman demonstrated, are undisguisedly hand-made. His means, probably the simplest since S.T. Gill's, were obvious even if intricate. From about 1940 he began to rule ink lines across his canvases, at first diagonally, but later with more complex interweavings. Spaces were sometimes left bare but more often they were tinted with minute modulations of hues within each area. He began some cityscapes with mosaics of monochrome greys and bistres — a slightly lighter palette than that used by the Cubists; and then employed most intricate juxtapositions of colour to form flickering mosaics that could look momentarily opaque but through which other shapes identified themselves. Miller wanted structure without the monumentality of a Rees or a Drysdale; so he re-introduced some elements of Impressionism; he wanted a controlled flux and a strictly ordered palpitation. As a result he created unprecedented paintings that are both sensuous and intellectual, strict and wayward, ashimmer with fluctuating light but as controlled as a stained-glass window.

His very early *Warrandyte* has kinships with David Davies, but what is remarkable is how this low-toned painting predicts the overall pulsation from edge to edge that was to distinguish his later and far less sombre work.

Landscape with Orange Cliffs is such a vivacious painting and when he negotiated its purchase, Laurie Thomas, then Director of The Western Australian Art Gallery, wrote to Godfrey Miller in September 1955: 'I agree with you that it could be one of the most important contributions to Australian landscape painting'.

Warrandyte
Oil on canvas mounted on board; c.1929; 24.7 × 30 cm.
Acquired: 1972
Australian National Gallery, Canberra.

Building and Trees
Oil on canvas; 1951-1953; 42.5 × 60.0 cm.
Acquired: 1953
Art Gallery of New South Wales.

Landscape with Orange Cliffs
Oil on canvas; c.1955; 66.7 × 100.3 cm.
Acquired: 1955
The Western Australian Art Gallery.

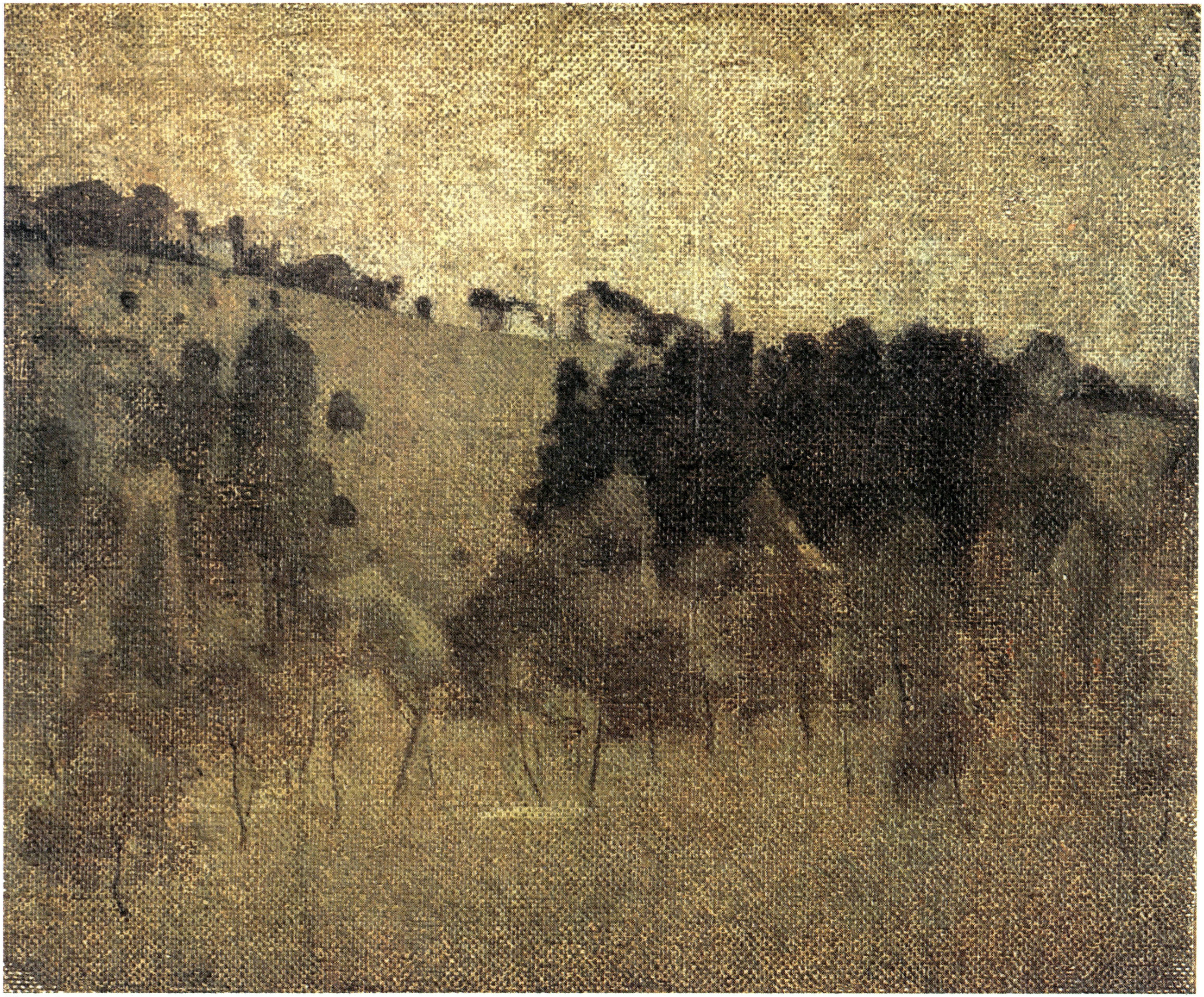

Warrandyte

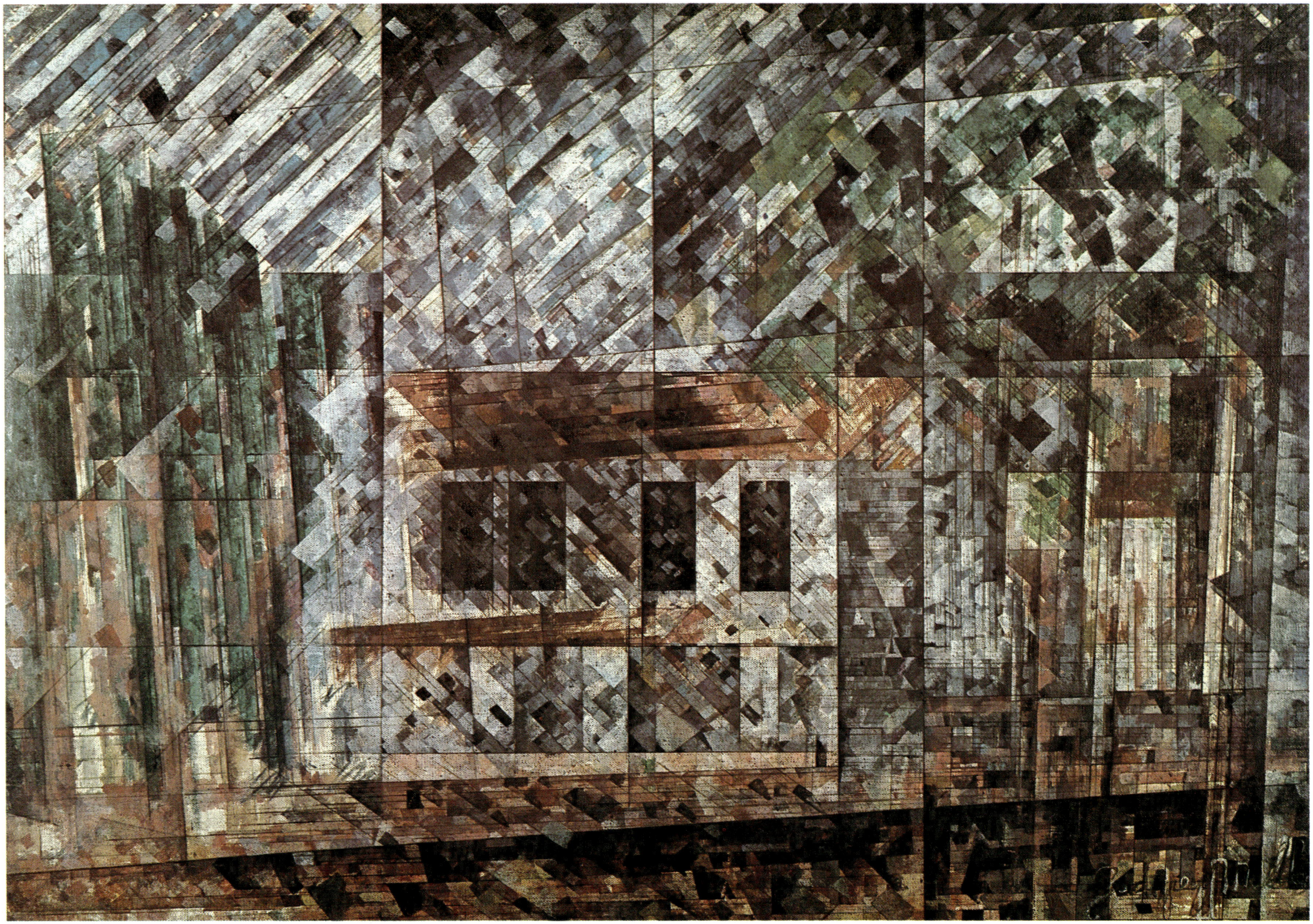

Building and Trees

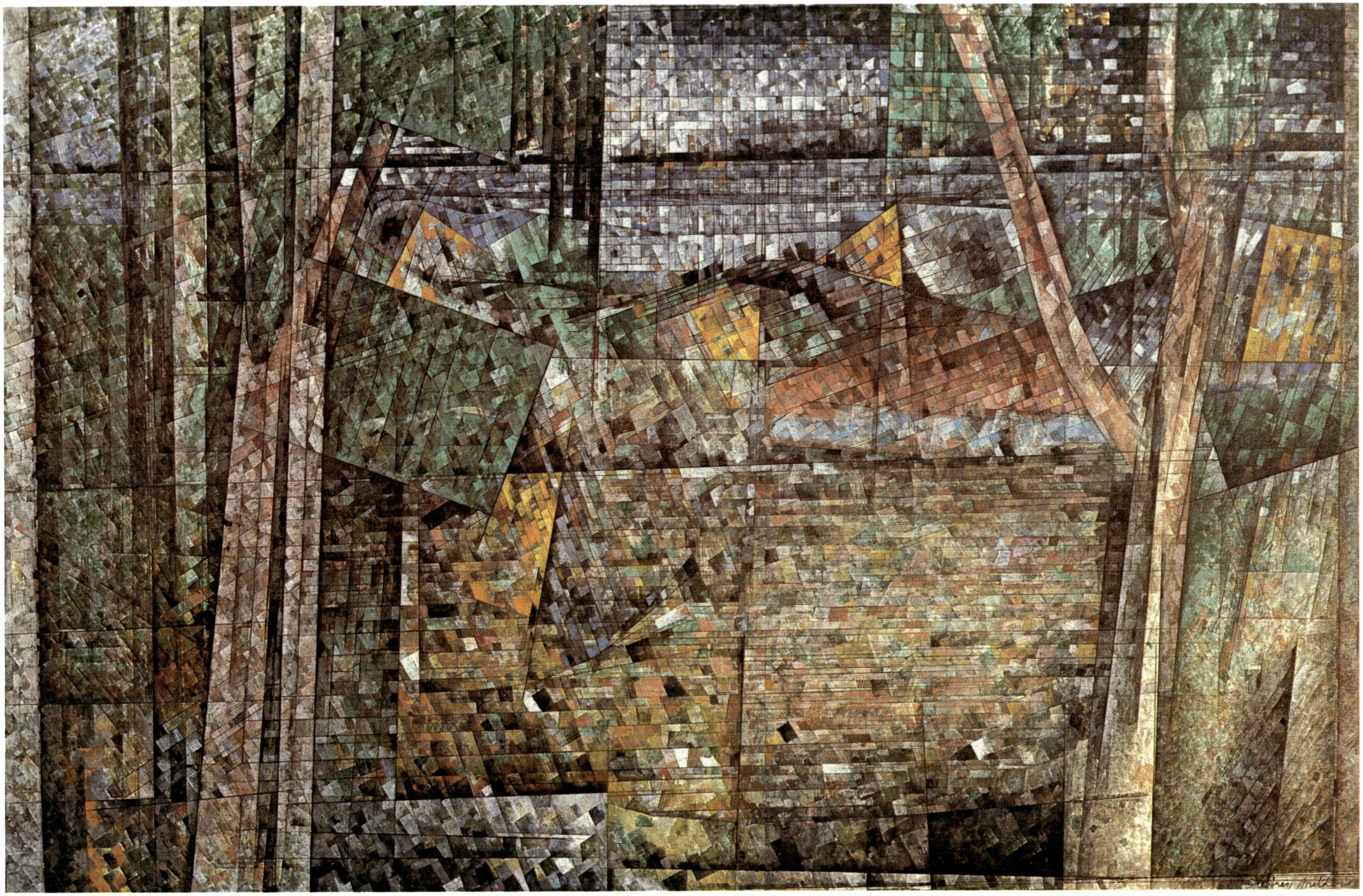

Landscape with Orange Cliffs

Guy Grey-Smith

Guy Edward Grey-Smith, born Wagin, Western Australia, 1916; lives in Perth.

Guy Grey-Smith's paintings are so solid and formidable that they remind the viewer that he was the only survivor from the crews of eight bombers on an RAF mission in May 1940.

In vivid oranges, furnace reds and electric greens, he formerly used conventional signs for plain, cliff, mountains and foliage; movement used to be dashing and spontaneous, but now his richly impastoed works of deeper, more resonant colour, are like myriad lava flows momentarily stilled. Areas are not coloured in, but are paint in motion; the surface is alive, shards of pigment thrust against one another, engage in jarring and abrasive encounters or dance in harmony. What was once crisp, bright and stylised has become tough and uncompromising.

The planes of colour derive from Cubism, that great seminal movement that engendered the blocky houses of Sali Herman, the flickering, modulated diamonds of Godfrey Miller and the crisp articulation of Rah Fizelle. It also prompted the paintings of Nicholas de Stael to whom Grey-Smith has been likened, but de Stael is more elegant, less closely knit, more nonchalant and vivacious. Guy Grey-Smith is dogged; he constructs as if with highly coloured ceramics, and is a potter. He wanted, he said 'to attain maturity in a form of art which is universal and at the same time completely expressive of our environment', for Grey-Smith is an expressive Cubist who feels the pulse of the earth beneath his brush. He thrusts an oblong of three blues through the sour and yellow greens of *Towards Ningham* and warms the cold olive and green fields with some orange and orange ochre areas that, however deliberated, look spontaneous because one of his virtues is to mesh the permanent with the transitory, which is a concern of all Australian landscape artists.

Towards Ningham
Oil on hardboard; 1974; 121.9 × 182.9 cm.
Courtesy of the Rudy Komon Gallery, Sydney.

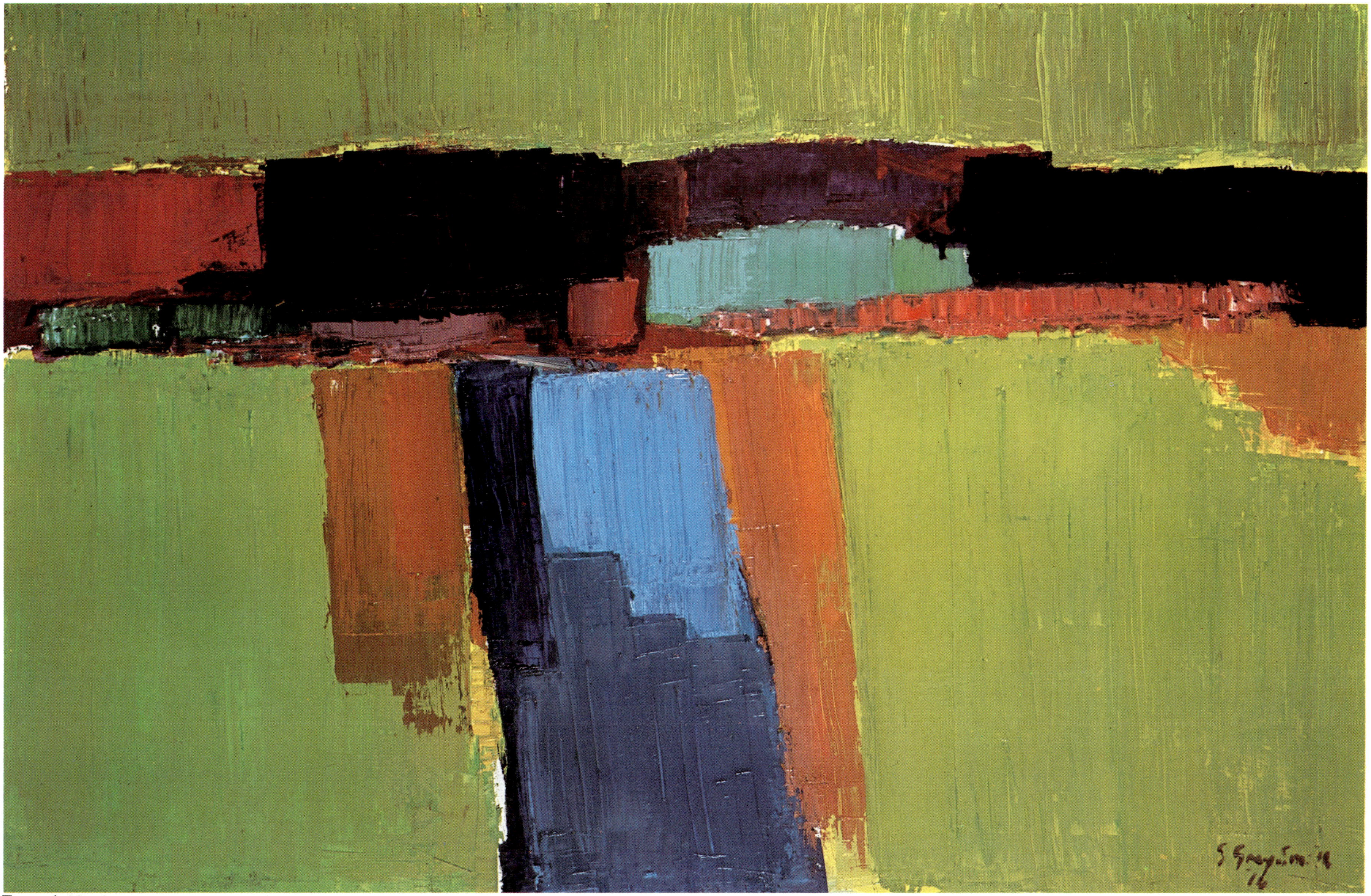

Towards Ningham

Jeffrey Smart

Jeffrey Smart, born Adelaide, South Australia, 1921; lives in Arezzo, Italy.

What man can do to the landscape frequently strikes Jeffrey Smart as odd, threatening and Surreal. He is never humorous, even if he is occasionally satirical; he is too detached an observer to distort the world through the unconscious imagery of the orthodox Surrealists. He does not create his paintings from fantasies and dreams; he does not invent, he discovers. The radar apparatus on top of a building, the freeway diving underground with obsessive determination, the Italian bicyclists riding in prim order in front of depersonalized high-rise blocks of flats, traffic islands, bathing sheds, a set of wide steps leading to some dynasty's obelisk and the lone sunbather in the dressing shed or on top of an apparently deserted building — all these results of man's activities are the subjects for his haunting paintings. The recent works are crisp, clean, clinical, austere, and none the less curious. It is as though an army of cleaners had washed down a 'pittura metafisica' painting by Giorgio de Chirico, removing deep shadows along with any object that was not quite appropriate to everyday reality.

Cape Dombey, painted in 1947, reveals the same mind at work that was later to consider that 'a dirt road is real, but an autostrada is Surreal'. In this desolate and isolated area in Victoria near the South Australian border, the square pyramid with its two horizontal bands of red and its vertical thrust emphasises that the world, which the signal is designed to help, is sliding slowly to the brink. Foreground, cliffs and slaty-grey indifferent sky are slipping out of control down a slight diagonal despite the warning from the pyramid. It is the imposition of this device that evokes the feeling of transience and impermanence.

Jeffrey Smart observes the curiosities of the new, man-dominated Australian landscape with the same fresh eye of John Glover who recorded it before man had barely scratched the surface.

Cape Dombey
Oil on canvas; 1947; 49.7 × 60.1 cm.
Acquired: 1975, the late Alan R. Renshaw Bequest.
The University of Sydney.

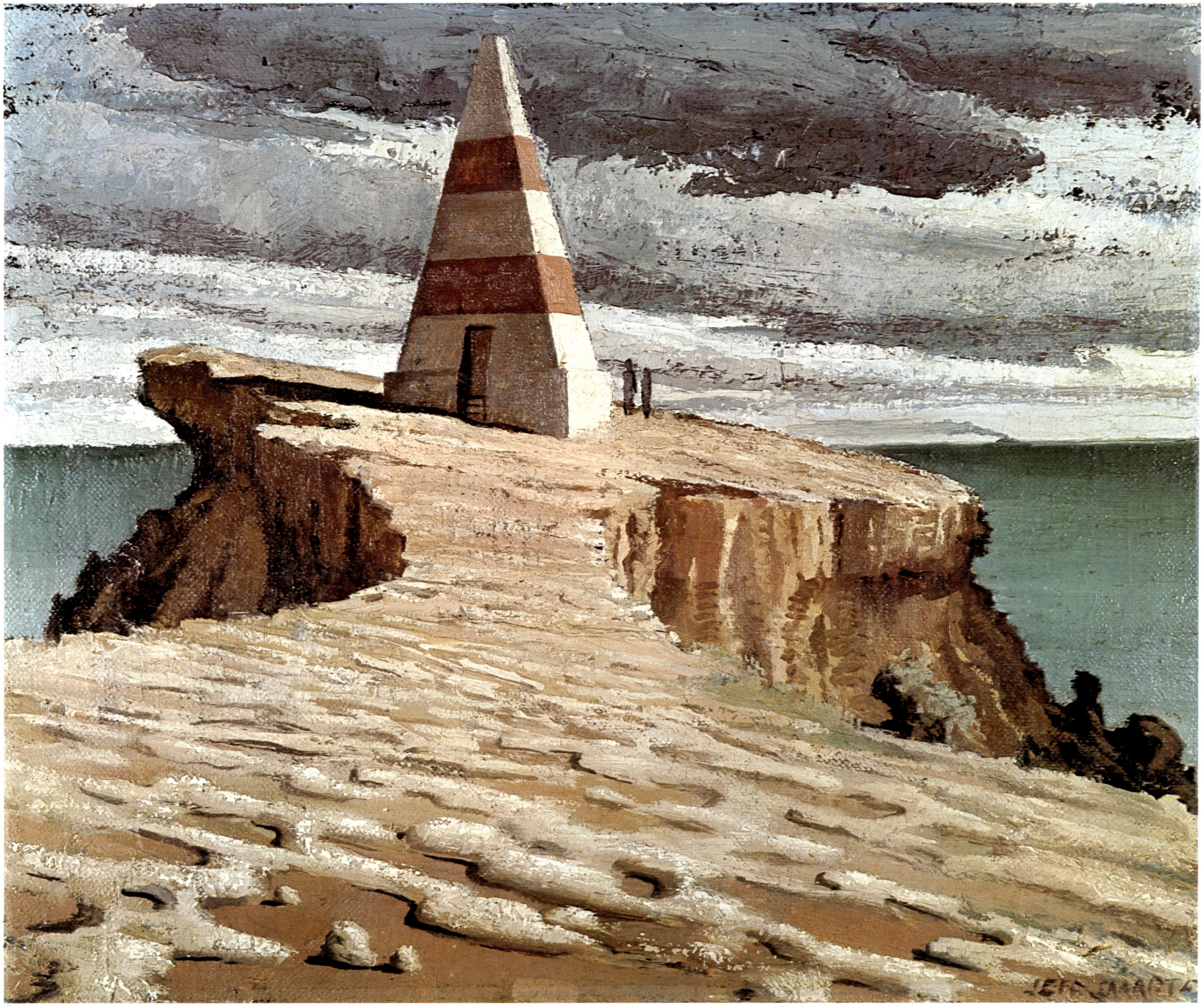

Cape Dombey

Sali Herman

Sali Herman, born Zurich, Switzerland, 1898. Arrived in Melbourne, 1937; settled in Sydney in 1938, where he now lives.

Not only did Sali Herman rehabilitate what were then called the slums of Paddington, Woolloomooloo and Glebe, but he also expanded the concept of art and landscape by winning the Wynne Prize for landscape painting with a view of McElhone Stairs which link a still dilapidated area of the wharves to Potts Point. He was to win this award again in 1965 and 1967, but the point had been made: to vistas, panoramas, beetling cliffs and seascapes could be added slum houses. Herman rehabilitated them not only in social esteem but also by making their worn, peeling and aged surfaces look like a seductive patina.

Long before there was the current concern with the preservation and conservation of historical buildings, Herman paid tribute, although with less of his customary impasto, to the simple, classical lines of the Law Courts, but there are the typical touches: two lawyers risking broken limbs by standing in a street usually thick with traffic and those trees that Herman saw clearly were not green but blue-green and sometimes slaty grey.

The Law Courts is almost a facade in itself; it hardly has any of the sudden, deep areas or the bare walls jutting like cliffs of most of his inner-suburb paintings, for it was the tactile facade of individual buildings that was to preoccupy him and of this, *Near the Docks* is a splendid example in richness and variation of surface. Not so Cubistic as many of his houses and far less monumental than some, the dwellings exhibit their own personalities. 'It's like *The Last Supper* by Leonardo da Vinci;' he once said to the writer, 'hot, cold, hot, cold, as you look along'.

Such paintings that once seemed so solid, stark and formidable, are filled with subtleties; hot surfaces are underpainted with cool tones; snowy-white plaster lies over burning reds. Again, the impasto and varied use of the palette knife, equally evident in securing the heat haze and undefined vastness of *Charters Towers*, give the surface an intimate liveliness that is aided by all those whimsical additives that Herman indulged in: window-boxes, women with brooms, nobody's dog or cat, and anonymous humans not daring to assert their personalities in the presence of these houses, each so full of character that Herman has been called the Australian Balzac.

The Law Courts
Oil on canvas; 1946; 61 × 81.5 cm.
Acquired: 1946, Felton Bequest.
National Gallery of Victoria.

Near the Docks
Oil on canvas, mounted on board in 1970; 1949; 49.5 × 95.2 cm.
Acquired: 1949
Art Gallery of New South Wales.

Charters Towers
Oil on canvas; 1968; 77.0 × 99.0 cm.
Privately owned.

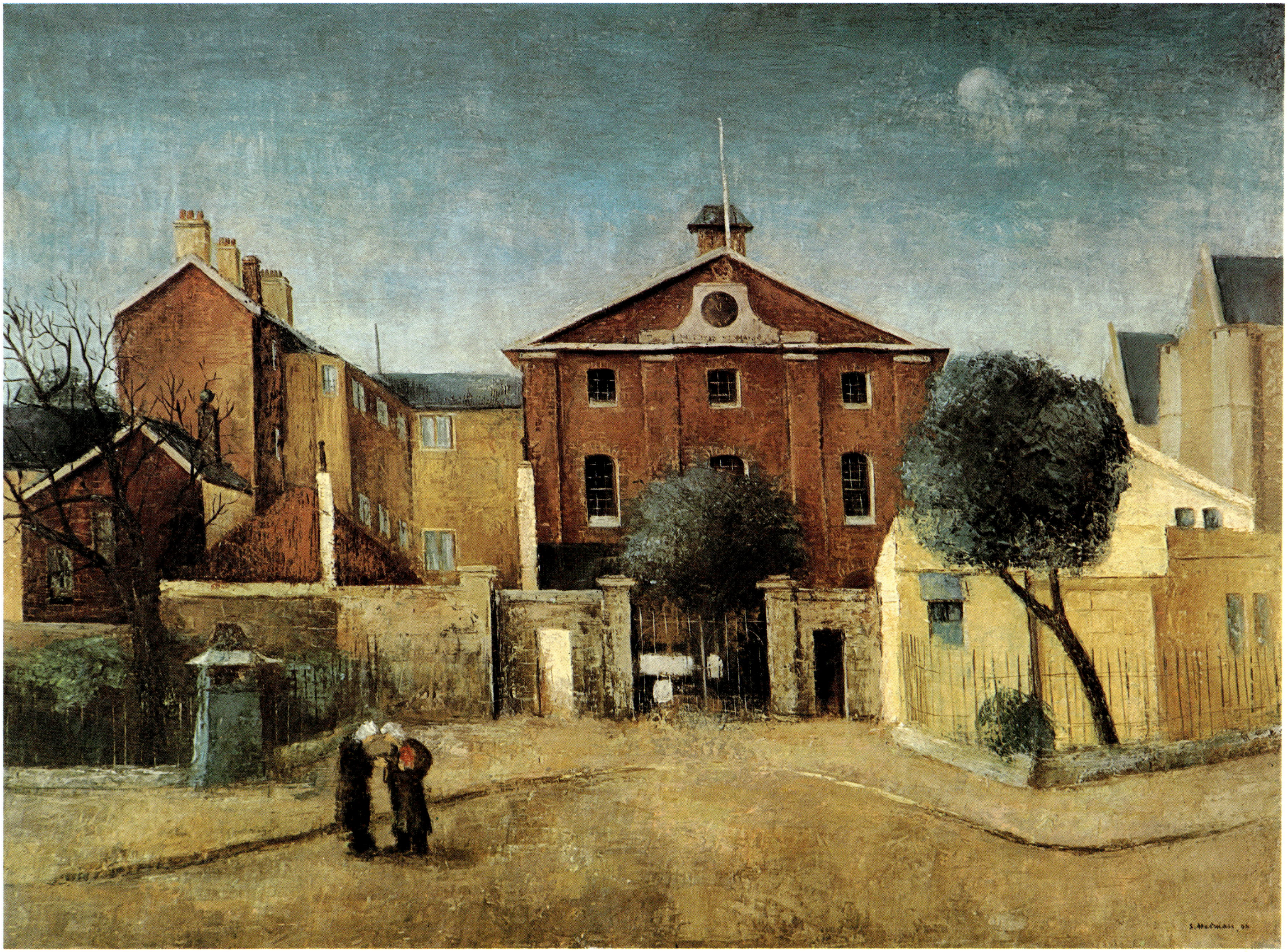

The Law Courts

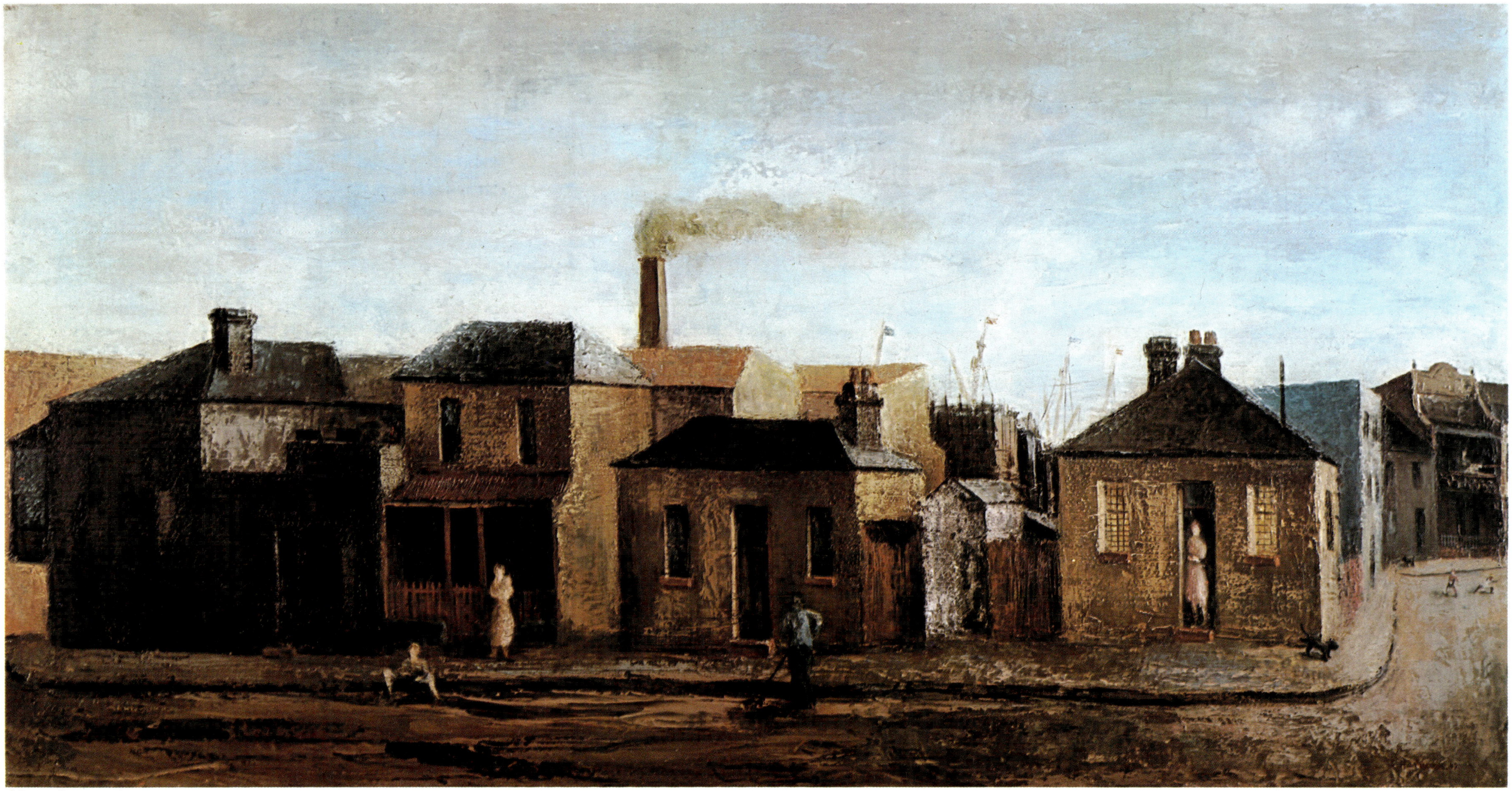

Near the Docks

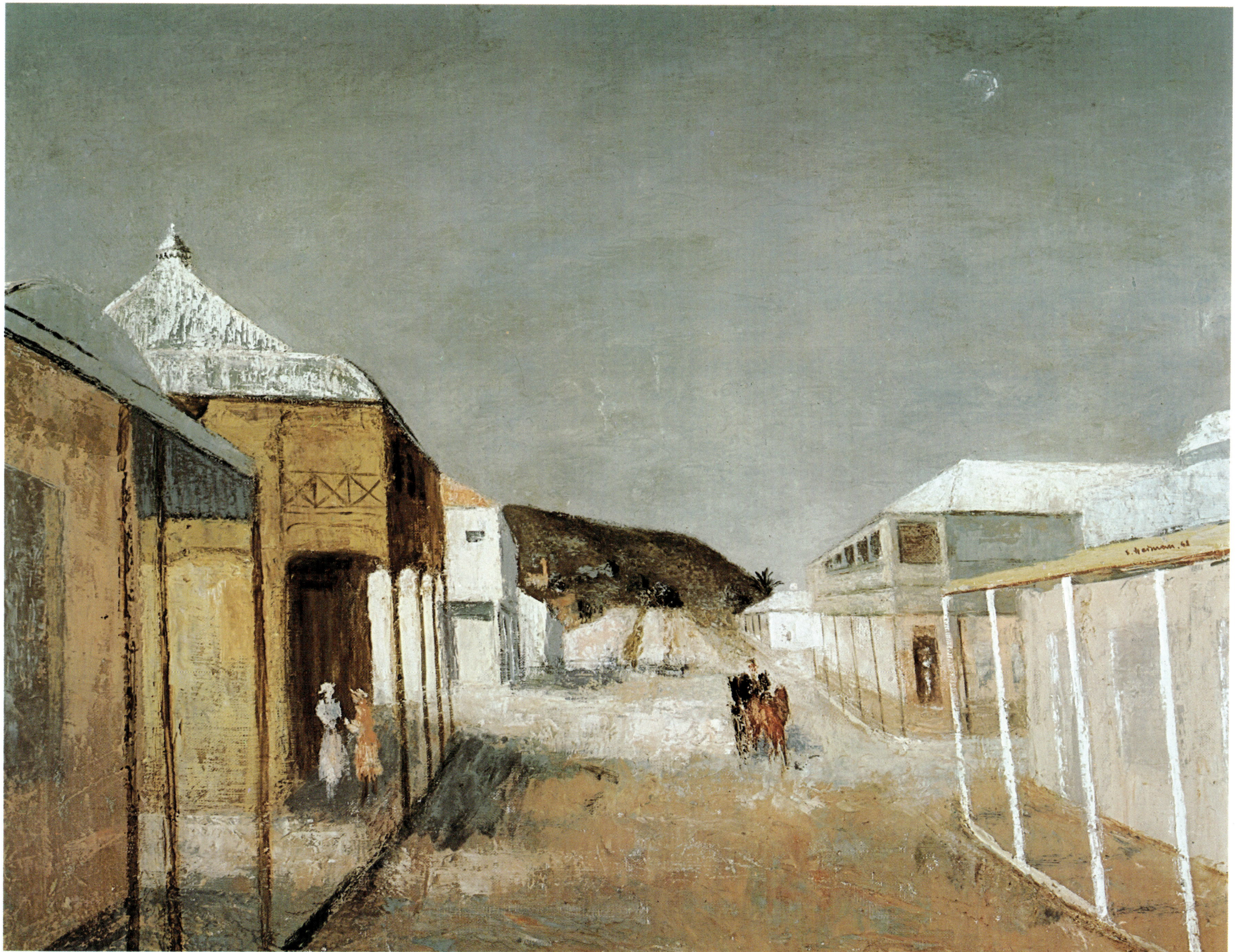

Charters Towers

Shay Docking

Shay Docking, born Warrnambool, Victoria, 1928; lives in Sydney.

As a child Shay Docking lived in the extinct volcanic region of Western Victoria and later in the south west of that State, a desolate area where one could only be conscious of the earth's basic structure. *Cape Dombey,* which Jeffrey Smart painted with a threatening loneliness and stark assertiveness similar to Shay Docking's, is in this area near the South Australian border. A no-man's-land, it lent itself to the Surreal interests of both painters; Smart was to discover a Surreal presence in the austere, dehumanised geometry of the modern city; Shay Docking, as in *Angophora on the Hawkesbury,* came to explore the unconscious, organic symbolism in waves, wind and water eroded cliffs, palms and the convolutions, fleshily smooth surface and groping movement of the angophora tree that should have been invented by a biomorphic Surrealist.

Shay Docking uses layer after layer of pastel on paper each layer being separated from the next by spraying with reworkable, matt fixative. The result is a subdued, even glow that suffuses the whole painting. Light does not fall on objects; no placement of colour creates it; its genesis is in the painting which has, therefore, something of the eerie lighting and isolation of 'pittura metafisica'.

There is no relenting, no softening of the insistence of the frontal, forceful images of fretted rock, harsh sky and tortuous encroachment of the angophora that clenches at the sky with more frenzied anguish than the tree roots in Russell Drysdale's *Rabbiters.* Both use natural growth as symbols, both have suggestions of the vision of Henry Moore and Graham Sutherland, but in Shay Docking's work the anxiety is almost solid and palpable. One would turn not to William Wordsworth but to Gerard Manley Hopkins for a poetic correlative:

'O the mind, mind has mountains; cliffs of fall
Frightful, sheer, no-man-fathomed. Hold them cheap
May who ne'er hung there.'

Angophora on the Hawkesbury
Pastel on paper glued to hardboard; February 1976; 77.5 × 96.3 cm.
Possession of the artist.

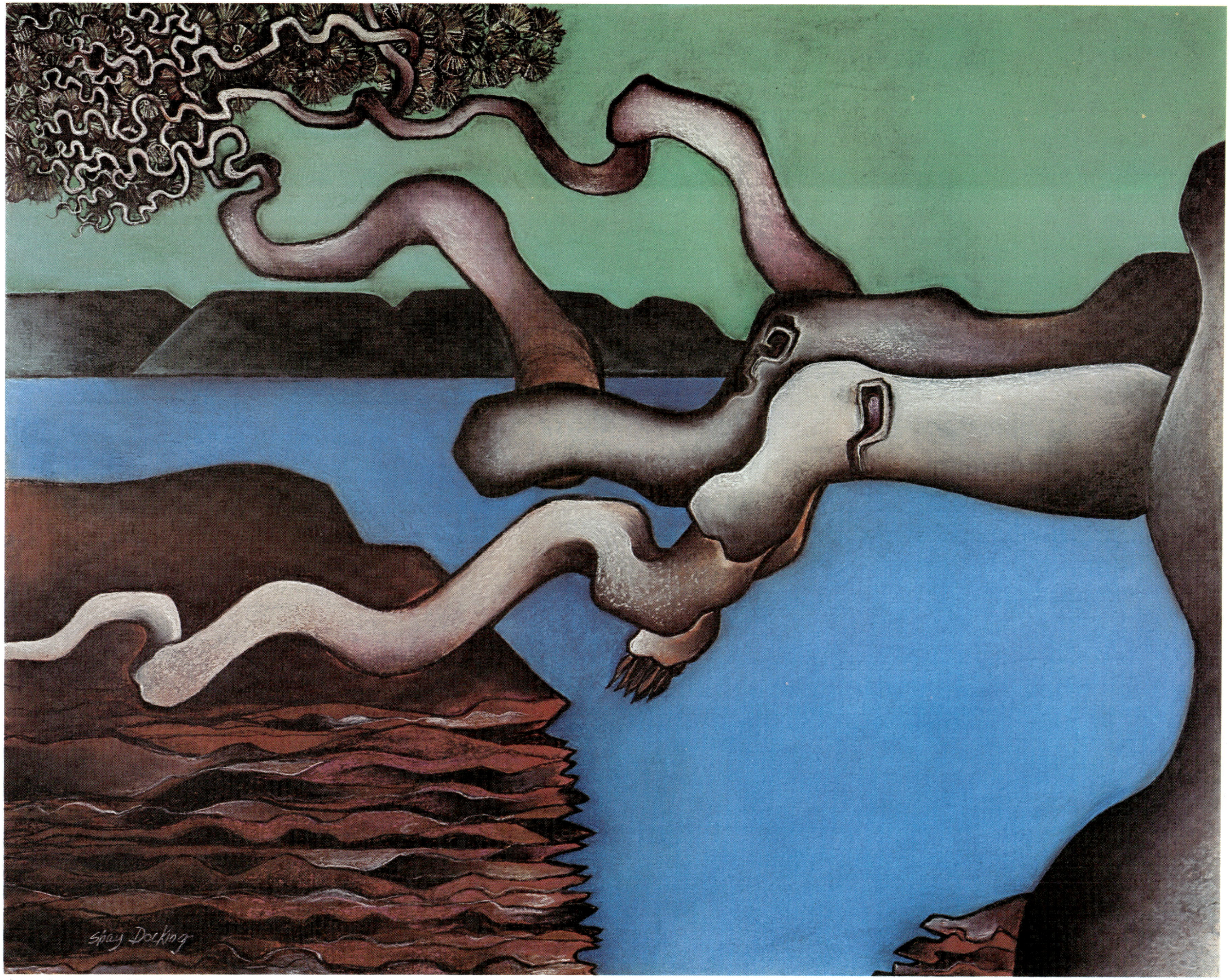

Angophora on the Hawkesbury

Desiderius Orban

Desiderius Orban, born Gyor, Hungary, 1884. Arrived in Sydney in 1939, where he now lives

In his ninety-first year Desiderius was given a retrospective by The Art Gallery of New South Wales; it included deeply felt romantic paintings of his work in Europe for he had painted in France, Italy, Spain, Germany, Austria, Rumania, Czechoslovakia and in his native Hungary.

In Budapest, he established a school: the Atelier Art and Craft Academie. Ever since he has remained a vigorous and stimulating teacher, enlivening his encouragement with anecdotes that sound like parables from a painting patriarch and permeate his latest restatement of his views, 'What is Art All About?' (1975): the painter, who is simply a craftsman, must be separated from the artists for only 'creativeness equals art'; 'Every work of art emanates a kind of spirituality' . . . 'the full responsibility of creativeness is rejecting the the help of outside influence'. Finally, as he has become more and more preoccupied with Zen, 'I repeat the words of the Chinese critic: "The spiritual rhythm is attained only when the artist forgets that it is he who is handling the brush".'

Orban's work deals in suggestions of mystery; whether it is a snowy landscape in Hungary, a village church in France, shadowy hills in Tasmania or a forest clearing on the south coast of New South Wales, there is a sombre depth and a sweet sorrow that has been called melancholy, but that is too negative a term for Orban's delight in the tenebrous and in the accumulation of the dark riches of the earth. Viewing an English landscape painting is like wandering through a park; to traverse a landscape painting by Orban is to recall the Russian poet who said, 'To live a life is not to cross a field'.

Orban's pastels are varied; strokes can be long and sinuous or short, broken and as abrupt as mosaics; the hues are both opaque and transparent as everywhere the hand traces the mood.

In his last paintings Orban's visions have become more mystical; the hand wanders with a will of its own; the gouge traces unpredictable and indecipherable calligraphy in the chip board on which he increasingly draws and paints. There is often an ebb and flow of religious feeling in Australian landscapes . . . a desert hell or a Utopian heaven on earth or a pantheistic solace, and in teaching and practice, Orban has become more and more involved with the notion of creation as in *The Separation of the Waters*.

Hobart
Pastel on black paper; 1944-46; 50.2 × 64.8 cm.
Acquired: 1968
Newcastle City Art Gallery.

South Coast Timberland
Pastel on paper; 1948; 48.7 × 64.1 cm.
Acquired: 1952
Art Gallery of New South Wales

Separation of the Waters
Mixed media on hardboard; 1972; 90.5 × 183.2 cm.
Possession of the artist.

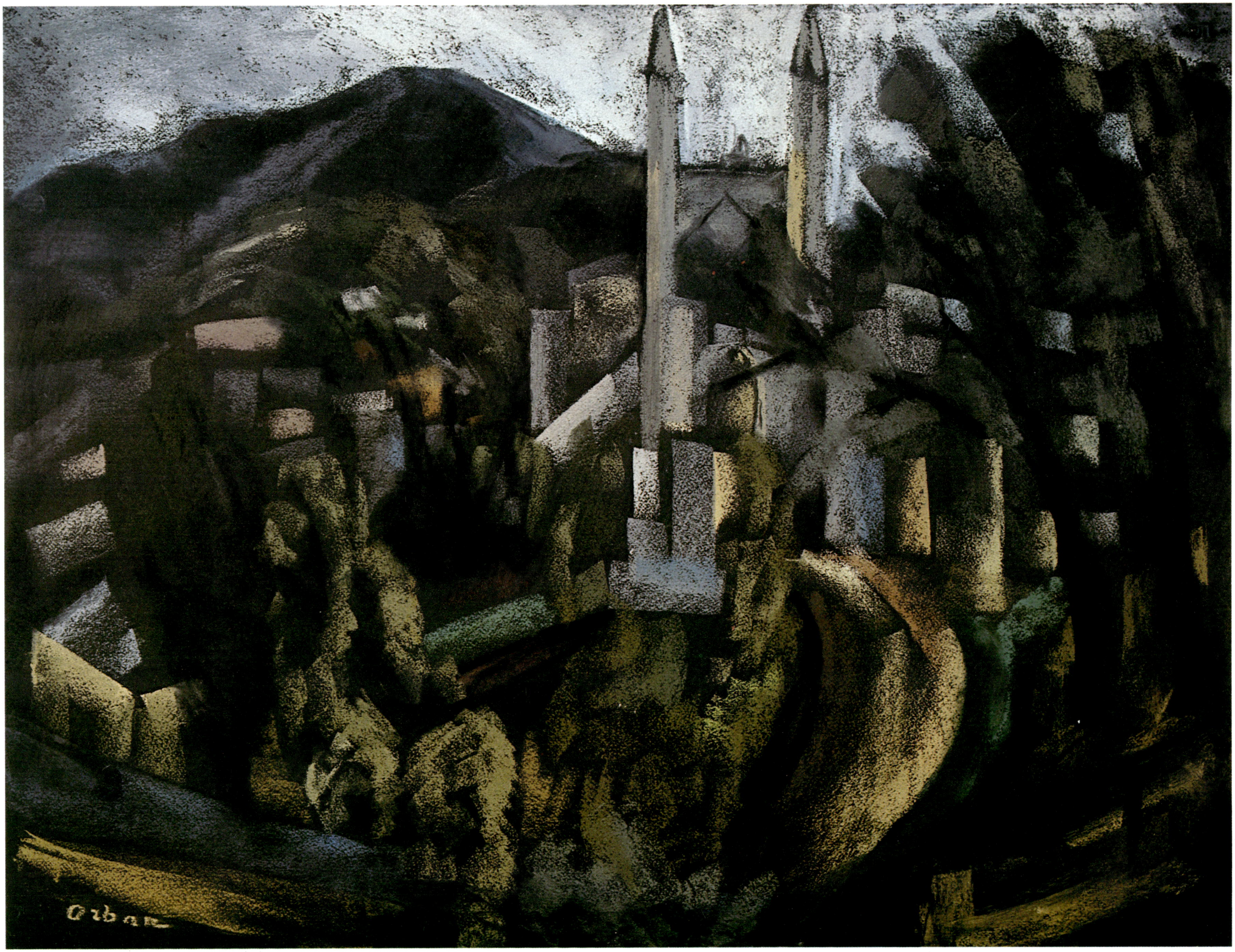

Hobart

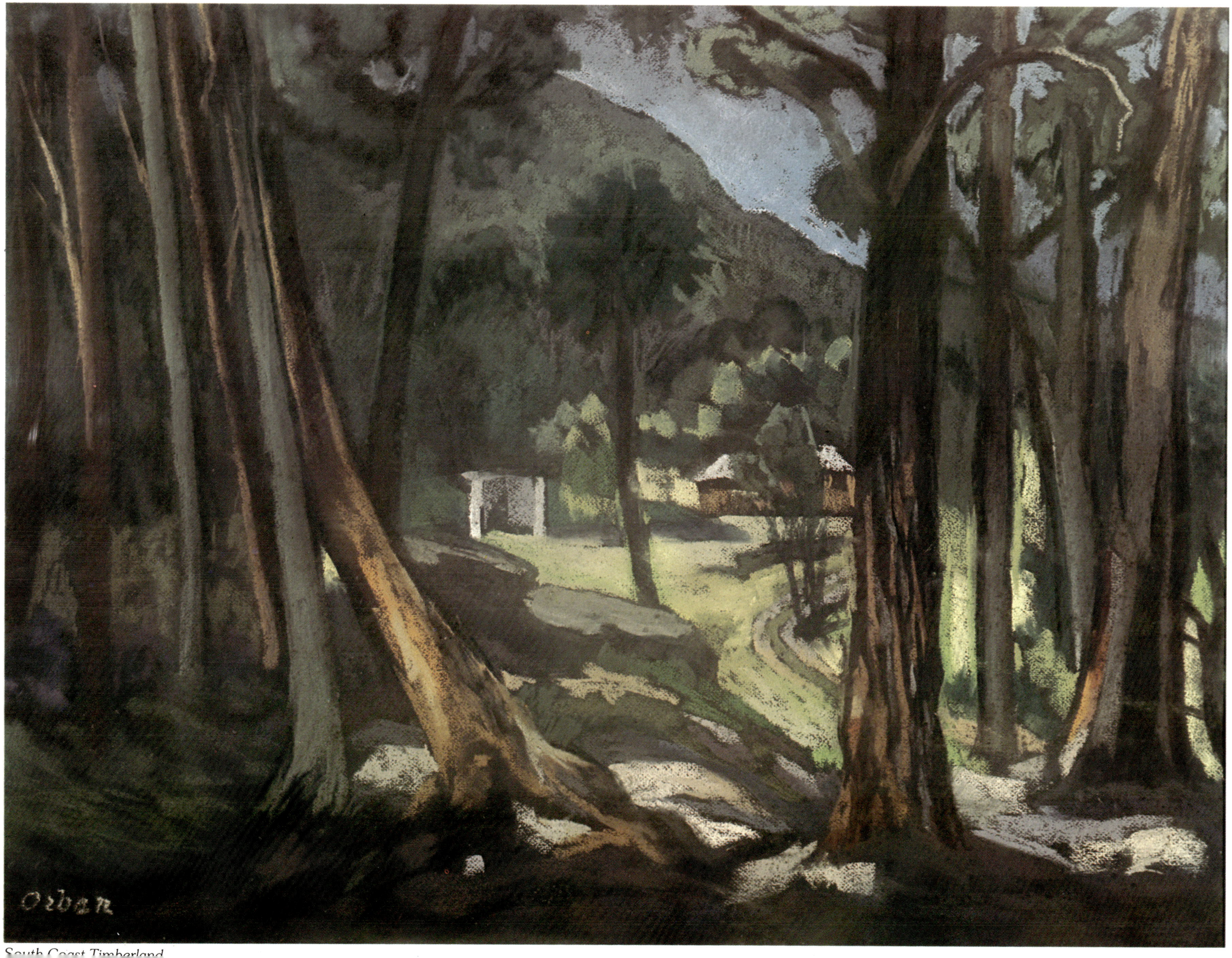

South Coast Timberland

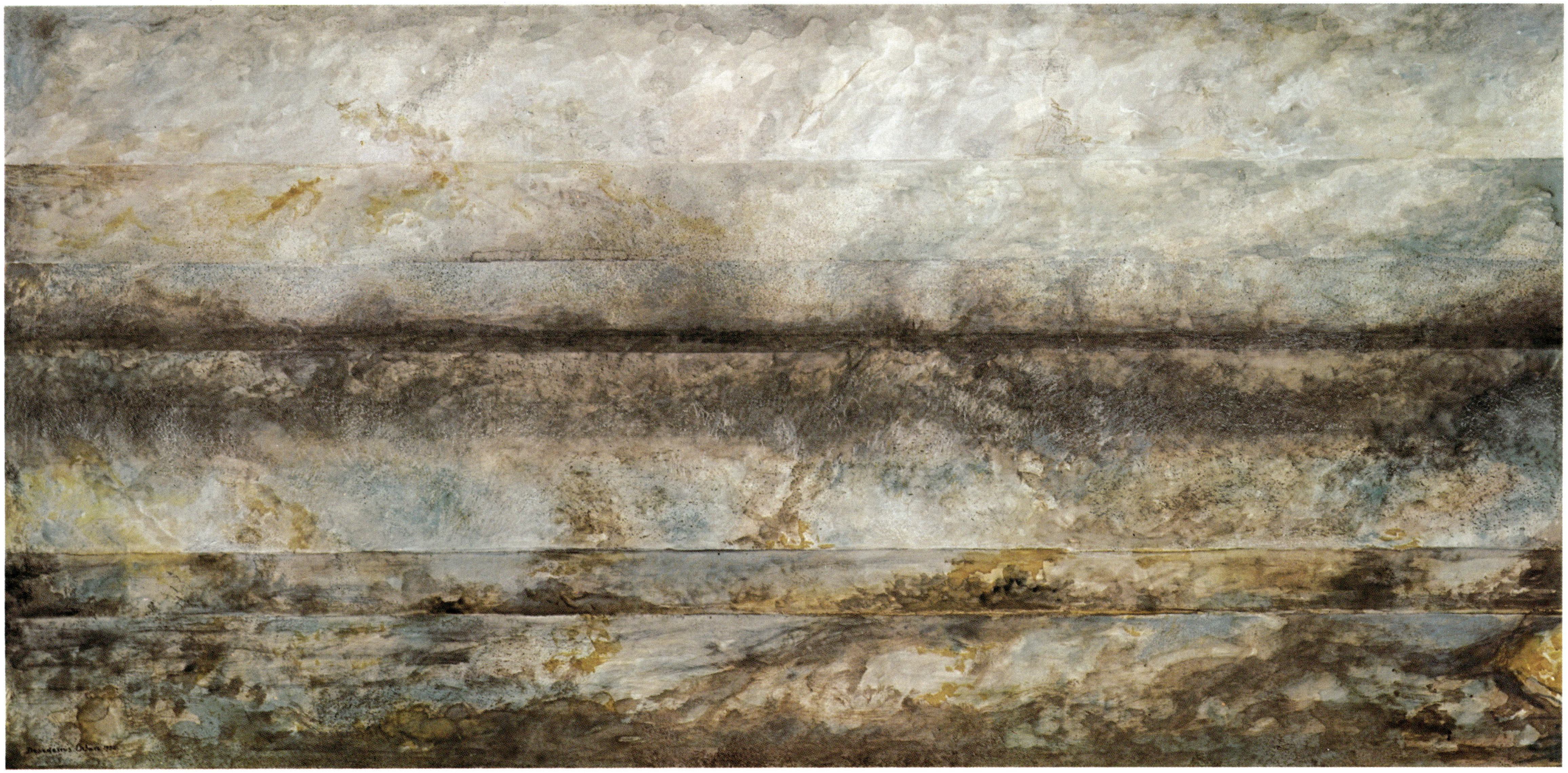

Separation of the Waters

Judy Cassab

Judy Cassab, born Vienna, Austria, 1920. Arrived in Sydney in 1951, where she now lives.

Judy Cassab, winner of the Archibald Prize in 1960 and 1967, may be better known as a portrait painter than a landscape artist, but since she arrived in 1951, having been trained in Hungary like her close friend, Desiderius Orban, she has been preoccupied with what was to her an exotic landscape. It remains exotic; and her latest works, like those of Orban and Lloyd Rees, portray it as mystical.

In *Orange Circumvision* she wishes to immerse herself in a landscape that entirely surrounds her; as John Olsen said of his painting, 'I am in the landscape and it is in me'; Cassab combines contemplation and simultaneity by fusing shape and movement. Movement runs through shapes and shapes give direction to movements. She is concerned with feelings, memories and observations partially obliterated by mood and atmosphere. Background and foreground, as in Orban's *Separation of the Waters,* have become one in the delicious drifts, veils and mists of colour. A large leaf-like orange oval or a fragile, blue disc may momentarily halt the flux of waters and rocks, but the mood is of mystical impermanence. Suggestions of rocky clefts waft up through the diaphanous shimmer of floating hues.

Canvases are crumpled on the floor to create bare hills and valleys, and are washed and stained with acrylic paints in a method that can be termed bas-relief improvisation. Colours collect in opaque lakes and flood thinly over raised areas. The canvas is then stretched taut and glazed, re-stained, dotted and impastoed; and again washed, rubbed, dappled and bruised with opaque or transparent colour. The landscape with a blue waterhole in an orange eye of a rocky depression becomes as full of incidents as a John Glover, but the mood, twilit and elusive, is that of David Davies: tremulous, subtle, low-keyed and dreamlike.

Orange Circumvision
Acrylic and oil on canvas; 1974; 157.5 × 204.5 cm.
Private collection.

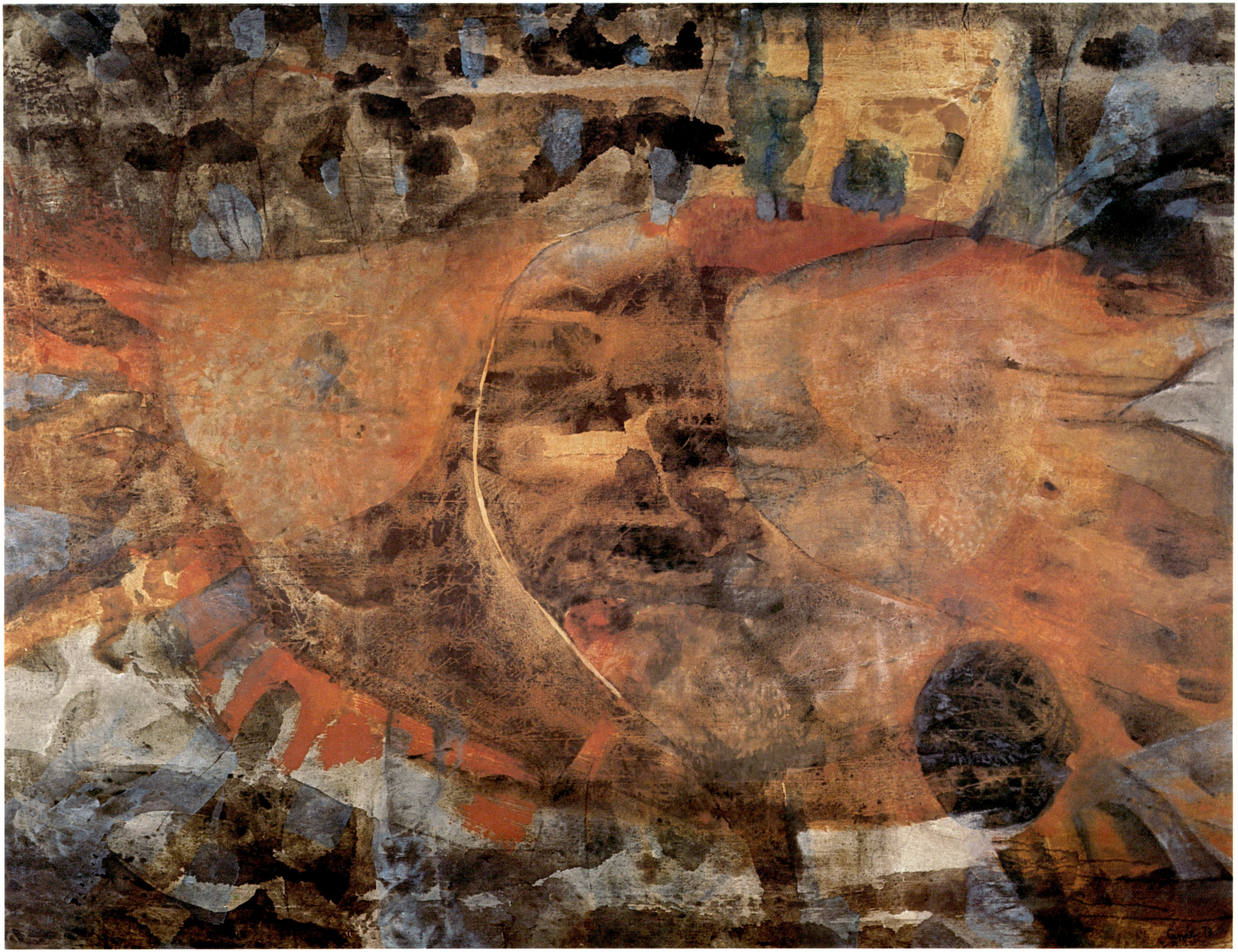

Orange Circumvision

Russell Drysdale

Sir George Russell Drysdale, born at Bognor Regis, Sussex, 1912. Came to Australia in 1923; lives at Gosford, New South Wales.

Like Lloyd Rees, Sidney Nolan and Arthur Boyd, Russell Drysdale preferred the still, the vast and the monumental. For him, no landscapes vibrating with planes and dabs of sparkling colour. He painted muted skies ravished by green-blue or veiled in golden dust; greys, deep thinly-painted browns, creamy ivories, ochres and faded yellows were his palette.

Though he transformed the deserts and their bare, eroded ridges into golden expanses, he discovered they were no Promised Lands; more often they were the scenes of man's vain endeavour, like *Emus in a Landscape*, where nature re-asserts itself, or like *The Rabbiters* with men so puny and their tasks apparently so fruitless that only their shadows have substance.

He has painted bush-heroes of a kind, but his landscapes are non-heroic; yet like Arthur Streeton's they are full of varied emotional content. *Road to the Black Mountains*, painted under the stimulus of the English Romantic revival, is replete with a gloomy urgency; the fitfully lit road is no Arcadian highway, for the painting is dominated by a brooding foreboding rarely achieved by his English counterparts. A similar uneasy loneliness is evoked by Donald Friend's *Brisbane River*, painted just after he met Drysdale during the Second World War.

For the first time since John Glover, an Australian artist was looking at his landscape through Claude's composition and suggestion of infinite vistas; to this Dyrsdale added sudden Romantic areas of intense shadow and equally intense areas of light on plain or mountainside; he also used the uncanny and eerie space of some Surrealists. He seems not to have been conscious of this and the Australian landscape, as in the eroded cliffs of *The Rabbiters*, is often Surreal. English critics have seen Drysdale's desert scenes as moonscapes, but here nature is anthropomorphic for the cliffs are enclosing jaws, and the root of the fallen tree is a gnarled fist of a blind creature groping in the empty sky. There are no Davies' or Withers' moons to bedew and bless the land; but not since Hans Heysen had an artist imbued the country with such grandeur and such symbolism, painted with delicacy *and* firmness. Drysdale also returned to the old masters in technique; the pervasive glow is a result of painting in a wax-linseed-oil medium over layers of strong colour.

The remoteness of the Outback is thus associated with the remoteness of history.

The Rabbiters
Oil on canvas; 1947; 76.2 × 101.6 cm.
Acquired: 1947
National Gallery of Victoria.

Emus in a Landscape
Oil on canvas; 1950; 101.5 × 127.0 cm.
Acquired: 1970
Australian National Gallery, Canberra.

Road to the Black Mountains
Oil on canvas; c.1952; 49.5 × 59.5 cm.
Gift of the Society of Women Artists, 1952
Art Gallery of New South Wales.

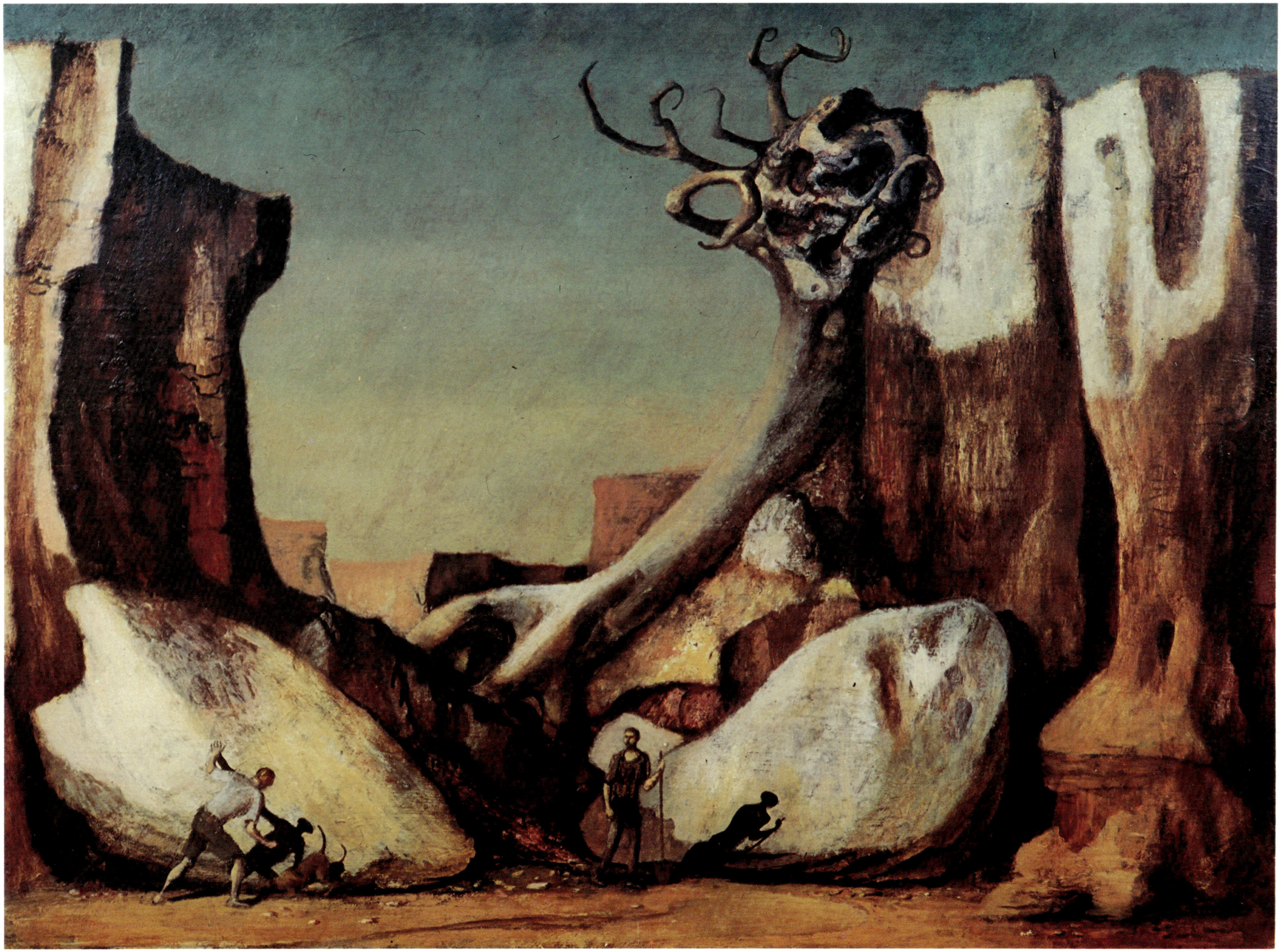

The Rabbiters

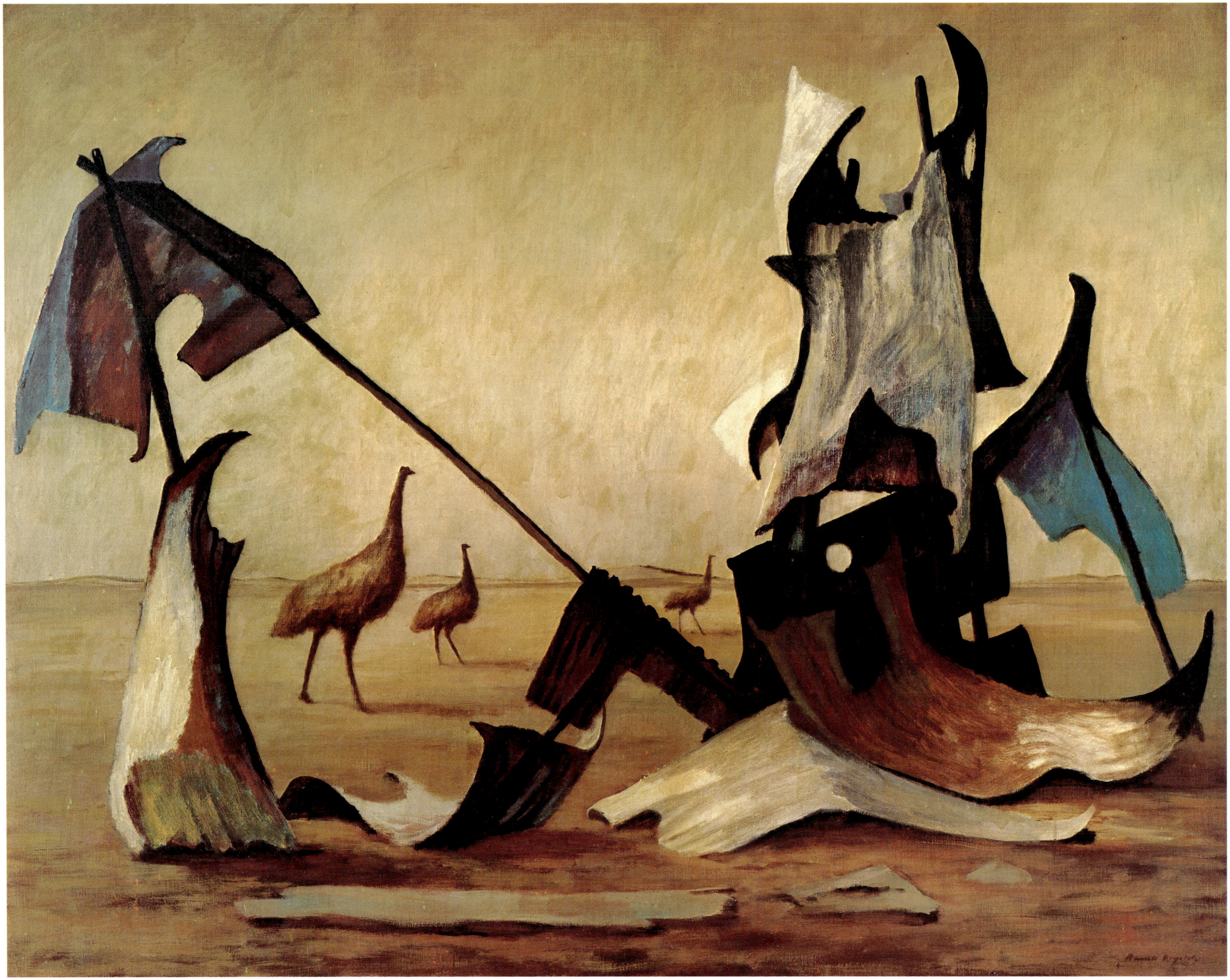

Emus in a Landscape

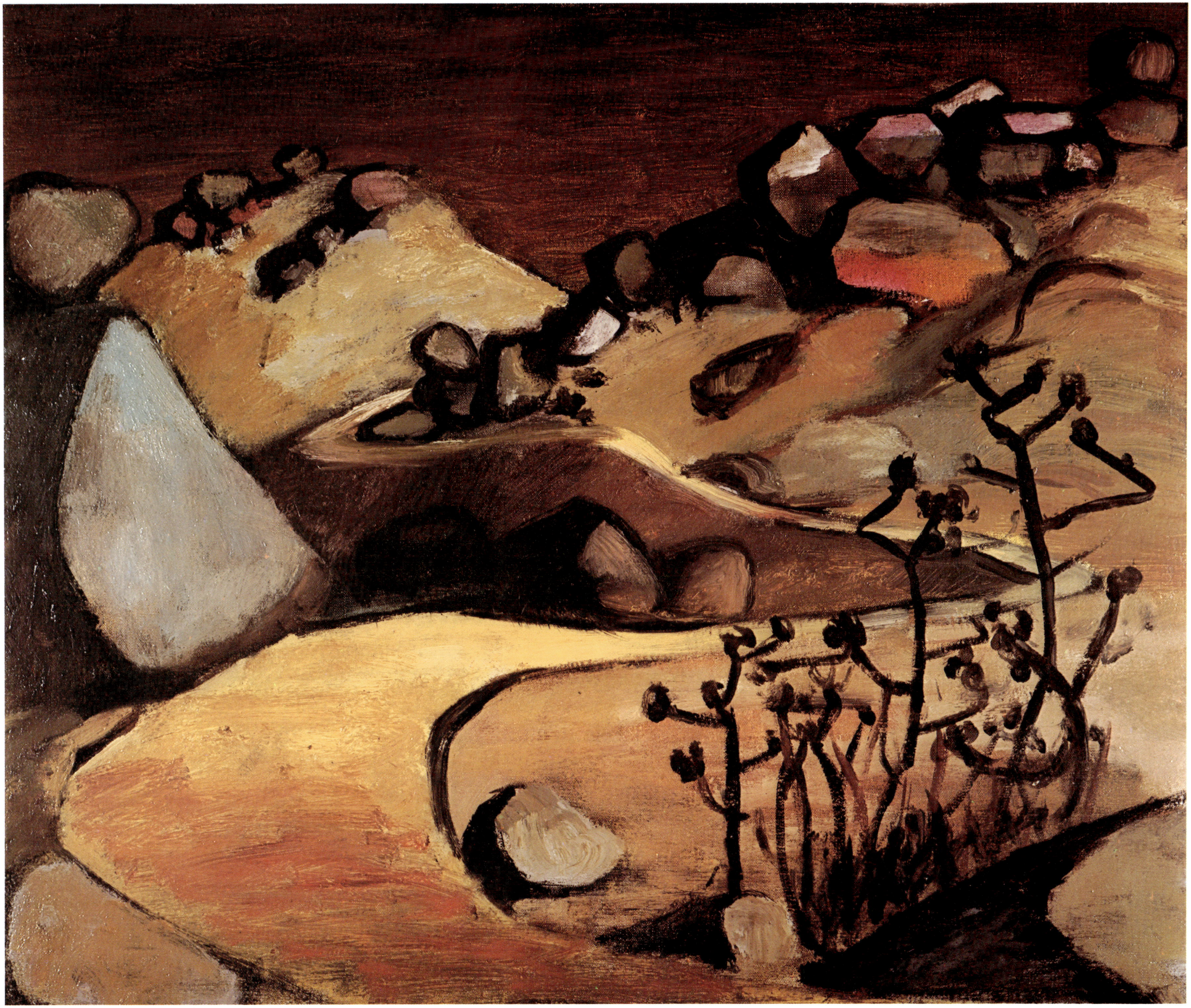

Road to the Black Mountains

Clifton Pugh

Clifton Ernest Pugh, born Melbourne, 1924; lives at Dunmoochin, Victoria.

Black in beak, white in tooth, talon and claw, cluttered with chaotic foliage and vegetation, scarred with rocks, wan and faded: this is nature to Clifton Pugh who presents the landscape as the domain of the scavenger and predator. Nature has formed a more neutral background to some portraits, but no more than neutral. When Arthur Boyd painted his series on Saint Francis of Assisi, the Saint blessed the world with glowingly beautiful hues; Pugh's Saint Francis roamed an inhospitable terrain that was enemy of the flesh and the soul.

Though Pugh has painted with artists like the optimistically boisterous John Perceval, Charles Blackman and Arthur Boyd, he rarely modifies his view of landscape as a theatre of the savage encounter.

The ferocity he depicts and implies in a decayed animal strung up in *Crucifixion* (1959), in *Memory of a Feral Cat* (1961) and *Dance of the Crows* does not depend on the bush as background but seems its natural product. To reinforce such an impression Pugh paints the ribs of the dead animal in this macabre dance as though they were extensions of the trees; a grey rock lies in the middle distance somewhat shaped like the carcass. There is, too, an equality of ferocity: the ribs, a hoof, the horns and the crows' beaks are all sharp and menacing.

Clifton Pugh has always tended towards semi-abstraction in certain areas to enhance the formidable solidity of his shapes; it is these, black and hardly varied, in *Dance of the Crows* that evoke a timelessness from a scene so compactly unified and intense that it drains the colour from the landscape which it leaves pale and disordered.

For Pugh such events give some order to the landscape which he, unlike some landscape painters, does not see as harmonious in itself.

Dance of the Crows
Oil on hardboard; 1960; 137.2 × 182.9 cm.
Courtesy of the Rudy Komon Gallery, Sydney.

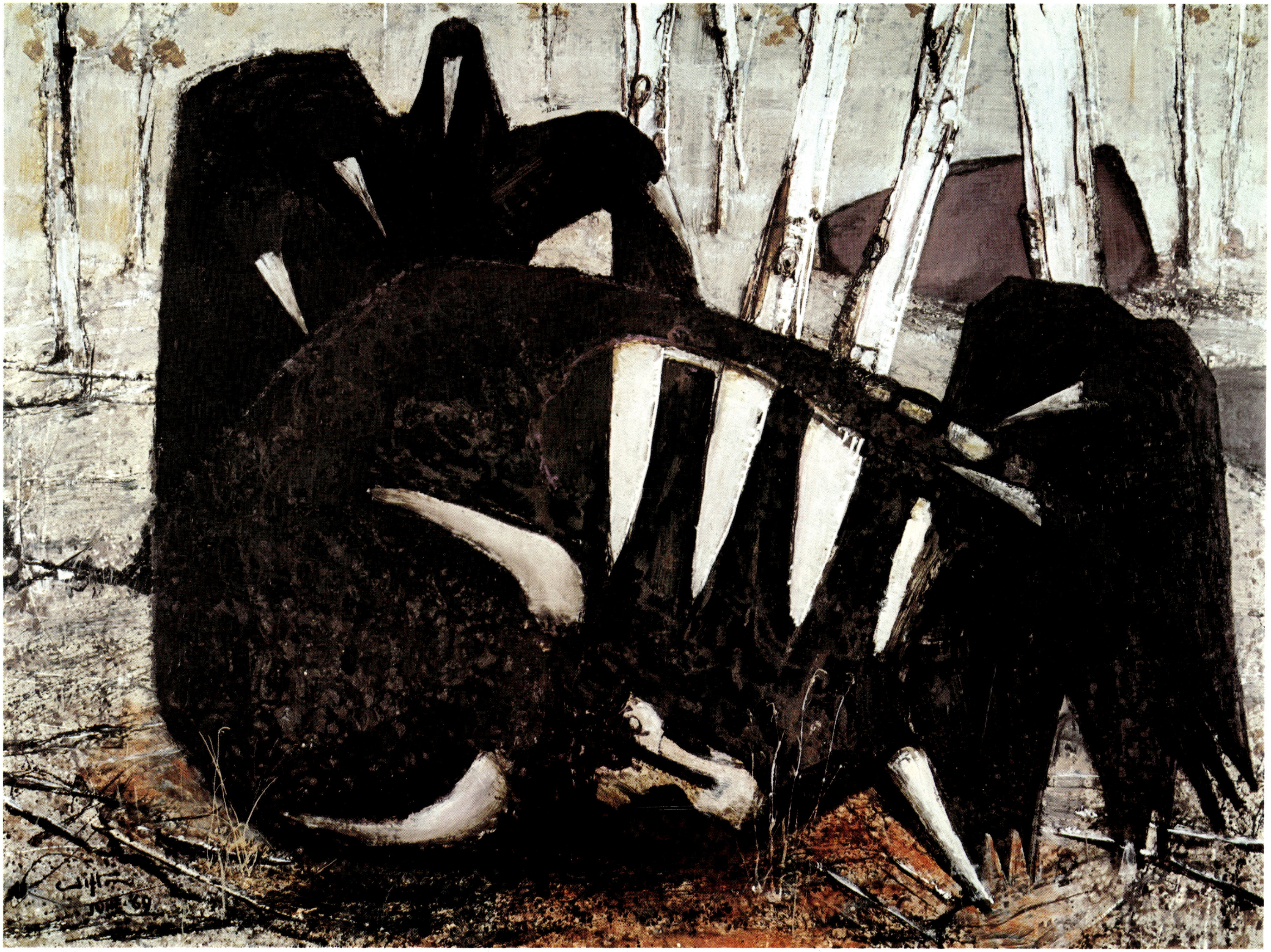

Dance of the Crows

Sidney Nolan

Sidney Robert Nolan, born Carlton, Melbourne, 1917. Has lived in England since 1951, making frequent visits to Australia.

Riverbend invites one to extend the quotation from William Wordsworth's 'After-Thought', that supplied Arthur Streeton with his title:

'as I cast my eyes,
I see what was, and is, and will abide;
Still glides the stream and shall forever glide;
The Form remains, the Function never dies;
While we, the brave, the mighty and the wise,
We men, who in our morn of youth defied
The elements, must vanish.'

The defiant, rumbustious and omnipresent Ned Kelly of the 1946-47 series had become a vulnerable, naked wraith by the mid-sixties; no longer the hero and hunter, he was as frail and lost as his victims. Except for the iron helmet, forged from plough-shares, there was little to distinguish victor and victim; each became, as in *Riverbend,* Lilliputian actors in a drama whose theme was not revenge, as in the early Kelly series, but the sad inevitability of retribution.

The palisade of trees, enclosing the scene and impenetrable to all but the fluttering light, creates a vast background against which Kelly and the trooper flit like the light itself. All is uncannily still in this oppressive forest that resembles the claustrophobic array of trees that Saint George faces in Albrecht Aldorfer's painting in Munich which Sidney Nolan did not see until 1970. Kelly is no Saint George; he haunts the river's edge like a ghost of his former self and disappears entirely from the last panels; that is, if we read the painting from left to right as though it were a set of pre-Renaissance panels unfolding a narrative simultaneously so that we can see all the stages of the story at once and also in a sequence.

While we trace the narratives of men and heroes, nature persists and here heralds its perennial rejuvenation by the fresh green at the top of the untidy trees.

One can almost hear a faint rustle of leaves, the shot ringing out, the dying echoes and then that eerie stillness of the Australian bush that so many writers and artists have commented upon. Meanwhile the noiseless, sluggish and opaque fawn-grey-green river floats on like the serene and majestic Oxus where, in Matthew Arnold's poem, Sohrab and Rustum fought alone.

Like Frederick McCubbin, Sidney Nolan has long been challenged by the almost formless nature of a close view of the bush and the curious way it percolates, rather than reflects, light. His Kelly has waded rivers and floodlands and has occupied the shores of a river as if it were the other side of the world. Conrad Martens and Lloyd Rees make a Romantic terrain of the foreshores, but for Nolan it is the other, the alien, shore.

The bush is for Nolan neither hospitable nor inhospitable; it is a grand, infinite and permanent location for a passing, melancholy encounter.

Riverbend
Oil on hardboard; 1966; nine panels each 154.4 × 121.9 cm; total width: 10.971 m.
(Another version, the same size, was painted on canvas, also in 1966.)
The Australian National University, Canberra.

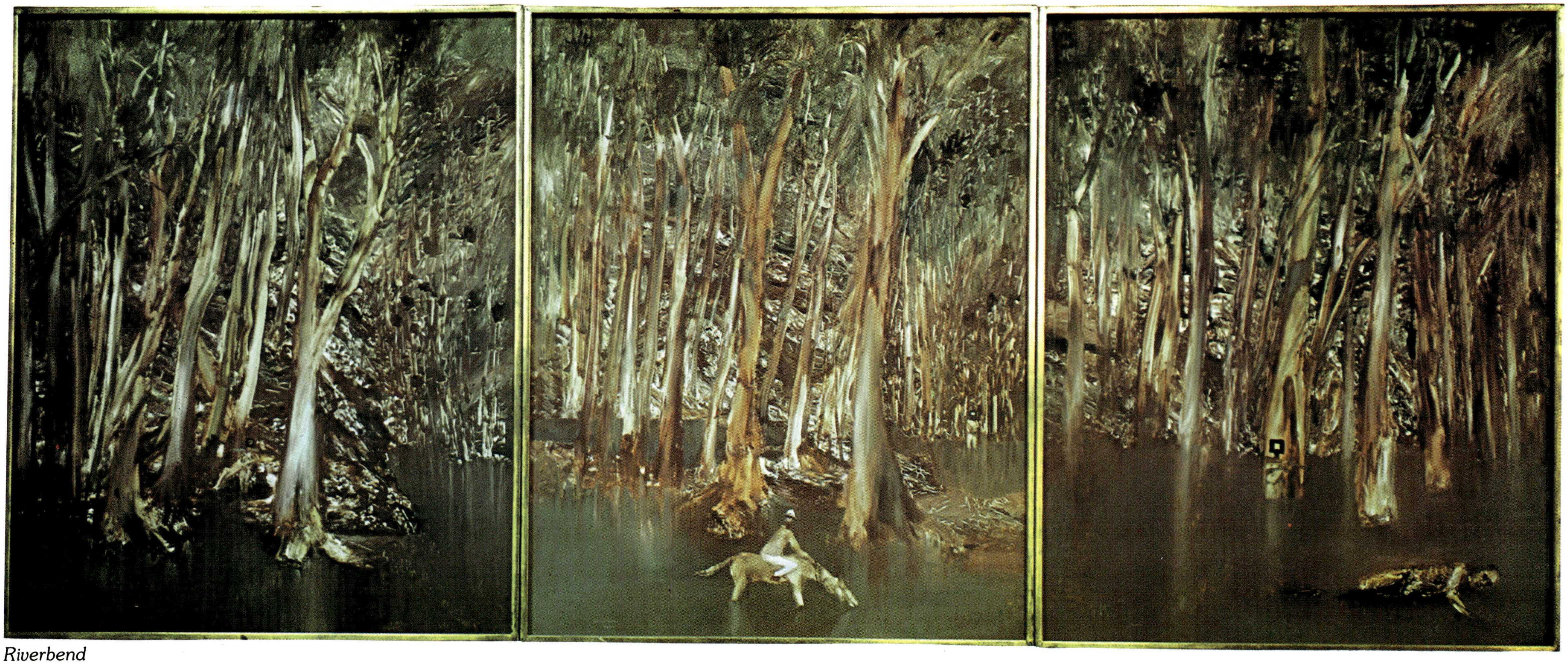

Riverbend

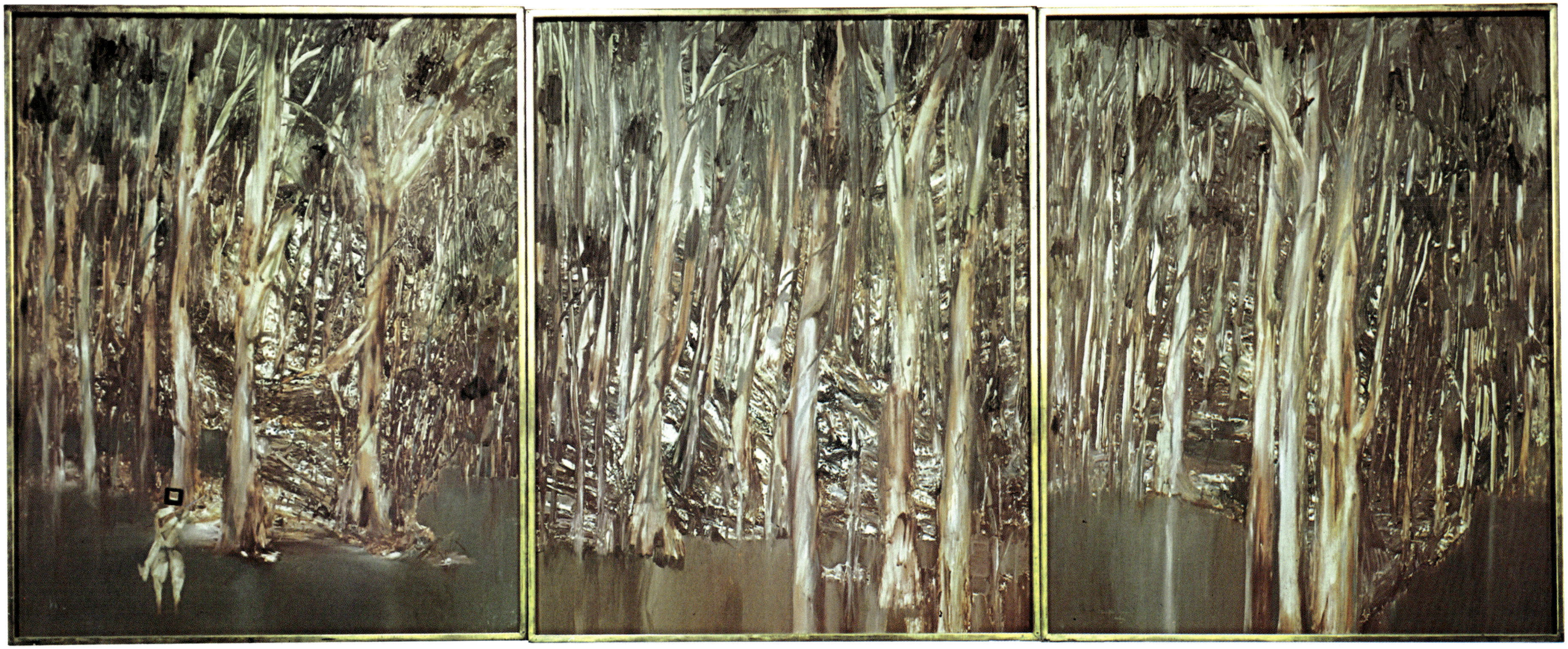

Riverbend

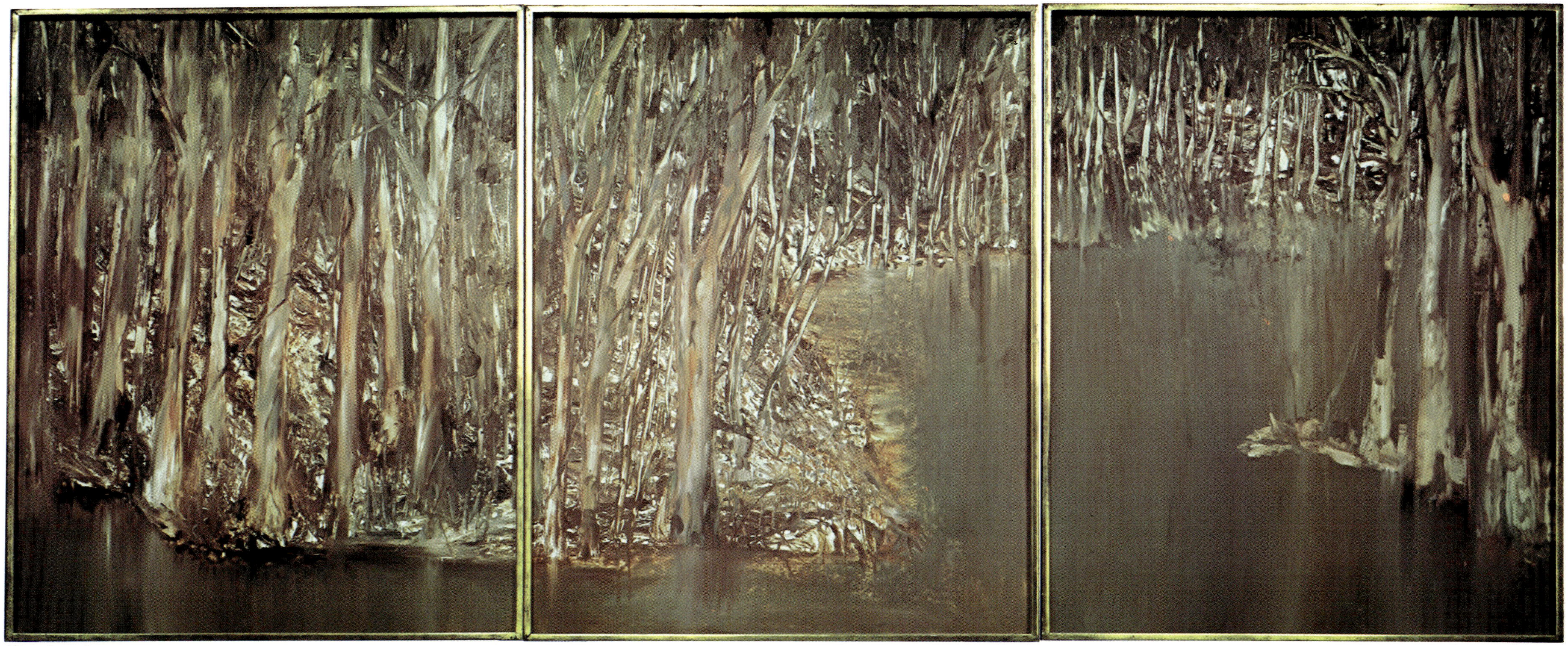

Riverbend

William Salmon

William Arthur Salmon, born Geelong, Victoria, 1928; lives at Little Hartley, New South Wales.

'My subject,' William Salmon has noted, 'is the Australian bush . . . I see the landscape intimately and not as something weird and exotic. It would be marvellous to be able to approach it as an aborigine without the prejudices of a western culture, but that is impossible'.

For Salmon the bush is not weird, exotic and symbolic; Nolan's palisade of trees has a purpose antithetical to Salmon's dancing frieze of slender limbs and tossed, sharp green foliage. Salmon is an observer of the lyrical elements of the bush, an attitude no doubt reinforced or influenced by the fact that he studied with Ray Crooke at the Swinburne Technical College; that Salmon watched Daryl Lindsay painting on his parents' property in Western Australia, and that in 1960 he went to Hill End painting with David Strachan.

For Crooke, Strachan and Salmon the landscape is a recorded experience; Salmon, writes of his training in 1951 at the Slade School, London, 'while freedom and adventure were encouraged, it was based on objective and unemotional study, styleless, and supposedly concerned with the tangible "realness" of things. I have since realised that the only reality which has any meaning is one's reaction and involvement, one's state of awareness'.

An inventive transcription is the result; the brush scatters touches that denote bark and foliage like chaff through the landscape. They become a set of crisp, independent notations adding to the vivacity of the scene. There are influences of the French Intimists and of *art nouveau* joined in a song lyric about the bush; trees, grasses, shrubs and cliff fuse with one another in a sprightly harmony, of which John Shaw Neilson wrote:

'Beauty is joy that stays not overlong.
Clad in the magic of sincerities
It rides up in a song'.

Cliff Face
Oil on canvas; 1975; 99.5 × 109 cm.
Possession of the artist.

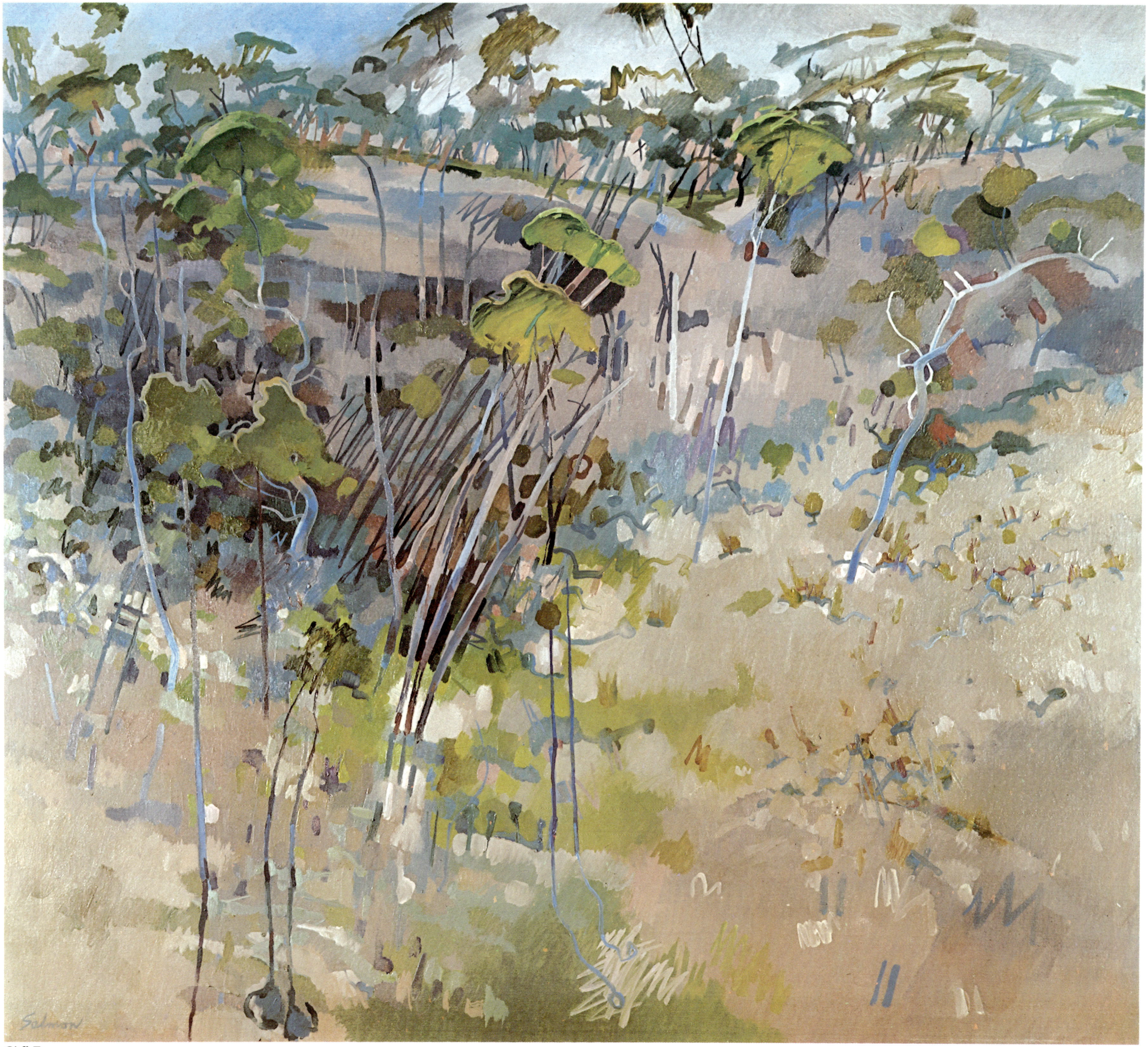

Cliff Face

Arthur Boyd

Arthur Merric Bloomfield Boyd, born Murrumbeena, Victoria, 1920; settled in London in 1959. Returned to Australia, 1975.

Arthur Boyd has peopled or, perhaps, infested his symbolic paintings with Surreal, hybrid creatures, becoming monsters or emerging from a monstrous state; in such paintings, the urbanscape and the landscape are so caught in a vortex of metamorphosis that they tend to lose their identity, for the forest and the plain are seen through the eyes of the dragonfly-woman or Nebuchadnezzar, maddened and desperate.

Three other kinds of his painting use the landscape quite differently: since the late 'forties Boyd has painted fresh, but bleached, Wimmera landscapes, in hues of pale and deep honey. Writing of Boyd's retrospective in 1962 at the Whitechapel Art Gallery, London, Robert Melville noted in 1973, 'This exhibition must have included some of the Wimmera landscapes, marvellously precise yet spectral under a downpour of light . . .' Of one work he recalled that 'It could have been painted by a precursor of Bosch before the invention of sin'.

With puritanical zeal Boyd presents far less serene scenes on the results of sin and evil; if he was interested in Bosch he was more involved with Pieter Brueghel the Elder, for *The Mining Town*, in true Brueghelian style, piles incident on incident to create a world in turmoil and polluted with proliferating wickedness and irrationality: the mine, rising like one of those curious mountains in Joachim Patinir, destroys the town; lovers cling in front of a graveyard; Christ's driving out the money-lenders is just another incident; the coffin lies on the ground; the pigs fall from the truck to inherit the earth; a naked figure climbs a tree; crippled men stalk the town; the broken tree clenches its fist and even the foreground shrubs with their sweet flowers are confined and distorted. But far away the open harbour and the open meadows indicate another world; scent of sea and mown meadows wafts over the savagery.

The other world was not always so pleasant as the Wimmera or the background of some of the Brueghelian paintings; in 1956 Boyd painted at Gaffney's Creek with John Perceval and their work became denser and gloomier. Boyd did a number of creek scenes, full of fallen timber, so subdued that they looked nocturnal and threatening, as though they were breeding grounds for his monsters. *Burning Off* with its delicately painted smoke is of this vintage, but more humanised. None the less, such is the ominous air, that one can speculate on what fires are being stoked. As James Mollison has written, 'Certain birds or beasts, tree or plant forms tell of the artist's mind impinging on what the eye sees'.

What the eye sees in such paintings as these three is a beautifully painted surface extracting all that tempera and oil mediums can afford. One of the tensions created in his work is the seeming divorce between significant meaning and the succulent, attractive and seductive paint. Boyd works in the tradition of the old masters: the most horrible disaster or the most golden, Arcadian landscape can be presented with equal beauty.

The Mining Town or Casting the Money Lenders from the Temple
Oil and tempera on hardboard; 1946-7; 87.2 × 109 cm.
Acquired: 1974
Australian National Gallery, Canberra.

Burning Off
Oil on hardboard; 1957; 91.1 × 122 cm.
Acquired in 1971 from funds donated by Mr Roderick Carnegie.
National Gallery of Victoria.

Wimmera Landscape
Oil on hardboard; c.1960-1963; 91.3 × 121.3 cm.
Presented 1968, Godfrey Phillips International Pty Ltd.
National Gallery of Victoria.

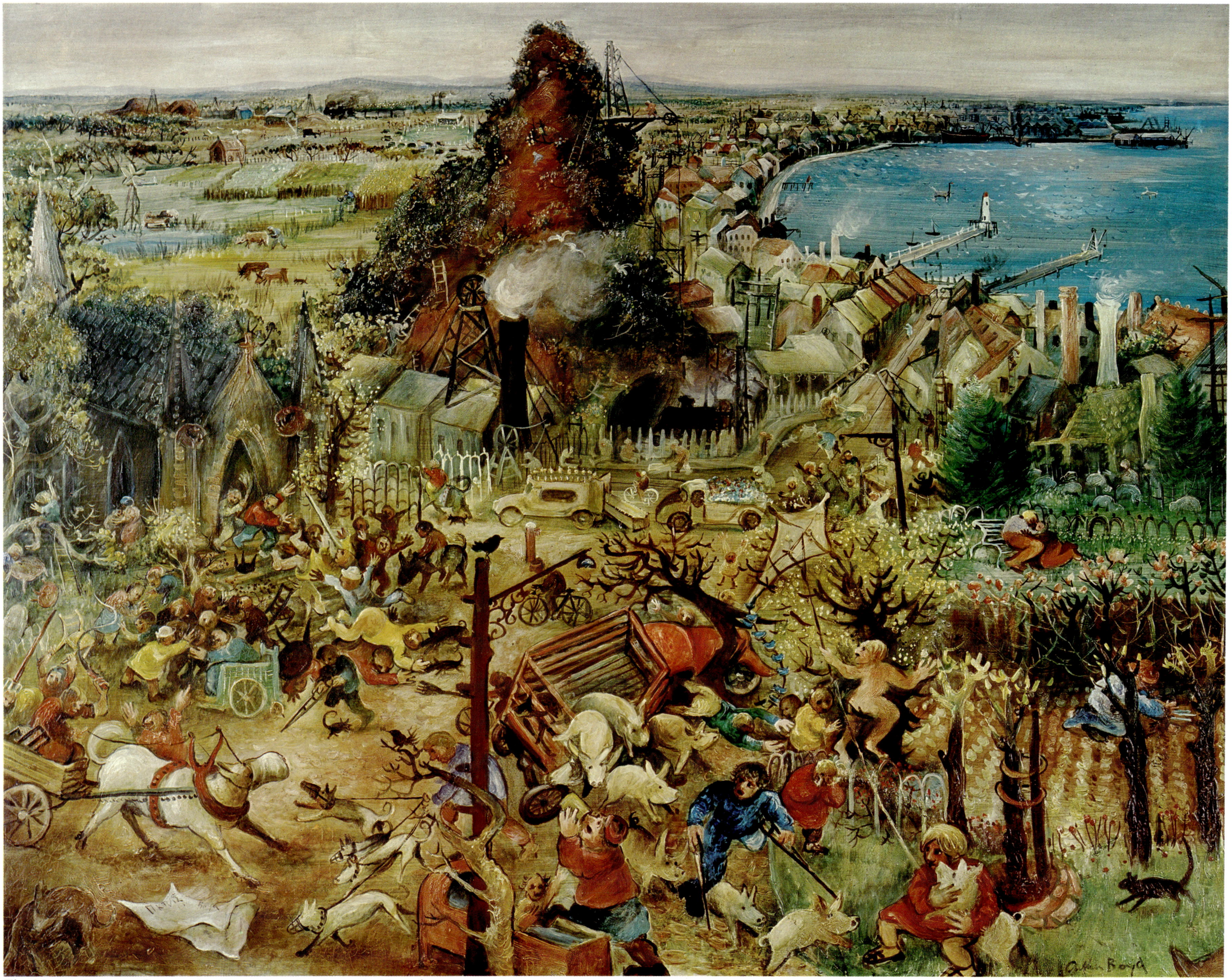

The Mining Town or Casting the Money Lenders from the Temple

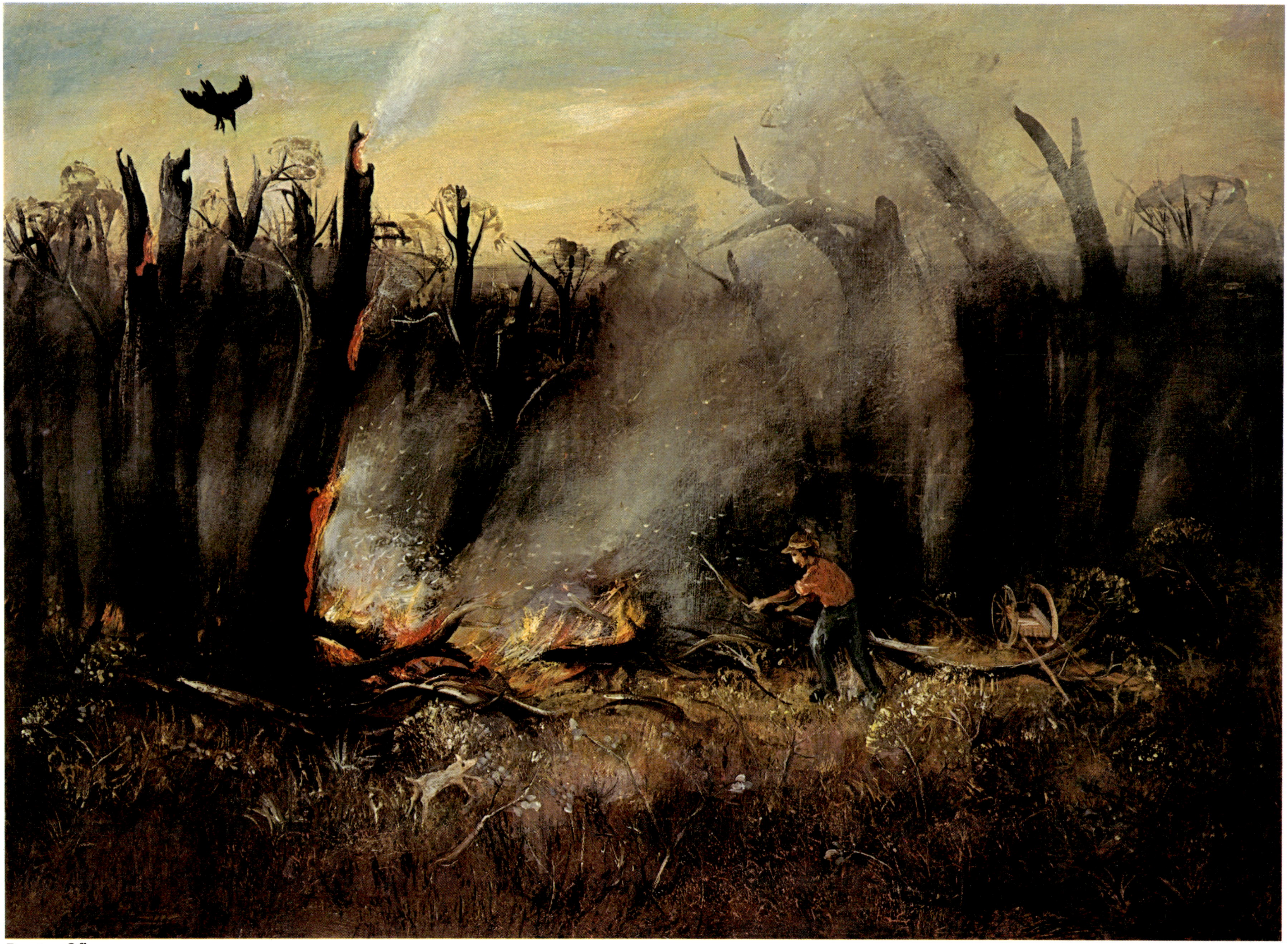

Burning Off

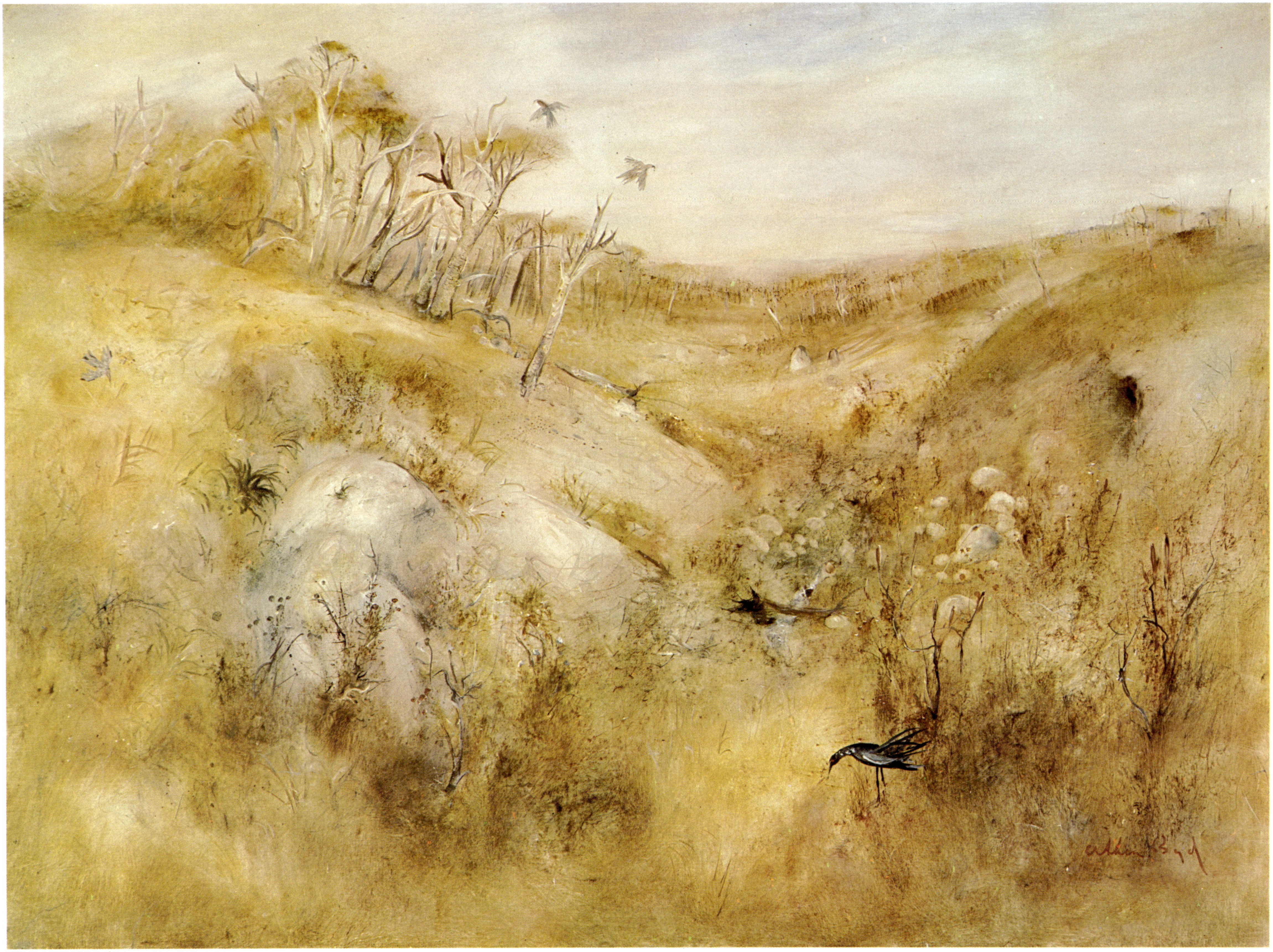

Wimmera Landscape

Michael Shannon

David Michael Shannon, born Kapunda, South Australia, 1927; lives in Melbourne.

Sali Herman's houses are patinated monuments and worn and ravaged personalities; they are homes and habitations; Blamire Young's *Rats' Castle* is an abandoned, haunted building only alive with memories; Arthur Boyd's *The Mining Town or Casting the Money Lenders from the Temple* is frenzied with human activities; Michael Shannon's city, as far as the eye can see down its street, is deserted and emptied of humans by the searing heat. The harsh light robs the buildings of individuality and all begins to shimmer in the summer sun. Shannon's customary deft and sketchy drawing with broken, black lines saves the buildings from heavy somnolence and evokes an atmosphere of dehydrated fragility. Further, lest the colours, beneath a dullish blue sky, look too uniformly hot, Shannon introduces soft pinks and acid greens.

Having studied with Fernand Léger in Paris, Shannon appreciates the dynamic formalisation of urbanscapes, but Léger liked the close frontal view; and, having studied at the Academie Florence from 1949 to 1952, Shannon preferred the panoramic view across shunting yards, rivers and wide streets. However formal his shapes they are always bathed in an atmosphere; a fresh wind blows through his Queensland houses; the air lies heavily over his railroad scenes; the sky can throb or be as still as a stone.

In *Summer Landscape, Melbourne,* Shannon cleaves the city with an empty street that symbolically divorces the city from life. Arthur Streeton's river in *Still Flows the Stream and Shall Forever Flow* moves through the centre in concert with the general harmony. If we look across the Yarra towards Melbourne with Frederick McCubbin, through the unpolluted air, it is clear what Michael Shannon's perspectival huddle is about, but such is his redeeming touch that he does not preach. Like Julian Ashton and S.T. Gill he inclines to nimble objectivity.

Summer Landscape, Melbourne
Oil on canvas; 1975; 121 × 182.5 cm.
Possession of the artist.

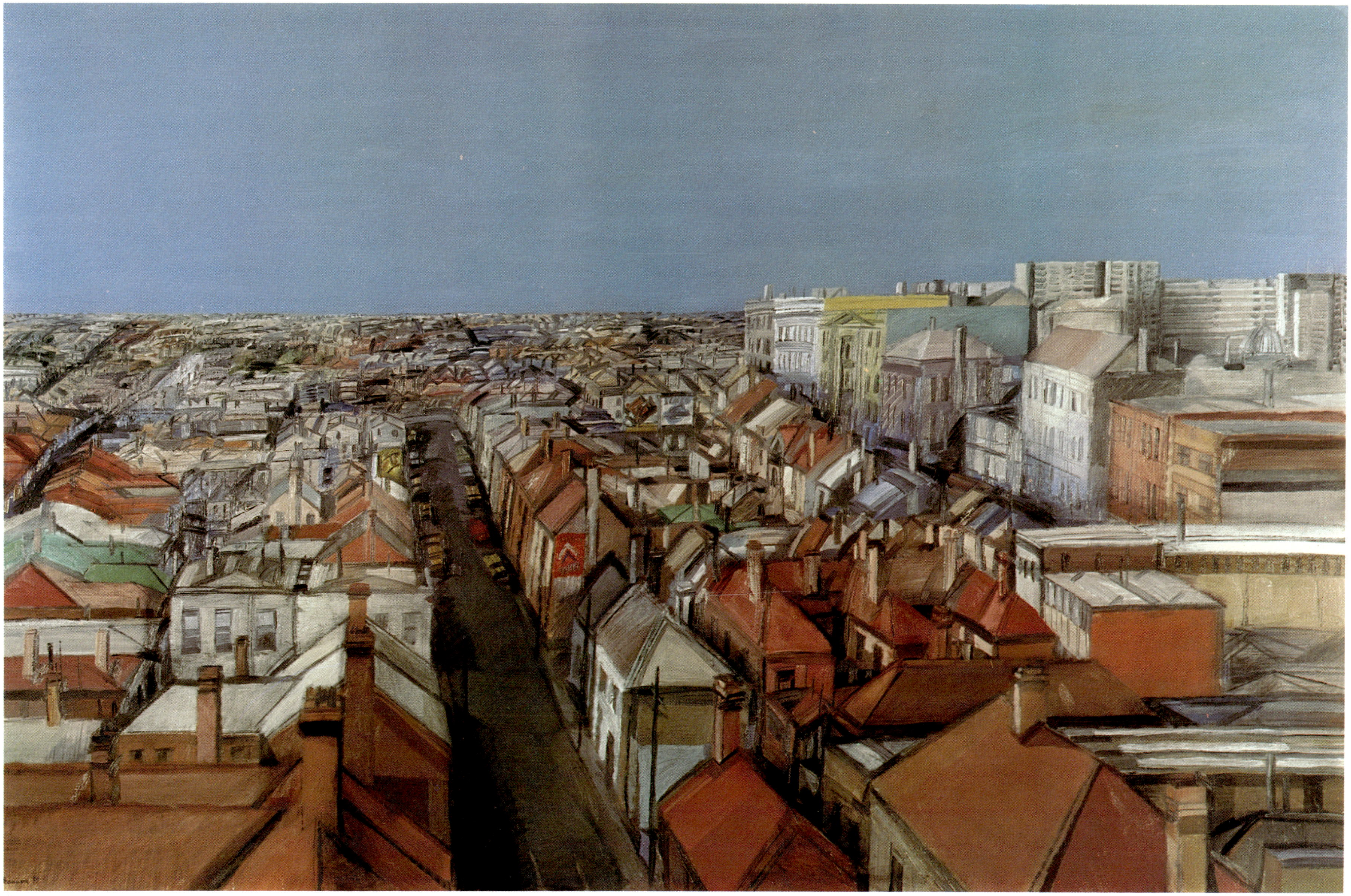

Summer Landscape, Melbourne

John Perceval

John Perceval, born Bruce Rock, Western Australia, 1923; settled in Melbourne in 1935, where he now lives.

For John Perceval, who married Arthur Boyd's sister, Mary, and who shared themes and painting sites with Arthur, the world is a whirlpool of ravishing paint. To preserve immediacy he usually paints outdoors with great speed. The farmlands, the forests, the creeks and the harbour advance upon one with a celebratory vivacity; the landscape is there as a physical presence. His early Brueghelian paintings seeth and toss more than Boyd's; he has no patience with the steadying horizon of a Fred Williams or of those vertical trees and solid houses that rivet sky to earth. In 1960, in *Homage to Buvelot* he did turn to the calm, stalwart tree, but he so scratched through the paint that the foliage could have been taken for wind-tossed water.

As he began he has remained; he accumulates incidents and paint; the early *Oakleigh Landscape,* from one of his first painting sites, crowds together all the features of rural life; despite the subdued colour, the scene is vigorously presented, for Perceval's landscape is no venue for retirement and serene contemplation. He gives the impression that life presses upon one and he renders its impact, urban or rural, with gusto and urgency. He is aware that this energy sometimes modifies reality but says, 'Of course a landscape can remain a landscape, a grandmother minding a child may still be that, even when the metamorphoses the paintings have gone through makes this not immediately apparent'.

Perceval's visit to Gaffney's Creek with Arthur Boyd in 1956 checked his jubilant bravura though the paint was as thick, swirled, scratched, heaped and fertile in enlivening images as ever; to convey the sense of the unfamiliar in *Black Cockatoo Flying Upstream,* he throws perspective out-of-kilter, the bucket and the cockatoo being almost in plane with the viewer. The world is out of joint; the bridge, with reddened girders, lies broken; the stream, seemingly blocked in its course, is equally frustrated; even the cockatoo wears a butterfly's tail. It is a menacing, shadowed scene, full of a black energy and, like Arthur Boyd's tangled forests and dark creek scenes, likely to produce monsters.

At about the same time Perceval was to discover Williamstown where the Yarra meets the sea. He said it was 'like finding Venice' and he meant the amalgamation of sky, land, ship and water; gannets dive, buoys bounce, boats bustle together and out of disorder create his busiest scenes. Boats, as in *Tugboat in a Boat,* give birth to boats.

The colour is Fauvist, but unlike John Rigby's, is blocky, heaped and swirled; the stroke is fractured and staccato; high-keyed as Rigby's palette is, the mood is of calm ecstasy; Perceval relishes turbulence.

Oakleigh Landscape
Oil on canvas; 1946; 57 × 84 cm.
Courtesy of the Rudy Komon Gallery, Sydney.

Black Cockatoo Flying Upstream
Oil on hardboard; 1956; 90.6 × 122.2 cm.
Acquired: 1972
Australian National Gallery, Canberra.

Tugboat in a Boat
Oil and enamel on hardboard; 1956; 73.7 × 121.9 cm.
Acquired: 1956
National Gallery of Victoria.

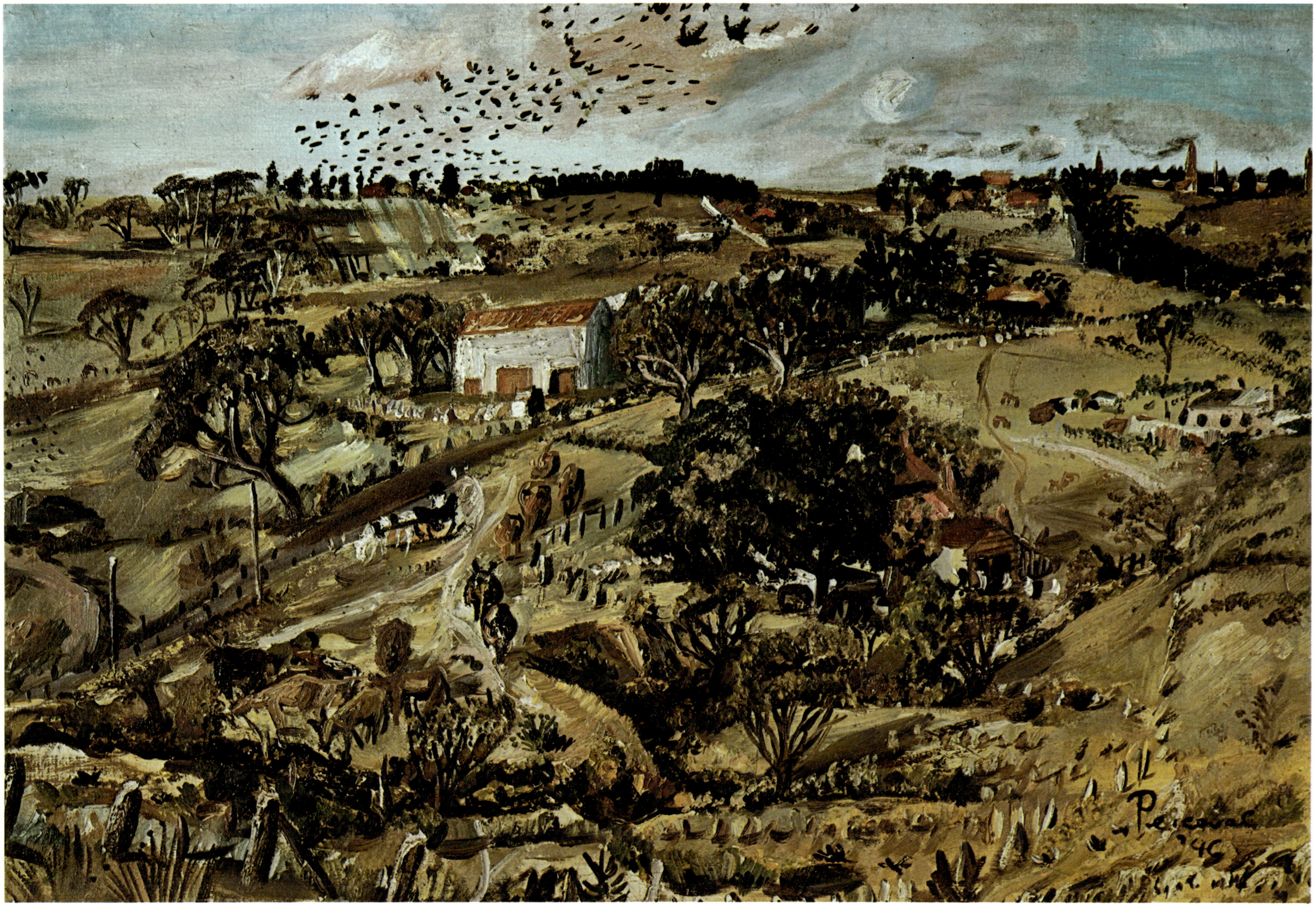

Oakleigh Landscape

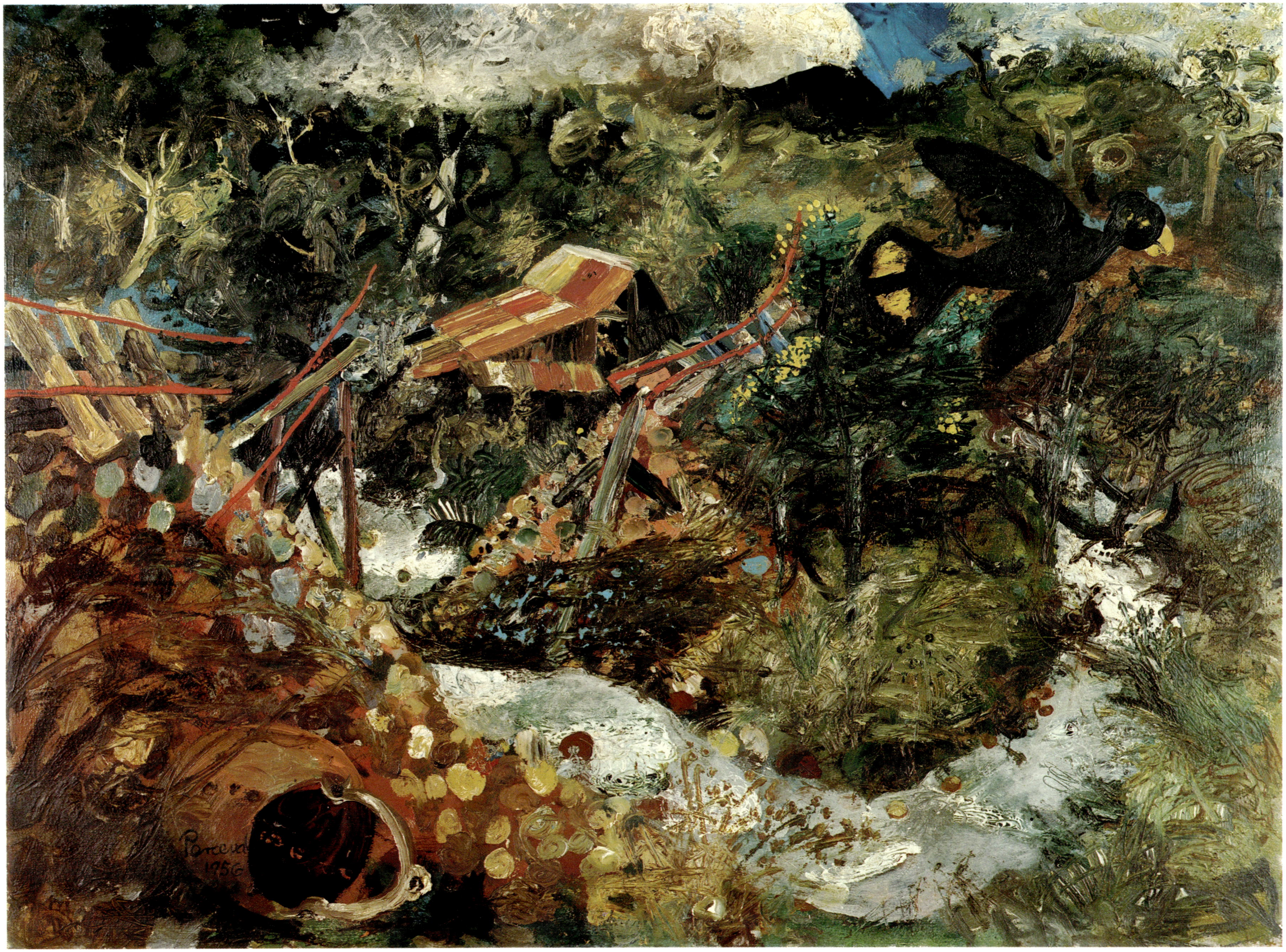

Black Cockatoo Flying Upstream

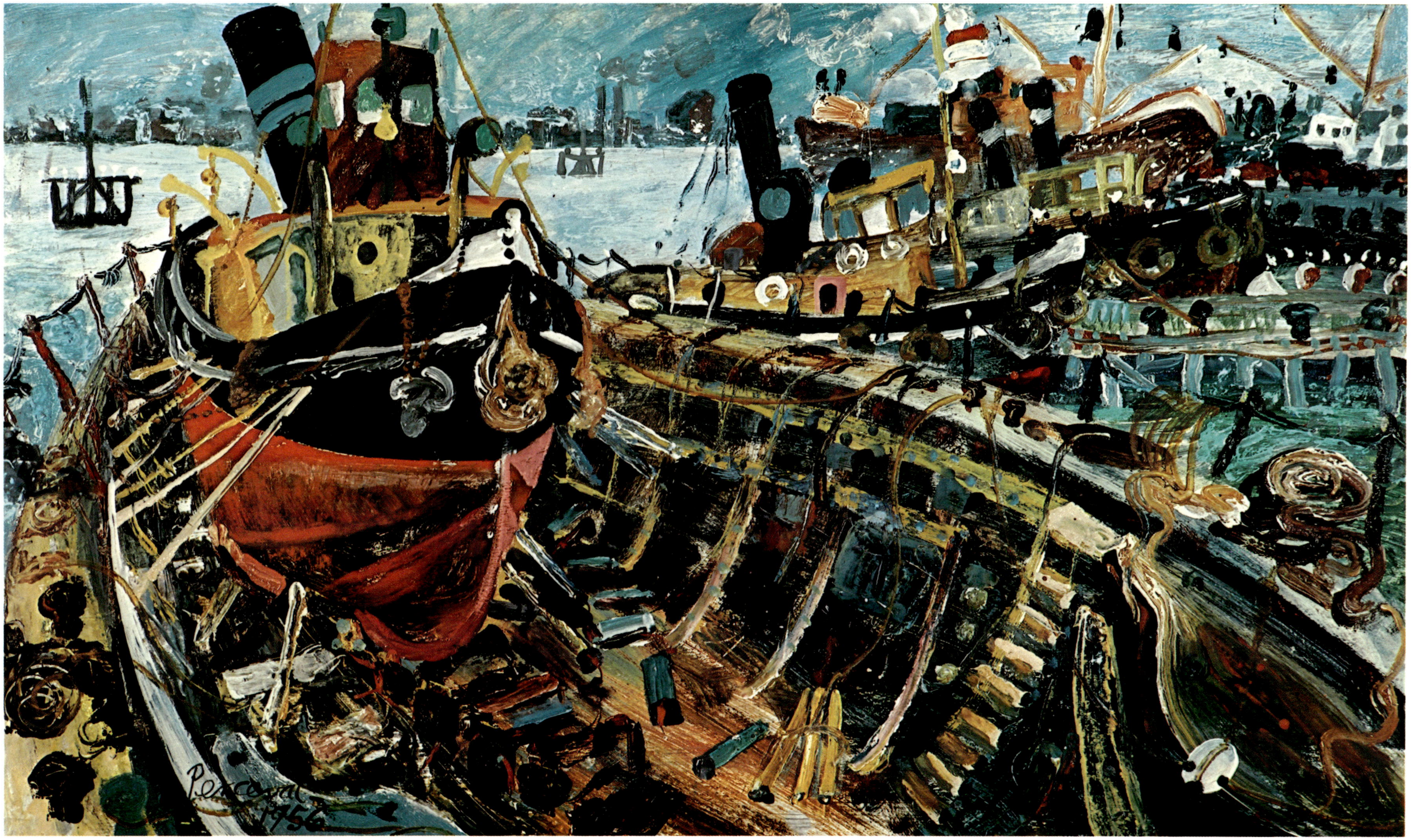

Tugboat in a Boat

John Rigby

John Thomas Rigby, born Brisbane, Queensland, 1922; lives in Pinjarra Hills, Queensland.

John Rigby's view of Moggill Village, near which he lives, is presented with a delight in the virtues of linear Fauvism; for Rigby, Fauvism's intense, subjective colour, its collation of primary hues and its ecstatic amalgam of foreground and background provide the appropriate mode for rendering the lush and lively growth and the compelling colour of Queensland's southern coastal vegetation.

Rigby pays tribute to the findings of the great Fauvists: Henri Matisse said it was a way of 'regaining the purity of our means'; in André Derain's hands 'tubes of paint became dynamite cartridges'; Raoul Dufy aimed 'to create the world of things we do not see'; it allowed Robert Delaunay 'To build up coloured phrases, colour acting as an almost independent agent'; and Maurice Vlaminck sought 'to reveal nature in freedom'.

For John Perceval the landscape is often a Fauvist whirlpool or vortex that churns and rotates thick pigment about his images; Rigby, even if there is an overall intensity of colour, wants separate areas to assert their differences, principally by a change in brush stroke; since the painting is about vital growth, the movement is vertical, the sky itself breaking into loose strokes that are like the dispersal or formation of flower petals.

William Salmon's song lyric, dedicated to a drier region, has restful pauses and painterly passages to provoke the imagination, but Rigby's sharp lucidity and exultant use of colour allow for no relief and no shadowy glades. Charles Blackman's drawing with collage is, in part, about the scientific divisionist approach to colour notation used by Georges Seurat. In contrast, Rigby's application is expressive and instinctive. He is not analysing the landscape into patches of complementary hues, but is achieving an exuberant and energetically elegant synthesis.

Moggill Village
Oil on canvas; 1975; 83.0 × 90.5 cm.
Possession of the artist.

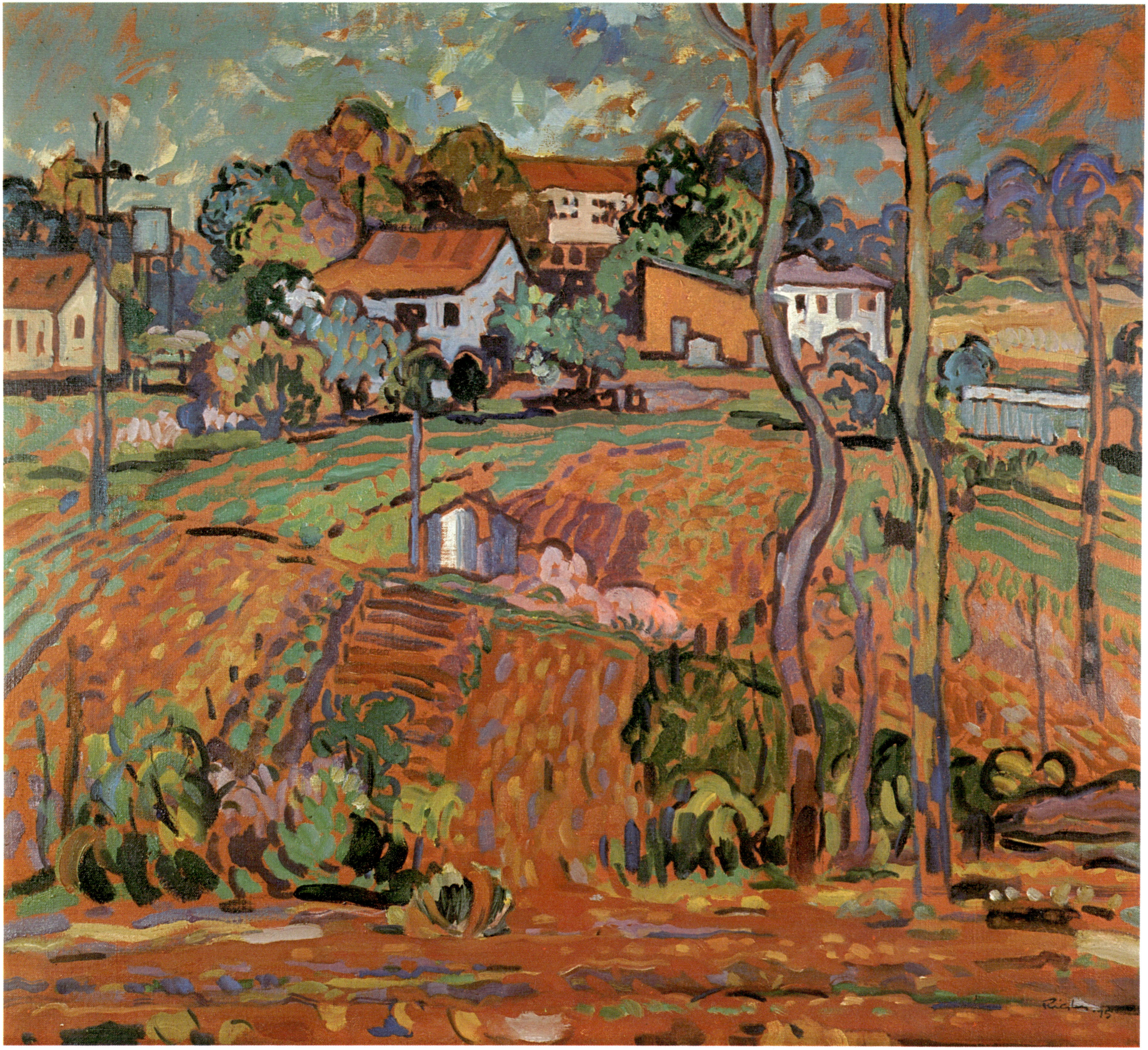

Moggill Village

Fred Williams

Frederick Ronald Williams, born Richmond, Victoria, 1927; lives in Melbourne.

Upwey Landscape exemplifies the most recognisable transcription of the bush that Fred Williams paints: a loose, seemingly random dispersal of rocks and trees, often like small eddies of succulent paint; complex and crowded notations; a ragged dotting and blobbing; an emphatic horizon line, often high in the picture and sometimes accompanied by other horizontals denoting riverbanks and plains; and an oriental elegance and fastidiousness both in the placement of summary signs for trees and scrub and in the subtle painting of delectable backgrounds.

Such paintings lie between *The Half Round Pond* and *Landscape with a Goose*; they were more intimate and delicate than his earlier work, which had a kinship with Henri Matisse and Paul Cézanne, and more strictly controlled than his later work which is intent upon a landscape independent of vertical-horizontal structures.

The Half Round Pond, like Nolan's *Riverbend*, shuts out the sky. It is gloomily claustrophobic like Perceval's *Black Cockatoo Flying Upstream*. Williams opposes a firm curve to the tall palisade of trees which resists the light and reflects it from pinkish patches; the pool is deep and forbidding. If Matisse added something to the trees, he has been eclipsed and plunged into darkness, but it is a darkness full of energy.

The pond's curve directs the eye to the lowering forest, where it resembles a frontier and barrier. The similar line in *Landscape with a Goose* leads one immediately to explore the light-hued and light-hearted bush; it is a return to the domestic landscape. Just as Sydney Long, Frederick McCubbin and Julian Ashton could decorate their paintings with the commonplace fowl, Williams, in an about-face from semi-abstract elegance and conventional signs for rock, branch and foliage, has added, with amusing defiance, a goose. It is, of course, tiny; it hardly intrudes, but it signifies Williams' desire to make the landscape more realistic, more immediately recognisable and, above all, less confined to verticals and horizontals and less dependent on the isolation of trees, trunks, branches, shrubs and fence posts. The landscape has become more cohesive; it is growing and bursting with Impressionist animation.

One no longer maps out the terrain; one enjoys a walk through it. The thin frieze of trees resembles William Salmon's in lightness and vivacity. Nolan's *Riverbend*, despite the flutter of leaves and loose bark, is majestically elegiac; Williams' road curves to the homely and solacing.

The Half Round Pond
Oil on hardboard; 1958; 103 × 72 cm.
Acquired: 1972
Australian National Gallery, Canberra.

Upwey Landscape
Oil on canvas; 1965; 147.3 × 182.9 cm.
Acquired: 1965, Felton Bequest.
National Gallery of Victoria.

Landscape with a Goose
Oil on canvas; 1974; 183.5 × 152.7 cm.
Acquired: 1975
Australian National Gallery, Canberra.

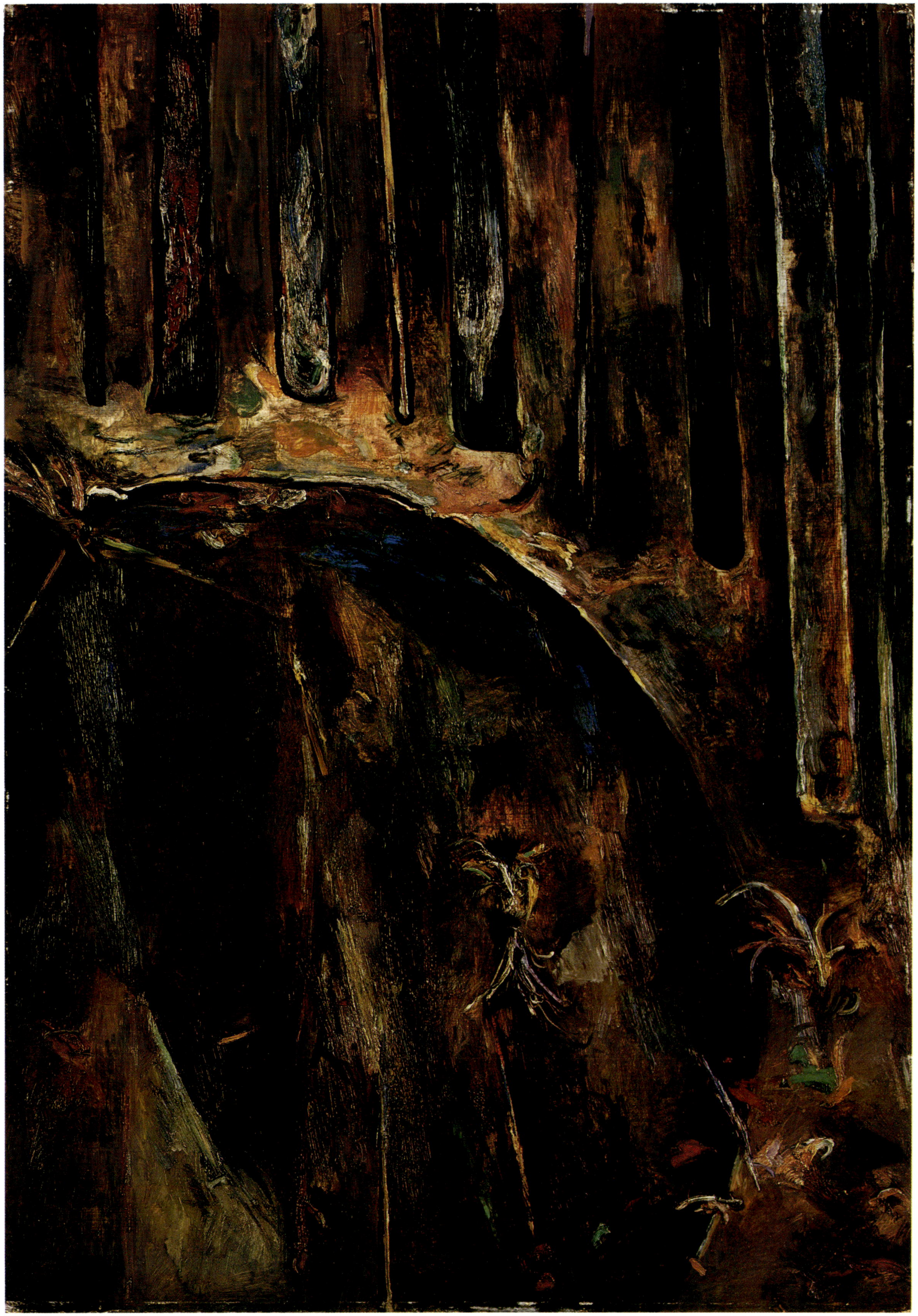

The Half Round Pond

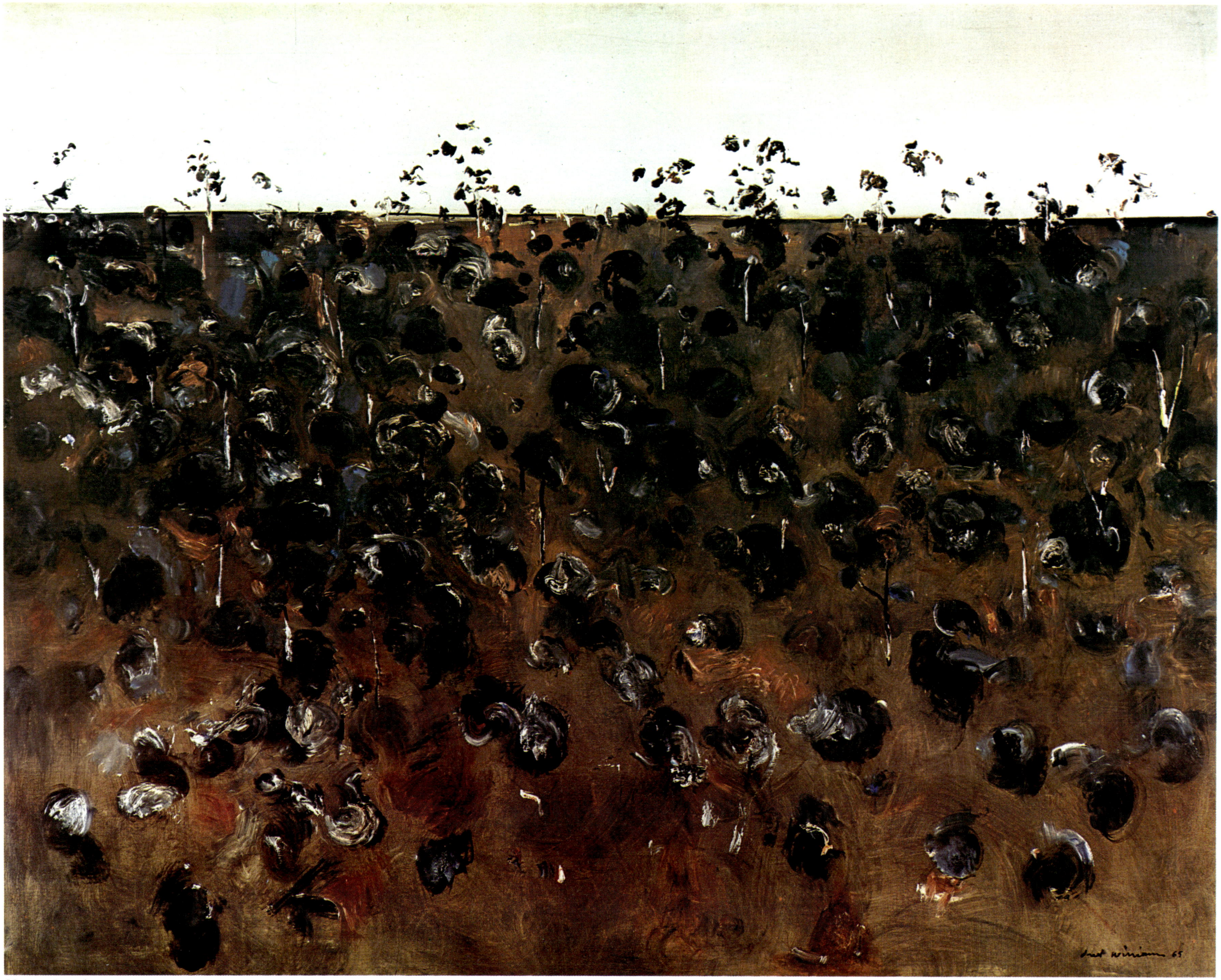

Upwey Landscape

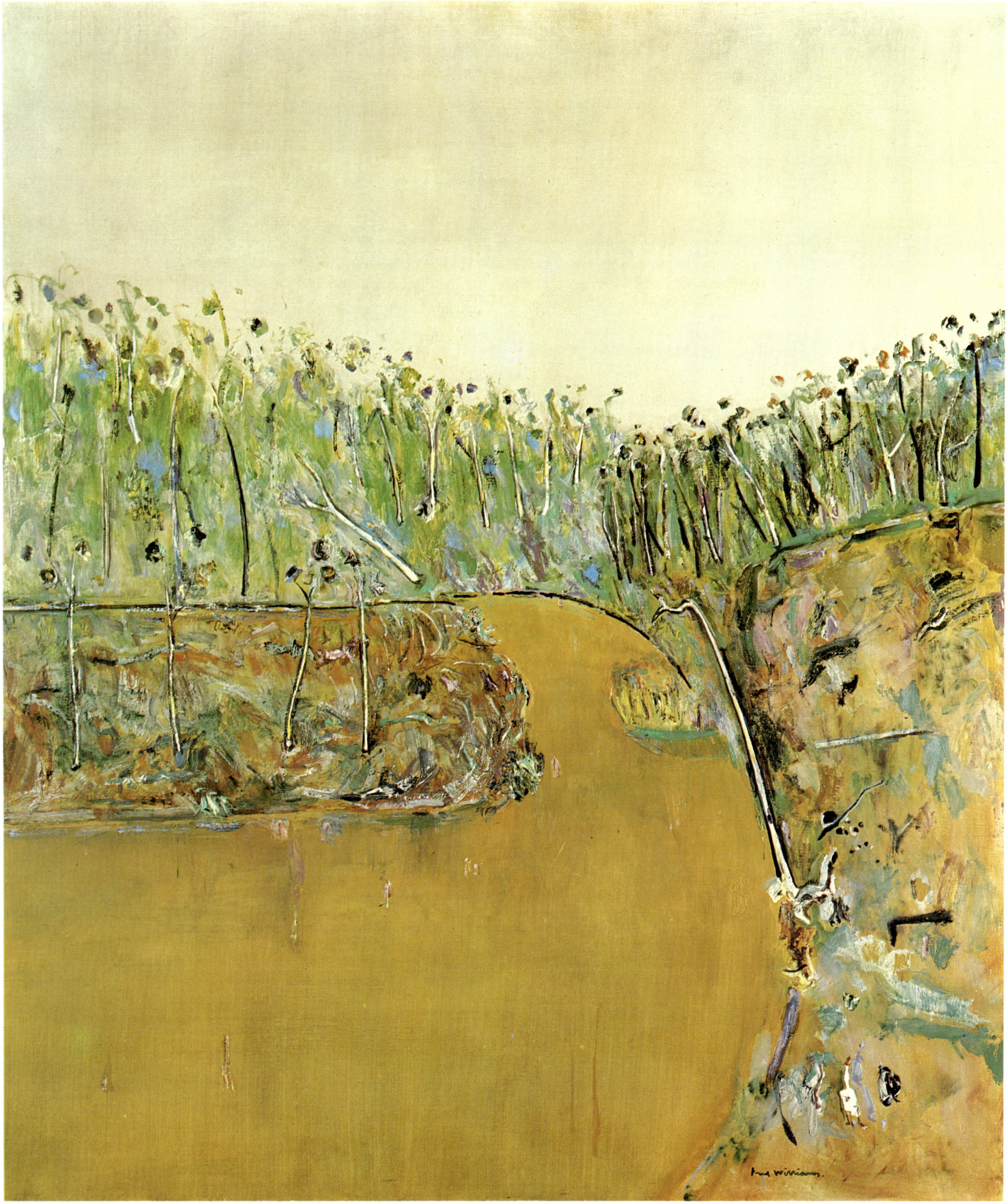

Landscape with a Goose

Julian Ashton

Julian Rossi Ashton, born Surrey, England 1851. Arrived in Melbourne, 1878; died in Sydney, 1942.

For some sixty years Julian Ashton was a major and beneficial influence on Australian art; he taught painters like Sydney Long and Rah Fizelle; he encouraged open-air painting as against academic practices and he taught in such a way that, like Desiderius Orban, he released rather than channelled potential. He praised and encouraged Blamire Young; he befriended Louis Buvelot and painted a portrait of him; when William Dobell returned to Australia in 1939, Ashton greeted his work enthusiastically; and the same enthusiasm persuaded the Art Gallery of New South Wales to purchase Arthur Streeton's *Still Glides the Stream and Shall Forever Glide.*

There is evidence of Ashton's early work as an illustrator in *Old Sydney, Cumberland Street;* he worked for 'The Illustrated Australian News', 'The Australian Sketcher' and 'The Picturesque Atlas'. In his autobiography, 'Now Came Still Evening On', published a year before he died, he tells how he went to Glenrowan to sketch the last scene of the Kelly Gang. A photograph of the corpse of Joe Byrne, propped up outside Seymour Police Station on 25 October 1878 still exists; a bowler-hatted Ashton is walking away from the unpleasantness. Those were the days before the Kelly myth could ignite the imaginations of Douglas Stewart and Sidney Nolan. Ashton relates how he was sketching Kelly at his trial when the accused turned his eyes upon him. Kelly's defence protested to the judge, Sir Redmond Barry, 'Your Honour, the prisoner complains that someone is making a sketch of him'. Sir Redmond replied, 'If anyone is making a sketch of the prisoner without his consent, this proceeding cannot be allowed in court'.

Julian Ashton dealt with plain, unvarnished facts; he did not try to ennoble the bush or the city; he was a recorder, and the personalities of buildings did not claim his interest as they did Sali Herman, Jeffrey Smart and Blamire Young. He painted the natural and unpretentious: a few fowls, some children in the gutter, rusted roofs; but his deployment of shapes and additive touches was skilful. Children, fowls and sheets are tellingly placed. Then, with a true artist-illustrator's gift, he uses the warm, grey brownish shadow to give substance to a faded scene.

Old Sydney, Cumberland Street
Watercolour on paper; c.1895; 36.2 × 48.5 cm.
Presented through The Minister of Works, 1902.
Art Gallery of New South Wales.

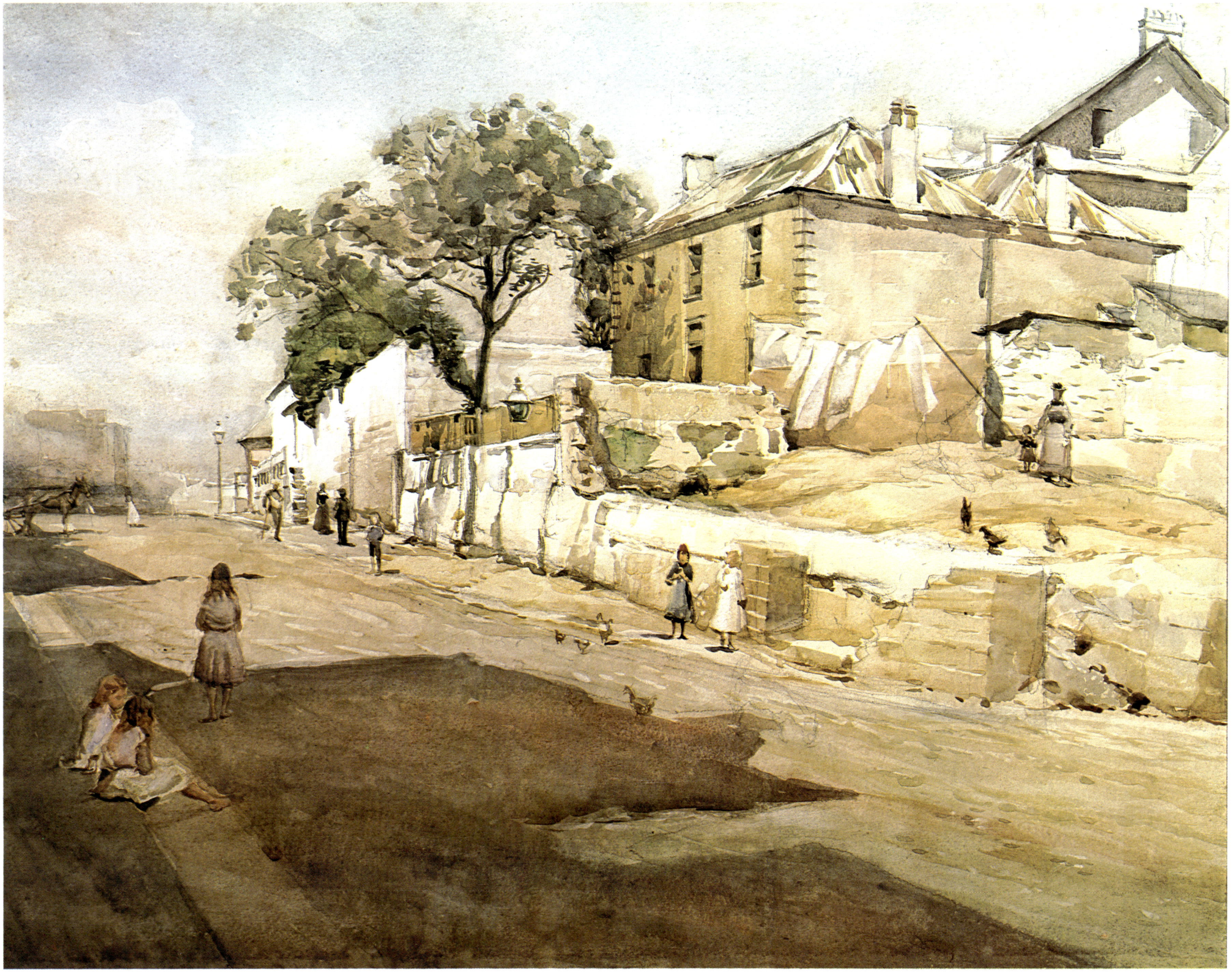

Old Sydney, Cumberland Street

John Olsen

John Olsen, born Newcastle, New South Wales, 1928; lives in Dural, New South Wales.

'It's all there — everything — ships coming in and out, the dawn, the sun, the great cranes, men working, traffic, movement — everything — I want to get it all down', said John Olsen in his more exuberant and less contemplative days. To get it down, he said, re-echoing Paul Klee, he took a line for a walk . . . but it was also a leap, a stroll and a dash. The line was not tracing shapes or giving directions; it indicated Olsen's immersion in the landscape. In a talk to the Contemporary Art Society of New South Wales on 21 August 1962, he said the landscape was not to be observed and delineated as in Renaissance paintings but was to render the totality and flux of the environment. The conveying of experience was the principal task, as in *Dappled Country*, with its wafting up a bird and head from wide and lean lines; 'I do not know where I have been; I only know I've been there'. Like Klee he wants to penetrate and present the organic life of trees and briars, grass and gulleys; so he aims at the intimate and the incidental, the fantastic and the whimsical and not at the sublime. It is little wonder that he admires and dots and isolated, sequential elements in John Glover and Henri Bastin.

The flux and bustling growth of *Fogg Dam* is celebrated, not confined, by a sliver of delicate off-pink on the horizon; this is unusual in an Olsen for the earth to him is an infinite carpet crossed by tracks and prints and dappled with shadows and soils of delicate hues. *Fogg Dam* could be accompanied by lines from Dylan Thomas' 'Poem in October' that Olsen read at his 1962 lecture:

'A springful of larks in a rolling
cloud and the roadside bushes brimming with whistling
Blackbirds and the sun of October
Summery
On the hill's shoulder'.

Pied Beauty, one of most dreaming, softly lyrical, wayward and relaxed of Olsen's paintings, its mood seeking comparison with the later works of Desiderius Orban and Lloyd Rees, is inspired by Gerard Manley Hopkins' poem of the same title:

'Glory be to God for dappled things —
For skies of couple-colour as a brinded cow;
For rose-moles all in stipple upon trout that swim;
Fresh-fire coal chestnut-falls; finches' wings;
Landscape plotted and pieced — fold, fallow and plough;
And all trades, their gear and tackle trim.
All things counter, original, spare, strange;
Whatever is fickle, freckled (who knows how?)
With swift, slow; sweet, sour; adazzle, dim;
He fathers forth whose beauty is past change:
Praise him.'

Olsen's achievement is to bring into the freshest harmony the disparate and his experience of its hidden order. The poetry he admires coalesces images as he does; the sudden disruption in their syntax parallels his intuitive innovations.

Dappled Country
Oil on canvas; 1963; 122.5 × 152.5 cm.
Acquired: 1971
Australian National Gallery, Canberra.

Pied Beauty
Oil on hardboard; 1969; 119.8 × 132.1 cm.
Acquired: 1969
Art Gallery of South Australia.

Fogg Dam
Oil on hardboard; 1974; 91.4 × 121.9 cm.
Courtesy of the Rudy Komon Gallery, Sydney.

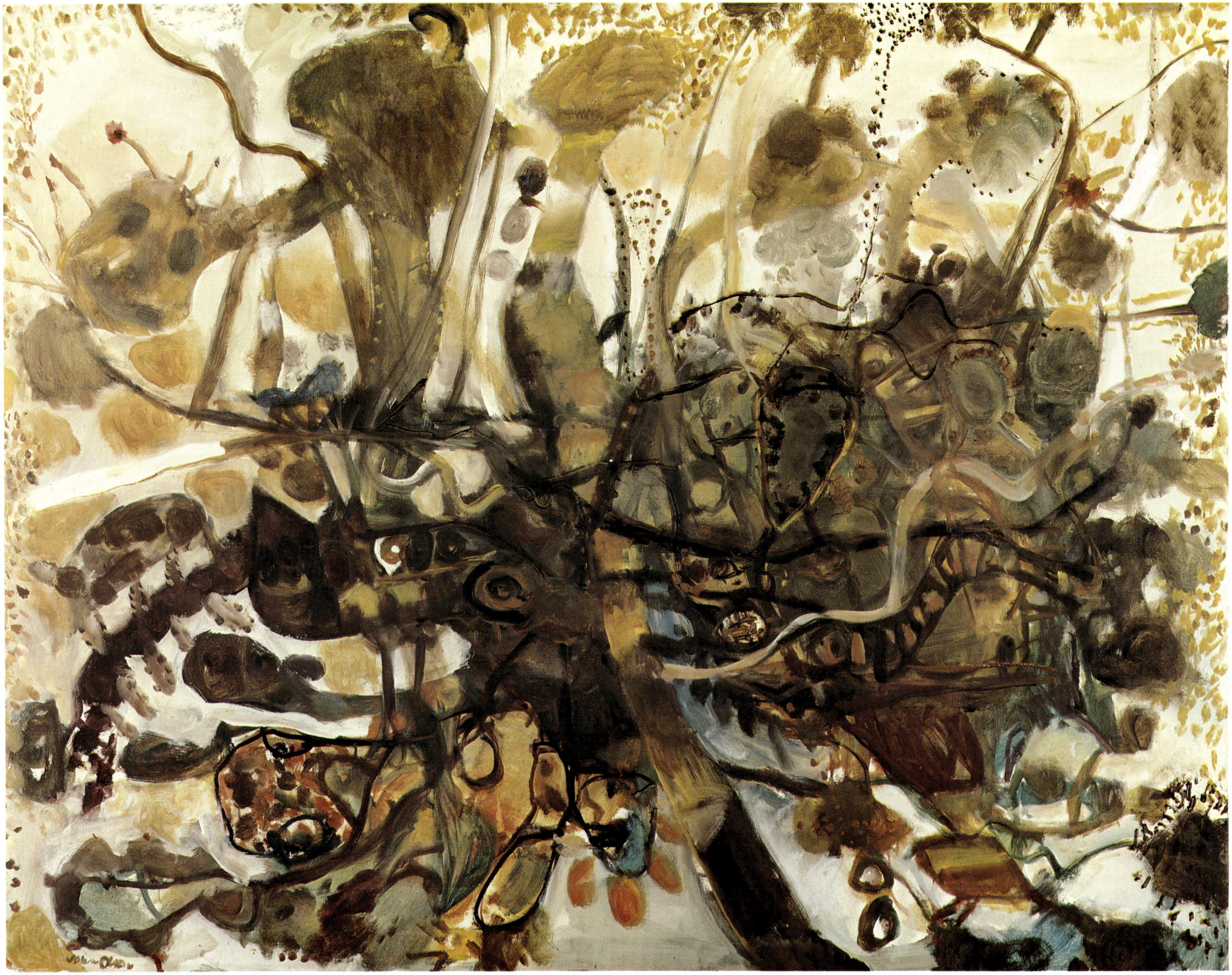

Dappled Country

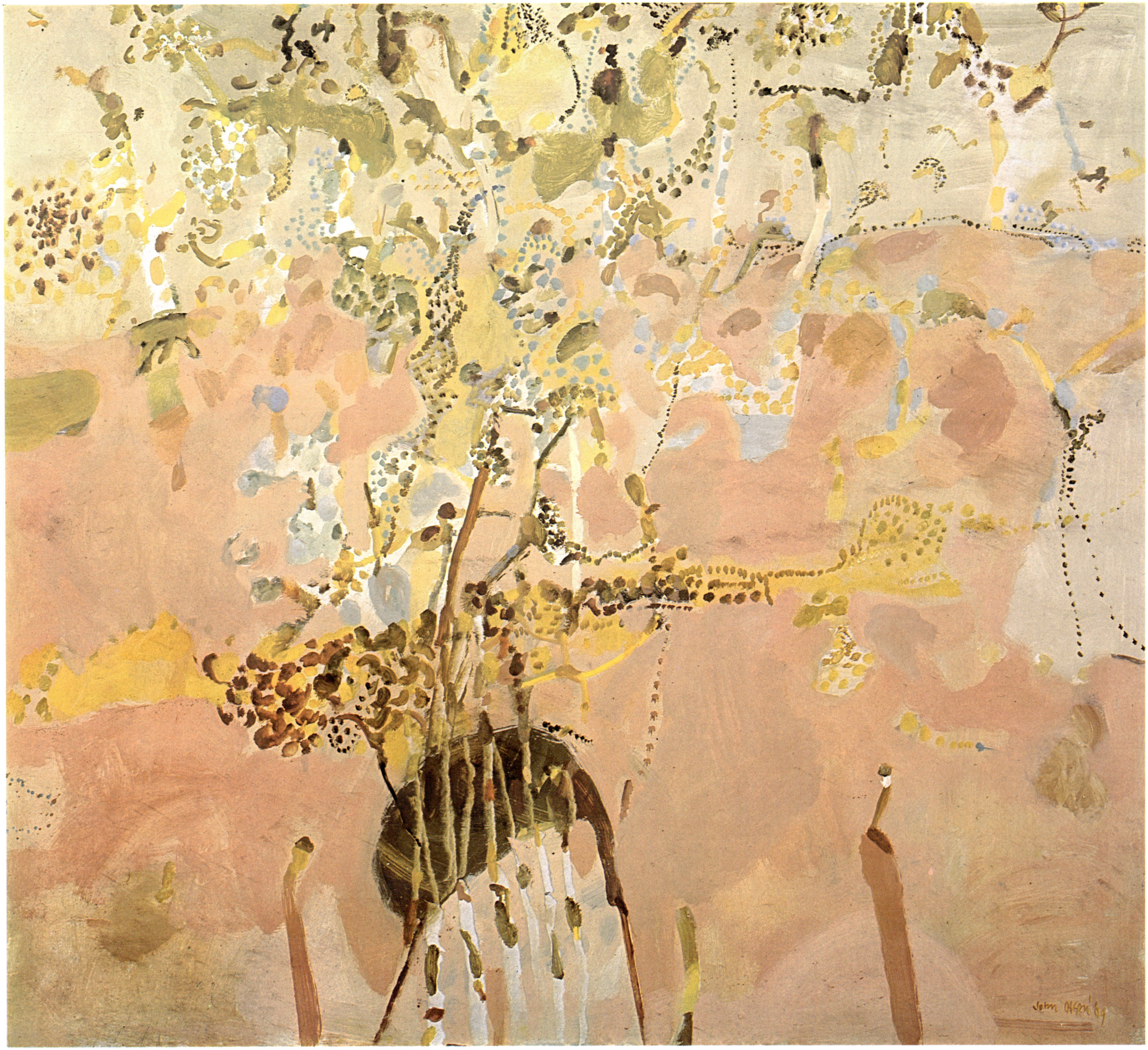

Pied Beauty

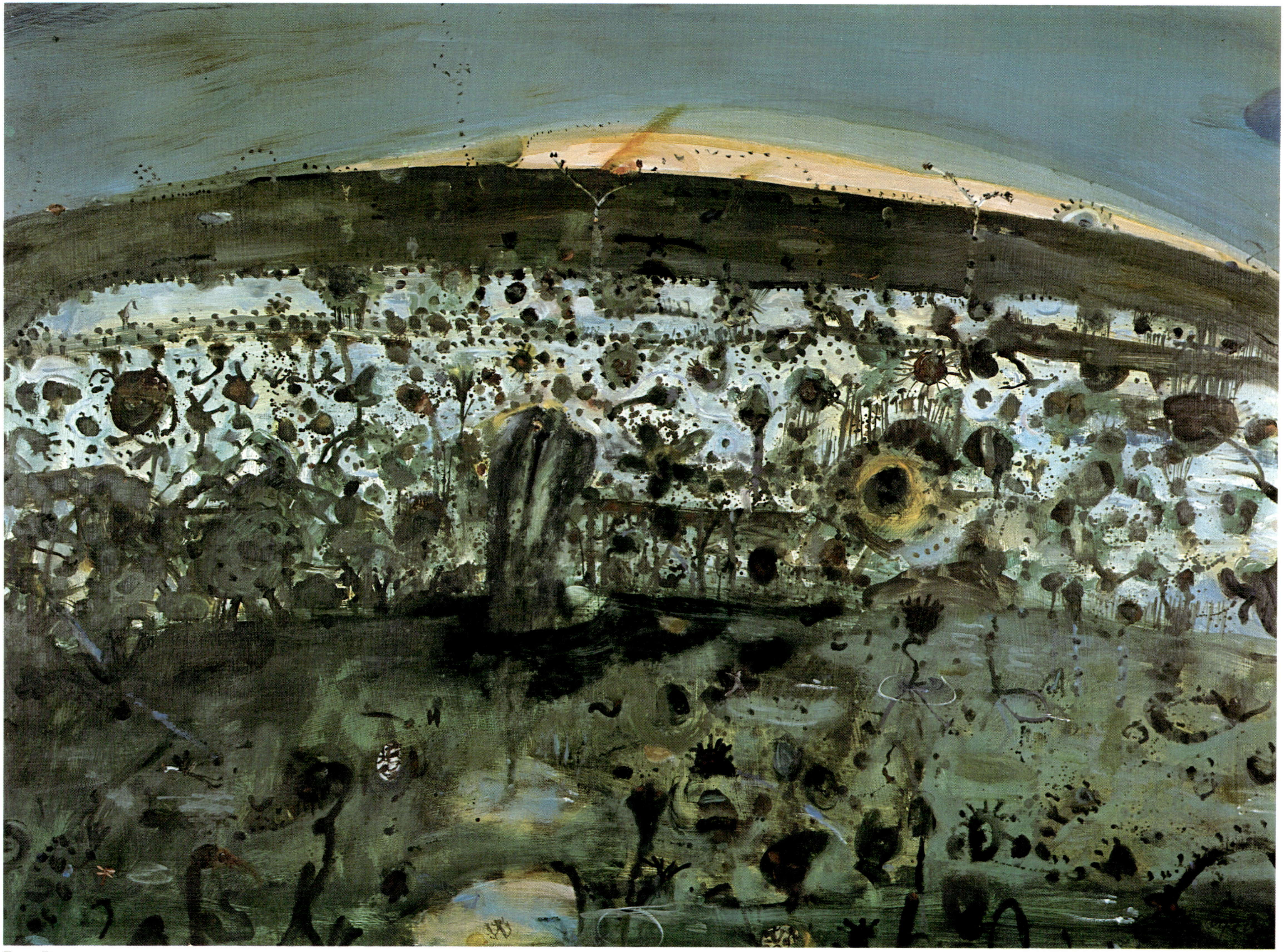

Fogg Dam

Henri Bastin

Henri Bastin, born Belgium, 1896. Arrived in Australia, 1920; lives in Queensland.

Henri Bastin, opal miner, whose favourite diggings are in an almost inaccessible area eight-hundred miles west of Brisbane, began painting while working for Major Harold de Vahl Rubin, a noted collector and dealer, who had once managed a gallery in Brook Street, London.

Like most naive painters, Henri Bastin paints what he loves; he titles his paintings *My Opal Mine* and *My Camp*. Naive painters, who have a particular perception of all things as separate but related entities, are not necessarily untutored and visually uneducated. Henri Rousseau, 'Le Douanier', knew a number of important painters, like Pablo Picasso, and certainly admired great paintings which he tried to emulate. In 1958 Henri Bastin, to let us know where his admiration lay, was pleased to title a painting, *Hommage à Rousseau*.

Of Bastin, John Olsen has written, 'He is a lone foxer — his world has a minimal use of human beings. He paints with a jeweller-like precision — pellucid stones are minutely examined and recorded in colours of mandarine, violet, emerald, green, bright blue . . . He loves to be close to the object, to feel the difference in colour of different layers of bark. His pictures are of a radiant stillness, a fixity in time. He is fond of portraying the disordered dottiness' of Australian trees'.

Olsen, Bastin, Glover and Williams are all, in separate ways, interpreters of landscape as dots, blobs, notations and touches that signal foliage, rocks, trees, stumps, tracks and fences.

Bastin, like Olsen in some of his works, shifts the beholder's eye around with a myriad of focal points; emphasis is equal and the distant cropped hill is as important as the foreground camp; the yellowish stones in the distance are almost as clearly delineated as those in the threshold of the painting.

The camp is set out like a picnic spot; everything is seen in its right place, as in an inventory. Indeed, Bastin sees the world as an inventory of objects, each sharply defined and set down, their addition celebrating the uniqueness of nature as a whole.

My Camp
Synthetic paint on hardboard; 1966; 91.5 × 121.3 cm.
Presented by Mr Patrick White, 1970.
Art Gallery of New South Wales.

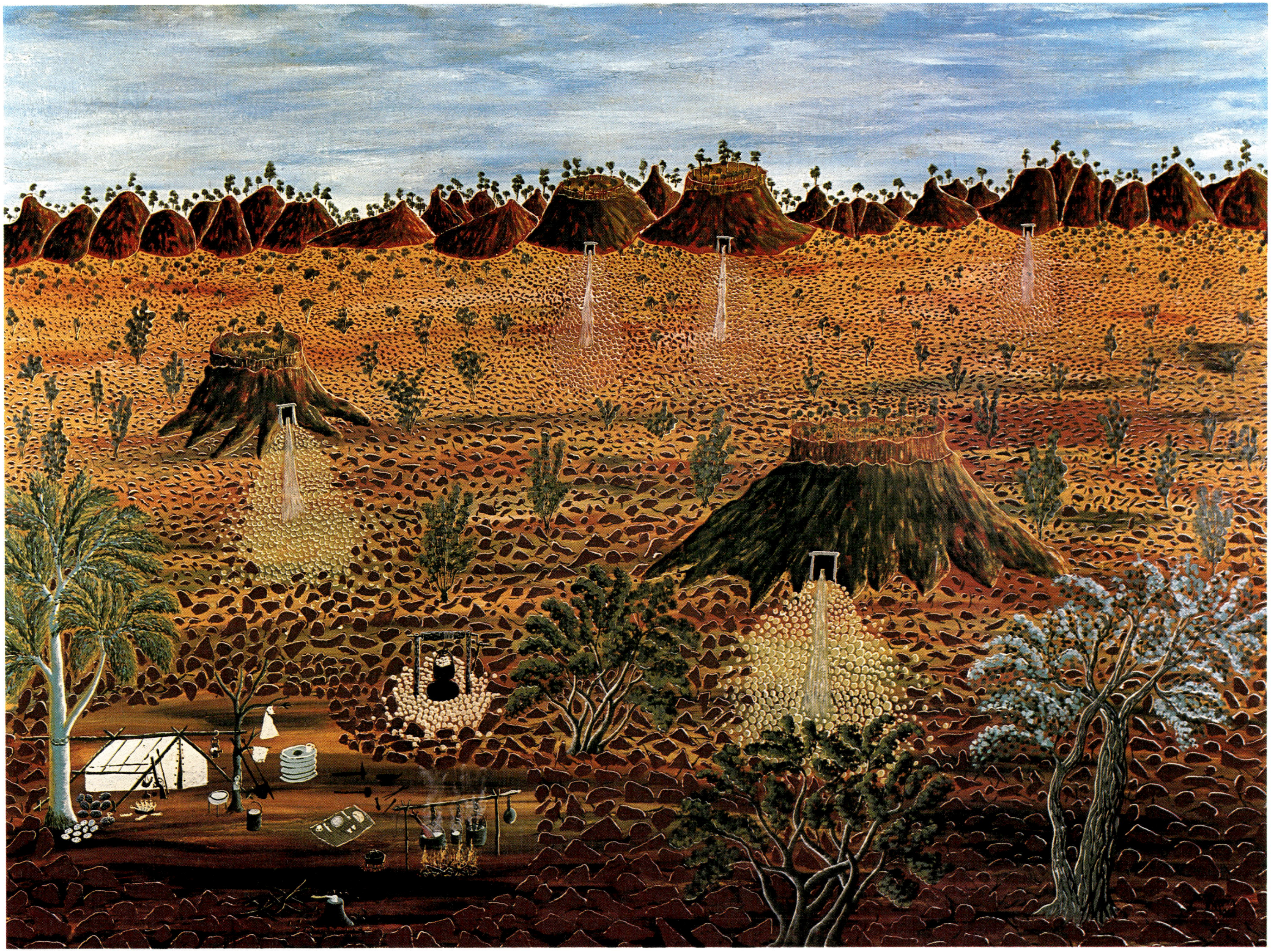

My Camp

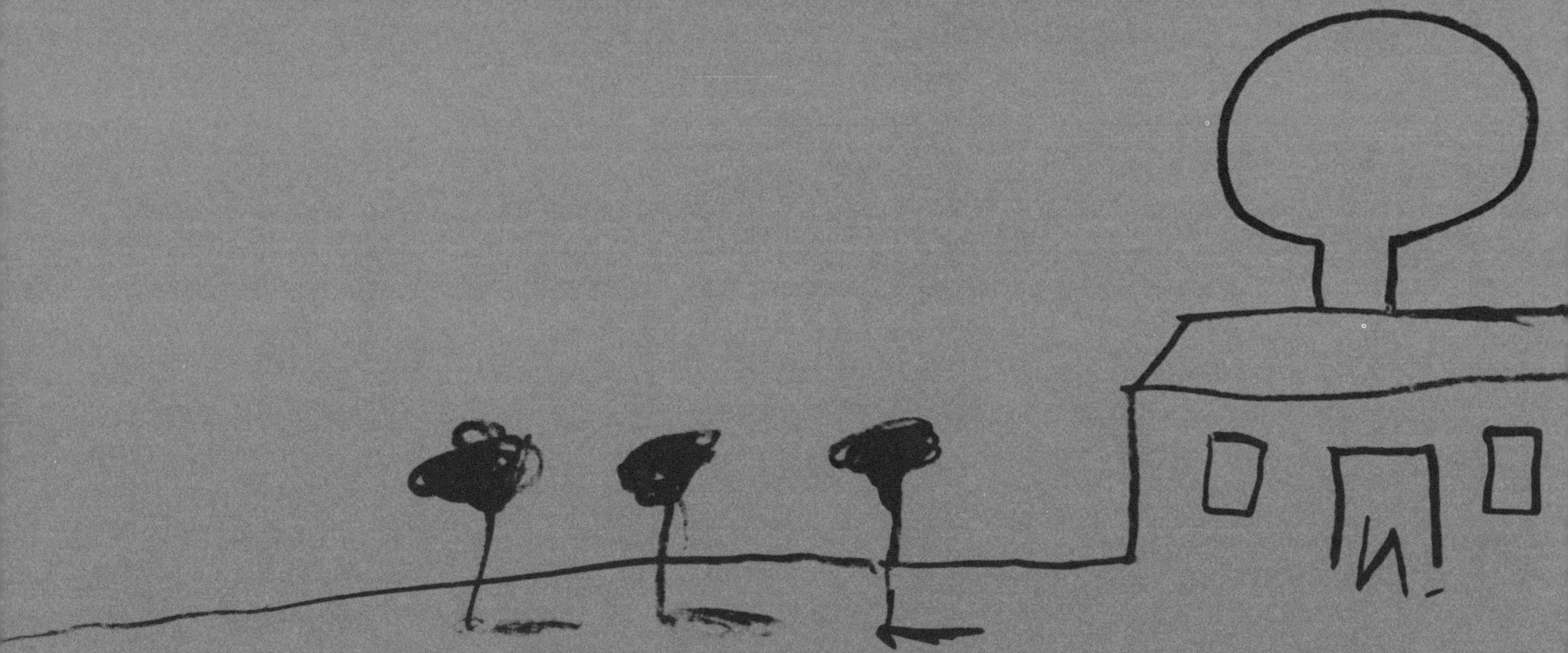